GLORY DAYS

MEMORABLE GAMES IN ALABAMA FOOTBALL HISTORY

TOMMY HICKS
FOREWORD BY MAL MOORE

SPORTS
PUBLISHING

This book is dedicated to the memory of Mal Moore,
one of the most genuine men I have ever met.

Sports Publishing books may be purchased in bulk at special discounts for sales promotion,
corporate gifts, fund-raising, or educational purposes. Special editions can also be created to
specifications. For details, contact the Special Sales Department, Sports Publishing, 307 West
36th Street, 11th Floor, New York, NY 10018 or sportspubbooks@skyhorsepublishing.com.

Sports Publishing® is a registered trademark of Skyhorse Publishing, Inc.®, a Delaware
corporation.

Visit our website at www.sportspubbooks.com.

10 9 8 7 6 5 4 3 2 1

Library of Congress Cataloging-in-Publication Data Hicks, Tommy, 1954- author.
  Glory days : memorable games in Alabama football history / Tommy Hicks ; foreword by
Mal Moore.
    pages cm
  ISBN 978-1-61321-362-9 (alk. paper)
1. University of Alabama--Football--History. 2. Alabama Crimson Tide (Football team)--
History--20th century. I. Title.
  GV958.A4H56 2013
  796.332'630976184--dc23
                              2013020797

Printed in the United States of America

Contents

Acknowledgments

This project has taken its twists and turns, but throughout the process I received great support, assistance, and guidance. As such, a lot of thank-yous and pats on the back are required.

The folks at Skyhorse Publishing made this book possible, and certainly the great work and patience of editor Julie Ganz deserves a high-five or two and more. Editor Jay Cassell and publicist Lauren Burnstein played key roles as well.

At my company, Alabama Media Group and AL.com, a number of people stepped forward in assisting with this book. K. A. Turner was of great help, and the same is true of Randy Kennedy, Izzy Gould, and Mark Heim.

The good folks at the University of Alabama were, of course, invaluable. Many, many thanks to Doug Walker, Jeff Purinton, and Josh Maxson, and of course the late Mal Moore. Kirk McNair of *Bama Magazine* offered assistance all along the way and is deserving of special mention.

Certainly, this project would be merely stats and scores without all those who offered their time and stories—some quite often—to the finished product. It is their stories, their play, and their words that bring these games to life again. Many thanks to all who participated in interviews and were so gracious with those memories and their time.

From a personal standpoint, there are a number of people whom I must thank publicly, and to whom I hope I have made clear privately of my appreciation for their love and/or support throughout this process. I have to start with Julie Jeter, who has provided encouragement and so much more every step along the way. The same is true of my daughter Maren, the best writer in the family. To my dad, known by everyone as Big E, and my brother Dean, sister-in-law Kim, and nephews Chance and Carson, thank you. Thanks also to Megan and Ryan Foster and of course to Damien and Trista.

Thanks must be given to a number of others, who can't all be listed here, though there are some whom I simply must note here: Ron Higgins, Kim Shugart, Bruce Gentry, Chris Stewart, Mark McCarter, Trish and Kevin Dougherty, Carly Dougherty and Kendall, Kristi and Dave Walker, Steve Richardson, Tony Barnhart, John Pruett, Jon Johnson, Gregg Dewalt, and Joel and Tina Erdmann. Thank you everyone.

Foreword

It is no small task to attempt to chronicle the biggest games in Alabama football history. The Crimson Tide is in the enviable position of having played many, many games regarded as "big games" because the importance of games is magnified with success. There are big games that everyone recognizes. In just about any season there are big games because of the opponent, its success and tradition, and the history of the game.

I've always thought of the Alabama-Tennessee game as being big for those reasons. And we always thought that if we could get by Tennessee undefeated, we would win the conference and have a chance to win the national championship.

The Tennessee game could affect the remainder of the season or the season itself. In 1990 we couldn't get off our goal line against Tennessee, but eventually we got a blocked field goal attempt by Stacy Harrison and a game-winning field goal by Phillip Doyle, and we upset the nation's third-ranked team, 9-6. That game put us on track and a couple of years later we won the national championship.

There are games that are big because of the consequences. A Sugar Bowl game matching the number one and number two teams, for instance, is a big game because the winner is the national champion.

To the coaches and players, every game is a big game, every game an important game. As a player and coach I went into every season thinking the most important game was the first game because we had to win that one to have a chance to play for the national championship.

Certainly Coach Gene Stallings had a point when he said that every game was a big game and that if one didn't think so one should experience the consequences of losing it.

One of the great things about Coach Bryant's teams was that they won just about every game they were supposed to win and they won their share of games against teams that had players equal to or superior to his ability. It was a strength of Coach Bryant that he prepared his teams for those situations and thus put his teams in position to win so many championships. It is fascinating to see not only how many championships his teams won, but also how many times he had his teams in position to win additional championships.

Many people believe the biggest win in Alabama football history wasn't a game that won the national championship, but a game that changed Crimson Tide football. That is the 1971 season-opening game against Southern Cal in Los Angeles. We were coming off back-to-back 6-5 seasons, and Southern Cal had beaten us badly in 1970 in Birmingham.

That was the year we went to the wishbone offense and it was my first year to coach quarterbacks. I don't think Coach Bryant decided to change from our Pro-style offense to the wishbone until about mid-July before the start of the season.

I was so focused on the job we had to do to put in this radical new offense that I didn't really think about how big the Southern Cal game was during preparation. I think I was more worried about whether we could make a first down. We had the element of surprise in that game and we scored the first three times we had the ball and won 17-10. Almost everyone talked about the wishbone, but our defense did a great job to hold a skillful Southern Cal team to only 10 points.

That game led to an undefeated season. It also gave everyone associated with Alabama football a shot of confidence that was desperately needed. That was Coach Bryant's 200th coaching victory. I believe that win may have energized Coach Bryant to continue coaching longer than he might have.

Sometimes a game becomes big for reasons beyond your control. Our 1965 team had a loss and a tie and we were playing Nebraska in the Orange Bowl. During the day the teams ranked ahead of us lost in the Sugar, Cotton and Rose Bowls and suddenly our game was for the national championship, which we won.

In 1992 we were undefeated, but we had to beat a Florida team in the first-ever Southeastern Conference Championship Game to have a chance to go to the Sugar Bowl to play against Miami for the national championship.

The Sugar Bowl was a big game, but so was the SEC Championship Game, which we had to win to have a chance to play for the national championship. It was fitting that Alabama, which is the flagship of SEC football, played and won the first SEC Championship Game. It was a bonus that we won in such exciting fashion with Antonio Langham's interception return for a touchdown.

We won some big bowl games and we also lost some. We played Notre Dame at the end of the 1973 season in the Sugar Bowl when we were number one and they were number two, and Notre Dame came out on top. That was a big game we lost. Of course, when we played Notre Dame in the BCS game at the end of the 2012 season we came out on top, winning our 15th national championship. That was another big game that we won.

We certainly have won our share, though, games like the 1978 Crimson Tide beating Penn State in the Sugar Bowl in a battle of number one against number two. Alabama was ready to play that game, and most of the big games we have played over the years.

Coach Nick Saban, with his process of preparation, teamwork, and attention to detail, has added to the list of Alabama's many great victories, and to its list of national championships, leading the program to national titles in 2009, 2011, and 2012.

The trick of the head coach is to get his team ready to play every game. You have to approach every game as though it is a big game, because it is. It's been said so often that it's a cliché, but it's also true that the biggest game is the next game and it doesn't matter what team it is against. A strength of Coach Bryant was that for every game he had the same routine, the same schedule for every game. His approach was to treat every game the same way. And he was able to get his players to perform at the same level, at their best, regardless of the opponent.

That preparation has led to a lot of big games and a lot of big wins.

Mal Moore,
Former Director of Athletics
University of Alabama

Editor's Note: Athletic Director Emeritus Mal Moore passed away in March 2013 at the age of 73.

CHAPTER ONE
1966 Tennessee

Alabama 11, Tennessee 10
October 15, 1966
Neyland Stadium
Knoxville, Tennessee

H e has photos, newspaper clippings, programs and other mementos of his sophomore season at Alabama, a season unlike any other for Mike Hall, who would later earn All-America honors. Many of the games and occurrences that took place that grand autumn of 1966 are as clear today for Hall as they were just days after taking place.

It was a special season and a special team.

Hall's memories of the games that season are pleasant. After all, the team finished the year unbeaten, winning each of the 11 games it played, each win cementing it as one of the finest teams in the program's history. It was a year of comebacks and easy wins, of big plays and big games, produced by a stifling defense, productive offense, All-America players and, in some cases, players some previously thought too small, too slow, or too something or other to be contributors to an undefeated team and season.

In short, the 1966 season had a little of everything and the Crimson Tide did whatever was necessary to produce a win each time it took to the field. It should have been, in the eyes of its players and coaches and fans, a national championship team. It should have been the Crimson Tide's third straight national championship team.

It wasn't.

Alabama's lone loss that season took place, not on the field of play but in the political arena. Politics—in this case, the Top 20 polls—proved to be the one opponent Alabama couldn't defeat. It was the one situation in which the members of the team couldn't entirely control their own fate by making a play on the field. That single defeat still stings today.

All the trophies, mementos and accolades from that season aren't enough to replace the one thing that's missing: a national championship, and the symbol of such an accomplishment: a national championship ring.

Hall and his teammates, who as a group get together twice every year and in many cases have remained close friends since their first day of practice, still long for the recognition they believe they should have received.

"We thought we should have a ring made up, but coach Bryant said, 'We're not going to have a ring made; we're not national champions,'" Hall recalled.

The 1966 team is often described with the use of alliteration: Undefeated, Untied, Uncrowned.

While posting convincing wins on the field, Alabama couldn't convince the pollsters it was the best team in the land. Voters didn't even see Alabama as the No. 2 team. The Crimson Tide finished the year ranked No. 3. Notre Dame was named the national champion, even though it had played for a tie in its regular season game against Michigan State, which ended the year No. 2 with a 9-0-1 record, the same mark as the Fighting Irish.

Notre Dame head coach Ara Parseghian elected to play for a tie on Nov. 19 in East Lansing, Mich., instead of playing to win, when his team faced the Spartans. He believed that the polls would keep the Irish No. 1 after its "Game of the Century" against Michigan State, even if it tied. He was right. The Associated Press poll and UPI poll both had Notre Dame at No. 1, the Spartans at No. 2 and Alabama—two-time defending national champion (and unbeaten and untied) Alabama—at No. 3.

Dan Jenkins, in an article for *Sports Illustrated*, wrote that Parseghian had "tied one for the Gipper."

Even when Notre Dame and Michigan State skipped bowl invitations while Alabama traveled to New Orleans for the Sugar Bowl, where it smashed Nebraska 34-7, the top three spots in both polls remained unchanged.

"It was devastating at the time," Hall said of the snub. "I'm still angry about it. I'm not wearing a national championship ring that I should be wearing."

To understand the disappointment that remains with Hall and his teammates is to know this fact: in the long history of college football polls, only once has a team that won the national championship the previous season, started the following season ranked No. 1, and won each of the games it played not been named the national champion. Alabama's 1966 team owns that distinction.

• • •

It was the third Saturday in October and everyone in the two states knew what that meant: Alabama and Tennessee would be facing each other in football. In 1966, Jim Stovall, then a freshman at Tennessee, couldn't wait for the game to be played. He was willing, as were the thousands who joined him, to sit in the rain to see the two teams play.

"The day was gray and the field muddy when the Vols and the Tide met in Neyland Stadium in 1966," Stovall wrote in 2006 on the University of Tennessee website known as the Tennessee Journalist (www.tnjn.com), which serves the university's School of Journalism and electronic media. "Despite the conditions, the players on both sides played like champions and produced one of the greatest meetings of the Alabama-Tennessee rivalry."

Stovall, a journalism major at UT that year and a staff writer for the school's student newspaper, *UT Daily Beacon*, as well as a self-professed die-hard Vols fans, noted the matchup featured strong play, but there was one unquestioned star and he wasn't wearing a helmet or shoulder pads. He was wearing a houndstooth hat.

"In 1966, we knew [Bryant] was good. We didn't know how good. On that rainy, muddy day, he gave us a glimpse," Stovall wrote.

"I remember seeing him down on the field," Stovall said in an interview. "You couldn't see that much, really, but he was a presence. Anybody who knew anything about football knew who he was and he already had things going at Alabama."

Bryant's success, nationally and against the Vols, only served to increase the stakes in the rivalry.

"At that time, Alabama was the game," Stovall said. "Florida might be the game these days, but then it was Alabama. There were big hopes for Tennessee football that season. I remember the week before [the Vols] went down to Atlanta to play Georgia Tech. I went to the university center early to stake out a seat to watch the game on TV. They lost 6-3 and it was a heartbreaking loss, a loss that increased the importance of the Alabama game."

Alabama quarterback Ken Stabler, a junior, knew the importance of the Tennessee game and was aware of the intensity of the rivalry. Just in case that fact had escaped him, some Vols fans offered him a reminder.

"Flying in there the day before [the game], we went by the stadium," Stabler recalled. "When we got to the stadium, there was a high construction crane and at the end of the crane somebody had hung an Alabama player in effigy, and [it] was wearing a No. 12 jersey." It was, of course, Stabler's jersey number. "That got my attention," he added. "That was the first time I'd really been there [freshmen weren't allowed to play in 1966; Alabama was the home team his sophomore year] and seeing that gave you a great sense of the rivalry. It certainly added more interest to the game."

In fact, the Alabama team had been greeted at the airport by members of the Knoxville Chamber of Commerce. The meeting would not be a Chamber of Commerce, warm-and-fuzzy moment. "They met us and gave everybody a keychain with a replica of the stadium on it," place-kicker and punter Steve Davis said. "When they got to coach Bryant and handed one to him, he threw it down on the ground. That got their attention."

Bryant was in town to win a football game, not exchange pleasantries.

"Coach Bryant respected Tennessee and he always saw the game, I think, as a barometer," Davis said. "If you could beat Tennessee, you could play in the SEC and you had a chance to win the SEC (championship)."

• • •

Tennessee started the game as though it had something to prove—to its fans, to Alabama and, in many respects, to itself. On Alabama's first possession, Vols defensive lineman Derrick Weatherford recovered a Leslie Kelley fumble at the Crimson Tide 23-yard line. Four plays later, on a 6-yard pass from quarterback Dewey Warren to tight end Austin Denney and the extra-point kick by Gary Wright, Tennessee led 7-0 less than four minutes into the game.

Wright added a 30-yard field goal 10 minutes later, putting the Vols in front 10-0, a score that would hold the remainder of the first half. The game was going the Vols' way, though both teams had managed less than 100 yards of total offense. Alabama had lost a pair of fumbles, the second coming at the Tennessee 6 when Stabler, who was 0-for-6 passing in the first half, fumbled and the Vols recovered, ending a possible touchdown drive.

As the Alabama players headed to the visiting locker room at halftime, they did so believing their head coach would be offering an unflattering evaluation of their play, and he would make his point in a direct and loud manner.

"I just knew coach Bryant was going to throw a running fit," Hall said of an anticipated halftime verbal assault. "There was no way I was going to be sitting up front. But that's not what happened at all. Coach Bryant came in and he tells us, 'We've got 'em right where we want 'em.' I was never more shocked in my life. It caught me off-guard."

Fellow sophomore linebacker Bob Childs was surprised, too. "We had seen coach Bryant get angry before," Childs said. "We thought he was going to knock the crap out of whoever he could get his hands on. But he came in humming a tune. . . . We thought, what in the world is going on? . . . He said the first half was theirs and the second half was going to be ours."

Offensive lineman Jim Fuller, who would later spend 13 seasons as an assistant coach at his alma mater (1984-96), said Bryant entered the locker room right after him and he expected his head coach to start yelling at the players right away.

"We came in, and it had been raining, not a heavy rain but constant, just enough so that you're just sort of miserable," Fuller said. "I was thinking, what in the world is he going to do? I was scared. I don't know if everybody was, but I was. Coach Bryant said, 'Managers, get these guys some dry jerseys and if there's anybody who wants to change pants, get those, too.' He called everybody up and told us to listen up. He then told the managers to 'Get these guys some Cokes.' He never raised his voice.

"We were really expecting him to come down on us. I was expecting him to come down on me. But he didn't. He was always a step ahead of us. I think he had a feeling of how to handle us in that situation. And he was right, of course."

Did Fuller believe his coach when he said they had Tennessee right where they wanted it? Or did he simply believe it was a crafty halftime pep talk? "I believed what he said. I always believed what he said," Fuller said. "He instilled that in our minds. That's the way we thought. If he said it, we believed him."

Stabler believed his coach, too. "We kind of looked at each other, then he said, 'Let's go back out there and play.' And that's what we did. . . . Coach Bryant always told us to keep doing the things we were doing, just do them better, anytime we weren't playing too well. We went out and did what we had been doing, we just executed better."

The calm halftime talk wasn't the only halftime surprise Bryant had for his team.

"Coach Bryant started walking around the locker room," Hall recalled. "He was taking a fist with one hand and slapping it against his other, open hand and he started singing 'What a Friend We Have in Jesus.' He was doing this, walking around, and one of the referees came in and said, 'Five minutes to kickoff.' Coach Bryant just said, 'Let's go get 'em.'"

Keith Dunnavant, author of *The Missing Ring: How Bear Bryant and the 1966 Alabama Crimson Tide Were Denied College Football's Most Elusive Prize* and *Coach: The Life of Paul "Bear" Bryant*, said Bryant's halftime talk proved the coach's strength well beyond drawing up Xs and Os. "That demonstrated what a master of psychology Bryant was," he said. "He knew the players didn't need to be mashed at that point; they needed to be motivated. They needed to know he believed they could win."

Hall agrees with Dunnavant. "He was a master psychologist. The old saying is if you want to plow the field you've got to be smarter than the mule. Coach Bryant was way smarter than the mule. He was a master. I can't put my finger on it, but a lot of it was intimidation."

The players, probably still dazed at the calm, but confident demeanor of their head coach during halftime, followed his instruction. "I know we were excited to get out of that door and get back on that field," Fuller said.

Childs said he stepped onto the field for the second half without any doubt as to the final outcome; Alabama was going to win because coach Bryant said so. "He got kids to do something they didn't think they were capable of doing," Childs said. "His speech, it wasn't a Knute Rockne-type speech, but he said the exact right thing for the time. It was exactly what we needed to hear."

• • •

The third quarter was scoreless but it was obvious Alabama was now playing with an extra skip in its step, especially on offense. On the first play from scrimmage, Stabler completed a 5-yard pass to Ray Perkins, his first completion of the game. He later connected with Wayne Cook for a 21-yard pass play. The defense came through, too, with end Mike Ford recovering a Charles Fulton fumble at the Vols' 46 late in the period. Hall, with Bryant's words still ringing in his ears, had hit Fulton hard, jarring the football from his grip.

Stabler went right to work, hitting Dennis Homan on a big pass play that, along with a penalty, moved Alabama to the Vols' 15. A second-down pass to Cook netted another first down to the Tennessee 5 where the Tide faced a first-and-goal situation. Kelley slammed off left guard for four yards to the 1, and two plays later, Stabler scored Alabama's only touchdown of the game.

To demonstrate his mindset—the score came on the second play of the fourth quarter, leaving plenty of time to play, Alabama's offense guaranteed of getting the football at least a couple more times—Bryant decided to go for the two-point conversion. Stabler tossed a strike to Cook on the attempt, trimming Tennessee's lead to 10-8.

"Players always want to go for it," Stabler said of Bryant's decision to go for the two-point conversion instead of having Davis kick an extra point. "But that wasn't our call. Whatever coach Bryant wanted to do, that's what we were going to do. There wasn't any discussion at all; it was his call. Whatever decision he made, that's what we went with and that's what we always believed was the right thing to do."

In the second half, Stabler would connect on 7-of-9 pass attempts for 72 yards and rush for another 17 yards. His steady hand and even steadier demeanor was a key factor in the comeback. On the drive that would put Alabama in the lead, Stabler directed the offense from its own 25 to the Tennessee 1, converting on three third-down situations, using a balance of running and passing plays.

The drive almost ended in disaster when Kelley fumbled at the Tennessee 12 on a second-down play, but Perkins recovered and the Tide actually gained five yards, moving to the Vols' 7. A quarterback keeper by Stabler gained three yards and a first-and-goal at the Vols' 3, but three plays later, Alabama had gained just two yards to the 1. Facing fourth-and-1 with less than four minutes to play, Bryant sent Davis into the game to put Alabama in front.

The difference was, Bryant didn't send in Bobby Johns, who had been the holder for Davis's field goal tries all season to that point. Instead, Bryant instructed Stabler to be the holder.

"I had been holding for extra points and field goals. Steve Davis and I were a combo," Johns, who would earn All-America honors as a cornerback, said. "I remember I was standing behind coach Bryant and coach (Sam) Bailey and they were talking about whether they should let Stabler hold, because he had been dealing with a wet football all day. I was thinking, *just let Stabler hold it.*"

Bryant decided to do just that, another decision his players, looking back on it, realize is another moment where their coach was two steps ahead of them and most everyone else. "(Stabler) got a low snap, but he made a great hold and Steve made the field goal," Johns said.

"You just rely on your instincts," Davis said of facing such a moment. "It's like shooting a free throw to win the game, (the approach) is almost automatic because you've done it so many times. It's routine. I'd always look at the center's hand. As soon as the center's hand moved, I would start my motion. You look for keys, and that was my key."

Perhaps wanting to emphasize the importance of the field goal, offensive lineman Bruce Stephens of Thomasville had a chat with Davis before the kicker reached the spot of the field where he would attempt the kick. "When I went out there I already stood out because my uniform was fairly clean compared to the other players," Davis said. "Bruce Stephens stopped me and he said, 'If you miss this field goal, I'll kill you.' I told him, 'I can promise you, I want to make this more than you want me to make it.'

"It wasn't a pretty kick; I didn't really get it very well. But the main thing was it went through. I was a happy camper when it went through."

Bryant had made sure his team was ready for just such a moment, just such a play. "That Wednesday afternoon (prior to the game) in the bright sunshine, our offensive team went through a practice with a wet football because coach Bryant had read in the Farmer's Almanac that that weekend there was a strong chance of rain in East Tennessee and he wanted us to be prepared," Jimmy Carroll, Alabama's center, said. "We stayed (at a hotel) somewhere on the river. We got up Saturday morning, looked out the window and you could see the stadium. Clouds started rolling in and it was getting dark. By the time we got there and went out for warm-ups, about halfway through them, it started raining, and it continued to rain almost the whole game."

So when Davis ran onto the field to prepare for the field goal, Carroll was ready, too. He knew what he had to do. "The most important thing was to get the ball to Stabler," he said. "You had to put two hands on the football and then worry about your blocking duties. . . . I tried to get [the referees] to get me a dry football, but I couldn't get it done. The snap was a little low but Stabler did a great job of grabbing it and putting it down and Steve, of course, kicked it through. . . . I can, with great joy, say that we didn't have a fumbled snap that day."

• • •

There was still 3:23 remaining to play and Tennessee only needed a field goal to win. Starting at their own 27, the Vols moved quickly up the field. Warren connected with Bill Baker on a 22-yard pass play on the first play from scrimmage, followed by a halfback pass to Denney to move the Vols all the way down to the Alabama 13.

"I remember running across the field thinking, that guy's going to score," Johns said. "Johnny Mosely made a great play and stopped him and we held them a couple of plays later."

In Mobile, Elliot Maisel, then a teenager and now a Mobile businessman, was involved in his usual weekend activity: caddying for his father Herman at the former Highland Country Club. He always took along a transistor radio so he could keep up with how his favorite football team was faring. Without an earplug, he kept the volume as low as possible.

As the round of golf and the game in Knoxville continued, Maisel became more excited about the football game on the radio than the golf he was witnessing. In truth, everyone within proximity of Maisel and his radio started giving more attention to first downs than par putts. As the game moved to its conclusion, the golf matches were suddenly abandoned.

"I'd been going to [Alabama] games since I was about four," Maisel said. "I was probably 11 or 12 years old at the time and I listened on this battery-powered transistor radio, which I have kept all these years, probably because of its history. . . . I always caddied for my dad on weekends and it was a weekly game for him and the others, probably seven or eight foursomes.

"It was just a little nine-hole course and there were a lot of intersections where you crossed each other. You could see other groups on other holes and tee boxes and what they were doing. If you were on the [number] three tee, you were close enough to see what was happening on the [number] seven green and the [number] two green. People knew I was listening to the game and it seemed like every minute someone was asking me, 'What's the score?'"

As the final moments were ticking away in Knoxville, the golfers in Mobile became more deeply involved. "We ended up sitting under this oak tree for probably 30 or 40 minutes, listening to the end of the game, everybody huddled around the radio," Maisel said. "They just forgot all about the golf game, and it was usually a serious game. There were all these grown men gathered around and they were running around, cheering.

"That's when it crystallized to me what Alabama football meant to a lot of people. Half of those guys were World War II veterans, but they were involved in this game. Remembering that day, it stills stands out to me today."

• • •

Just as Alabama had done a few minutes earlier, Tennessee got close, reaching the Alabama 2, but couldn't punch in a touchdown. With only a few seconds remaining to be played, Vols head coach Doug Dickey called on place-kicker Wright, who had nailed a 30-yarder earlier in the game, to win the game with a 20-yard field goal.

With all the back-and-forth of the game, the pep talk, the comebacks, the rain and mud, the outcome of the game came down to a single play, with a twist. Wright, an Alabama native who chose to walk on at Tennessee rather than seek to play at Alabama, would attempt a field goal to win or lose the game.

The snap and placement were good and the kick was well struck, but it had a right-sided bend. It slipped just right of the uprights, leaving Alabama with an 11-10 win and Wright with a nickname he heard often the rest of that season and from time to time since that day: Wide Wright.

"I remember watching it," Davis said. "Dude Hennessey was the coach [in charge of scouting Tennessee] for that game and I remember when they got ready to kick the field goal, he turned his head and refused to watch. He couldn't watch it. I watched the ball. I watch where the ball lands. Usually, that's a good way to tell if the kick is good or not. I saw where it landed and I thought he had made it, but the referee signaled it was no good. I was surprised. It couldn't have missed by much. It had to be close."

Davis could empathize with the heartbreak Wright was feeling. "Kicking can be tough," he said. "If you make a kick like that, you're the hero; if you miss it, you're the goat. It's that simple."

• • •

Some have suggested over the years that Wright simply pushed his kick to the right. Others have said the unsung hero on that rainy, muddy but happy day for Alabama was Donny Johnston. Called on to rush the field goal try, Johnston came close to blocking the kick, but arrived a fraction of a second too late. Or did he? It has been said that Johnston's charge forced Wright to hurry his kick or at least it altered the direction of the kick.

Bryant would later tell reporters that if the kick hadn't been off-target "Donnie would have blocked it," and that either way, Alabama wins the game.

"He was kind of a utility guy on the team," Dunnavant said in describing Johnston. "He was known as one of the quickest guys on the team. Bryant sent him in to try and block the kick. On his way out, Ray Perkins stopped him and told him, 'You block this and you'll get my tickets for the next game.' That meant something, because guys would sell their tickets for spending money. He didn't block it, but he was a guy who almost became really famous."

Johnston has learned to live without the fame. "Coach Bryant put his hand on my shoulder and he said, 'You know what to do,'" Johnston said of the words of his coach just before he sent him into the game. "I had been practicing blocking kicks by diving into a sawdust pit at practice. I practiced it all the time.

"I lined up next to Bobby Johns and I went off his movement. I remember looking right down at [Wright's] foot. The ball went right by my fingertips. If he had kicked it straight, I would have got it. I know I would have got it. I dove and landed on my left hip and I got a hip-pointer. It hurt like crazy. In the locker room after the game, reporters were interviewing coach Bryant in the taping room, so I couldn't go in there. The managers just put me on equipment trunks to take care of me."

Johns remembers the play clearly, too. "I had never seen it done before," he recalled, "but he looked right inside at the ball. He took his cleats and he drew a line in the mud to get a line on the ball and he got in a four-point stance real early. Then he just charged in there. I thought he was going to block it."

Bryant's confidence in Johnston gave him confidence in himself, he said. "He could get you to do things you didn't think you could do," Johnston said. "He'd be in the locker room and it was always noisy and loud, but when coach Bryant said 'Listen up,' you could hear a pin drop."

As was proven that afternoon in Knoxville, even when he spoke calmly, Bryant's message was received by his players.

Following the game, Bryant was quick to give his players the credit for the win. "Needless to say, I've never been prouder of a team," he said. "They certainly proved to me they have class. It takes a lot to come back, come back, come back and then keep coming back. They were well-prepared and I guess it was a great game. It looked like it."

CHAPTER TWO
1967 Auburn

Alabama 7, Auburn 3
December 2, 1967
Legion Field
Birmingham, Alabama

Every time Ken Stabler looked out the window, the view was the same: it was raining, usually a hard rain, and it didn't appear it was going to stop any time soon. The view was the same across the state. Iron Bowl fans, glancing out the windows of their homes or cars, saw the same thing all day—rain, rain, and more rain.

No matter what role those heading to Birmingham's Legion Field that wet, chilly December day would have—player, coach, fan, reporter—one thing was absolutely certain: it wasn't going to be pretty.

Then again, beauty is in the eye of the beholder. As they headed back to their respective homes following the game, soaked, cold, and generally uncomfortable, Alabama fans found it easy to smile. They had witnessed a 47-yard run by Stabler, actually sloshing more than running, that would never leave their memory banks.

It is a memory still so fresh today that some fans, witnessing it between the raindrops and thousands of umbrellas in use, can describe it as though watching it live. The mud and Auburn's defense wouldn't be able to keep Stabler out of the end zone, nor Alabama from winning a game that would play out as Crimson Tide head coach Paul "Bear" Bryant had predicted.

• • •

This most certainly was not a "beautiful day for football." Constant rain and wind, even tornado warnings, should have kept many ticker-holders at home. These days, the game might have been postponed and its start delayed. That wasn't the case in 1967. It was a miserable, nasty day, but it was a scheduled game, and the game, like "the show" in Hollywood, must go on.

The teams went through their usual routines, though doing so in unusual circumstances. There was no question as to what kind of conditions would have to be weathered. Yet even in pregame warm-ups what the game meant to fans of both teams was abundantly clear.

Despite the terrible conditions, the fans arrived as they always did for the rivalry. They huddled together as though they had collectively and unexpectedly been caught out in the rain. For most, the weather didn't lead them to change their wardrobe plans. Men wore suits and ties and women were adorned in dresses, as was the attire of the day when attending games, especially *that* game. The only change was the addition of raincoats and ponchos and any other clothing worn over the suits and dresses that might provide a bit of protection from the elements. For the most part that particular day, the effort was futile.

On the field, both teams continued to push themselves and the opponent despite the conditions. Ball control and field position were the rule of the day and one mistake opened the door of opportunity, which Stabler, later named to the school's All-Century team, ran through—or more accurately, sloshed through—for the game-winning play. It is a play that remains one of the most famous in Alabama's long football history, now known simply as the "Run in the Mud" as artist Daniel Moore would title his painting depicting the play.

It was a game in which former *Huntsville Times* sports editor John Pruett, a member of the Alabama Sports Writers Association's Hall of Fame, would take a walk in the mud. "From a weather standpoint, it was the worst game I can ever remember covering," he said. "Several of us from the paper drove down from Huntsville to Birmingham that morning. It started raining around Cullman and seldom let up the rest of the day. It was pouring by the time we got to Legion Field."

• • •

Bryant preached to his players the importance of field position and was ready to take whatever means necessary to make that a priority throughout the game. He also told his players that in conditions such as the ones they were about to face, as few as three or four plays would likely dictate the outcome, telling his players to be ready for those plays. Bryant also mentioned something that Stabler, Mike Hall, Dennis Homan and most of the other players clearly remember—he said that Auburn would make a mistake in its kicking game, and when it did the team needed to take advantage of that mistake.

When the Crimson Tide players headed out to the field to begin the game, they saw the stands completely filled, with more umbrellas in one place than perhaps anywhere else in the world. Stabler wasn't surprised.

"It's the Iron Bowl," he said with a tone that suggested it was the only explanation required. "It's Alabama versus Auburn. Half the place [Legion Field] was filled with Alabama fans and half the place was filled with Auburn fans. I wasn't shocked the place was a sellout. In the old Iron Bowl days, and today too, you expected it. And not a soul left [early]. It was really nasty weather and not a soul left."

Auburn owned the first half, yet even though the Tigers had three scoring opportunities, they failed to collect any points. Alabama had four possessions in the first period, punting on third down on each of the possessions as Bryant sought to avoid making a mistake such as fumbling the football or throwing an interception deep in his team's territory, where it spent all of the first half, failing to gain a first down and never pushing the ball to Auburn's side of the 50-yard line.

Alabama started its four first-quarter possessions on its own 1, 21, 6 and 2. After booming 57- and 50-yard punts in his first two tries, punter Steve Davis's 29-yard punt from the Alabama 12 on a third down-and-4 kick gave Auburn its first possession in Alabama territory at the Crimson Tide 41. The Tigers moved toward the end zone, producing a first down-and-goal at the Alabama 5, but an incomplete pass and a pair of 1-yard gains left them with a fourth-and-goal at the Alabama 3. Auburn chose to go for the score, but halfback Richard Plagge gained just a yard, giving Alabama the ball at its own 2.

Three plays later, Alabama punted the ball back to the Tigers, who started their possession at the Alabama 40. This time Auburn got to the 13, but a sack cost it nine yards and the Tigers eventually faced fourth-and-15 from the 18. Kicker John Riley's 35-yard field goal try sailed wide right. Late in the half, Auburn was knocking on the door again with a first-and-10 from the Alabama 15. Three plays later the Tigers faced a fourth-and-2 at the 7 and chose again to go for the touchdown. Once again, Alabama's defense denied the Tigers, Mike Hall making the stop on Allen Giffin after a one-yard gain.

"Coach Bryant had pretty much psyched Auburn out the week before because he told the media he didn't think Auburn could score a touchdown against us," Hall said. "It worked. They got inside our 10- yard line four times and all they got was a field goal."

Alabama had managed just 36 yards of total offense in the first half, while Auburn, despite its three scoring chances, had managed 130 yards but no points. Field conditions, awful at the start of the game, worsened as the game continued. At halftime, Bryant made an adjustment, not to the game plan, but with the equipment.

Defensive back Bobby Johns said, "It was one of those games, because of the weather and the field, that as a defensive back you were always worried about slipping down or letting your man get behind you and scoring. I was worried about that a lot."

In order to help with that, Bryant told the team's managers to take off the cleats that were being used and replace them with longer cleats, giving his players a better chance of keeping their balance. Bryant also had his players put on clean jerseys. "It took a pair of pliers to get those cleats off and put the others on," said Finus Gaston, Alabama's senior associate athletics director and chief financial officer, who was then a junior at Tuscaloosa High School and would later become the team's head manager. "And it took us until three or four o'clock in the morning to wash all the equipment off so they wouldn't ruin."

Based on Alabama's improved performance in the second half, the strategy was successful, or at least offered enough help to allow Alabama to make enough plays to win the game, though the start of the second half favored Auburn. The Crimson Tide opened the third period on offense but ran three plays and punted. Auburn, starting at Alabama's 40 after a 16-yard Davis punt, advanced the ball 19 yards to the 21, where Riley connected on a 38-yard field goal to give the Tigers a 3-0 lead.

Another third-down punt and a fumble after a completed pass on its next two offensive possessions seemed to suggest this would not be Alabama's day. Following the fumble recovery at the Alabama 23, Riley returned to attempt another field goal on fourth-and-8, but a miscue on the play thwarted the opportunity and Alabama took possession. After both teams punted, Alabama had the ball again but turned it over to the Tigers when a Stabler pass was intercepted, setting up Auburn at the Alabama 41. One play later, the third period ended. Alabama had 15 minutes left to win the game.

It was on that Auburn series that Bryant's prediction came true. Auburn advanced to the Alabama 24 but two plays later faced fourth-and-14 at the Tide 31. Auburn set up to punt. The snap to punter Tommy Lunceford was low and slipped through his fingers, finally coming to rest at the Alabama 46 where Alabama took over possession.

"I was 30 feet from [Lunceford] on the sidelines," Davis said of his Auburn counterpart. " . . . The ball, when you're punting in that kind of weather, a lot of things can go wrong."

Stabler smiled. Not only because his team had the ball in its best field position of the day, but because he kept hearing the words of his head coach. "The first thing I thought, when they made that mistake, was *coach Bryant was right,*" Stabler said. "He said they would make a mistake in the kicking game and we had to be ready. It was happening exactly like he said it would. We had the field position that coach Bryant, with the third-down punts, was playing for all day."

Three plays later, Stabler would slosh his way into Alabama football lore. A 5-yard gain followed by a 2-yard gain moved Alabama to the Auburn 47. Facing a third-and-3 situation, the call was for an option play around right end with Stabler either pitching to the trailing back or keeping himself. The Crimson Tide was looking to get the first down, to get some offensive momentum. It got a whole lot more. Stabler considered pitching, but spotted an opening and tucked the ball under his arm, slipping defenders and reaching the right sideline.

"Man in motion right. Here's Stabler keeping himself," Alabama radio play-by-play announcer John Forney told his audience. *"Stabler now cuts in . . . He's at the 40 yard line, he's at the 30, he's at the 20, he's at the 10, he's at the 5. He scores! Kenny Stabler takes it in! . . . A fantastic run by Ken 'Snake' Stabler on the option play."*

The touchdown was a credit to Stabler's athleticism, as well as key blocks produced by Dennis Dixon, Dennis Homan, and others up front.

"As an offensive player, you always think you can make a play, but we believed in coach Bryant," Stabler said. "If he had said we needed to punt on first down that's what we would have done. So we played conservative. We knew our defense—it was a great defense—would hold Auburn. We played a real estate game. It was what coach Bryant said to do."

Auburn's Yearout didn't see Stabler's run as a thing of beauty amidst the mess; he saw it as the result of a penalty. He claimed, and others on Auburn's team offered their vocal support, that Dixon had held him on the play, allowing Stabler to escape his grasp and work his way to the end zone. But the referees didn't see the hold and the play stood. On the Alabama sidelines, hearing the complaints of Auburn players, Homan, whose solid block at first opened a path for Stabler, asked Dixon if he held Yearout.

"I couldn't have stopped him any other way," Homan said Dixon replied. It would be several years before Dixon would repeat that statement to anyone other than a teammate. By then, as was true that afternoon, all that mattered to Alabama players, coaches, and fans was that officially, it was a touchdown.

"We used to kid [Dixon] about it all the time," Davis said. "We'd say to him, 'Show us your blocking technique.'"

Homan was happy with his technique on the famous play. "I've kidded Snake about that play for years," Homan said. "One time, in talking with Daniel Moore, the artist who did the *Run in the Mud* painting of that play, I said to him, 'Daniel, you got it all wrong; it should have been called the 'Block in the Mud.' Snake told me it was the only block I threw all year, but it was a good one. I love that play. Coach Bryant, on his [TV highlight] show the next day, kept talking about that play and he said he could watch it all day. I could too.

"My assignment was to make a block. I could tell they didn't see me at all. Anybody could have made that block. I landed on my back, but I could see Kenny going down the sidelines. I was laying in mud, but it wouldn't have mattered if it was quicksand, having it finish the way it did. That was just a great feeling."

Standing on the sidelines, center Billy Johnson, who shared time all day with Terry Kilgore, watched as the play unfolded. "I came out [of the game] the play before Stabler scored. I was on the sidelines watching and when he took off, all I could do was watch and pray. Terry had a good block on the play. . . . When I was in there, I wasn't worried about blocking as much as I was worried about getting the ball back to Stabler, so that's all you thought about all day. I thought, *just get him the ball then try to get in somebody's way for a little while*. But I was thinking I had to get the ball to Snake first. That's what mattered most."

• • •

Alabama had the lead, but the game was far from over. There would be a combined eight more offensive possessions before the final second ticked off the Legion Field scoreboard clock. Alabama's defense would have to continue its strong play. It would be ready for the challenge.

The Tigers would punt on its next two possessions, but Alabama's offense fared no better and each time had to return the favor. Late in the game, after a 31-yard Davis punt sailed into the end zone for a touchback to the Auburn 20, a pass by quarterback Loran Carter was intercepted by Alabama's Bob Childs. Taking over at the Tigers' 36, Alabama could only gain eight yards. Instead of risking a mistake on a field goal try in the wet conditions, Bryant sent Davis out to punt again—his 13th punt of the day. He delivered a 28-yarder into the end zone for another touchback. Once again, Carter hoped to pass Auburn from deep in its own territory toward a game-winning touchdown. On the first play he connected on a 31-yard pass play. He tried another deep pass, but again, Childs intercepted, giving Alabama the ball with little time left to play. The Crimson Tide ran five plays and faced a fourth-and-4 situation at the Auburn 41. Davis set up to punt, but instead Stabler carried the ball for 14 yards and a first down, erasing the game's final seconds in the process.

"That was a great game," Childs said. "Coach [Ken] Donahue [defensive coordinator] put in something special for that game that allowed a gap for me to run through. I must have called that stunt 50 times. Nobody ever touched me on that set up. I called it a few times on that first series and I heard somebody [on Auburn's team] say, 'Here comes that S.O.B. Childs.'"

When Alabama had secured the victory, a few of Hall's friends found their way to the field to congratulate him. "They were wearing their coats and ties and they wanted to celebrate," Hall said. "I told them, 'Don't jump on me, I'm nasty.' They said they didn't care. . . . I picked mud out of my ears and nose for two weeks after that game. It was just awful."

And as the celebration continued, Hall recalled Bryant's words, not just the ones predicting an Auburn kicking game mistake, but his words from days before when he told reporters he didn't believe Auburn's offense could score a touchdown against his defense. As it turned out, Bryant was right about that, too.

"He didn't say that to us," Hall said. "He said it for [Auburn]. But it didn't matter if he said it or not. When the other team gets inside your 10-yard line, one, they shouldn't be there in the first place, but two, when they get there you need to tighten up your chinstrap and keep them out of the end zone. We tightened up our chinstraps."

In the end, Alabama's offense, with just four first downs and 176 total yards, scored enough points to win the game, while its defense, which allowed Auburn 216 total yards, refused to surrender the important yards. Alabama, which punted on third down six times, including its first four possessions in its field position-first approach, cashed in on an Auburn mistake.

As a reward, Alabama's players tuned into coach Bryant's show the next day, as Alabama fans all across the state did on a regular basis, and listened to their coach talk about the victory, especially Stabler's "run in the mud" that accounted for the game-winning play.

"Here comes the big one," Bryant said before the highlight film showed Stabler's dance down the right sideline. *"Fourth quarter, Stabler . . . watch Dennis Homan here, makes the block. There's a big block by Dennis Dixon. (David) Chatwood makes a big block. Stabler turns it on. . . . Kilgore's down there with him. Actually, it's down the sidelines*

and I can't see it. . . . A great play, a great run by Kenny Stabler who puts it in there. We go out front 6-3."

A replay of the run then appears on the screen and Bryant is only too happy to describe the action again. *"Here it comes again. Stabler, there he goes again. Here's the block by Homan. There was a block by Mike Hall back there, too. . . . and Stabler turns it on. I could watch that all night."*

CHAPTER THREE
1969 Ole Miss

Alabama 33, Ole Miss 32
October 4, 1969
Legion Field
Birmingham, Alabama

When then-15-year-old David Cutcliffe made his way to Legion Field to watch his favorite team, the No. 15 Alabama Crimson Tide, play SEC rival and No. 20 Ole Miss in early October of 1969, he knew the game would be special.

And why not? The Alabama-Ole Miss rivalry was one of the best in college football, Ole Miss quarterback Archie Manning was developing into an All-America player, Paul "Bear" Bryant was one of the country's best college coaches, and Legion Field at the time was known as "The Football Capital of the South."

In fact, the game took on historic meaning before the kickoff. It was the first-ever college football game played at night to be televised nationally. Alabama and Ole Miss introduced prime time college football.

What Cutcliffe didn't know was just how historic the game would be. He, like the other more than 62,000 fans who filed into Legion Field, knew to expect an offensive showcase, but they couldn't have imagined the offensive show that would take place, especially when the first half of play offered little indication of what was ahead.

The matchups were terrific: Manning vs. Scott Hunter, Bryant vs. Ole Miss head coach Johnny Vaught (a combined 360 wins going into the game), receivers George Ranager of Alabama (who grew up in Mississippi) vs. Floyd Franks of Ole Miss, SEC records vs. NCAA records.

The combination of talent and TV cameras, tradition and Deep South football combined to produce an outstanding football game, one that wasn't decided until the final moments. These teams were ready for the prime-time spotlight.

"Being there in Legion Field for that game, it was bigger than life to me," Cutcliffe said. "I had been a big fan of [former Alabama All-America quarterback Joe] Namath and watching good quarterback play. Being there for that game was special to me."

Cutcliffe said he didn't mind that his seats were several rows up; it provided a good view of what was taking place on the field and he could see everything that took place on each play: blocking assignments, receivers' routes, quarterback movements and defensive adjustments. What he saw was offenses and quarterbacks playing at optimum speed and efficiency.

Cutcliffe—who would later serve as a student assistant under Bryant in the early- to mid-1970s; serve as head coach at Ole Miss and Duke; and coach Manning's sons Peyton (as offensive coordinator at Tennessee) and Eli (as head coach at Ole Miss)—loved the view.

"It was amazing," he said. "I remember coach Bryant pacing the sidelines and coach Vaught, such a classy guy, working too. I was at the game with Bobby Johns [former Alabama All-America cornerback, then a coach at Birmingham's Banks High School, which Cutcliffe attended and where he would later coach]. It was a special time."

• • •

The game, despite its wide TV-viewing appeal, started later than was originally scheduled. It was an 8:30 PM start, pushed back because of a bandleader and his clout. "Lawrence Welk had the most popular show on TV at that time and he was live on Saturday night and he had a nonpreemptive clause in his contract, which meant the game couldn't start until after his show," Hunter recalled.

Former Jackson, Miss. *Clarion-Ledger* sports editor, the late Wayne Thompson, had to wrestle with tight deadlines during a time when copy was produced on portable typewriters and getting the stories back to newspaper offices was a slow and tedious process, addressed the issue. "So if you want to know who's running this country," he wrote, "it's a bunch of little old ladies who like to watch Lawrence Welk."

"A-one, an a two . . . "

The game started quickly, with both teams scoring on its first possession, but in the final quarter, it seemed the teams scored every two minutes.

Ken Haines, then stationed at Fort Rucker but with a couple of days of R&R, found himself at Legion Field that night, but his incentive for attending the game differed from most who were on hand. Army buddy Ed Crick, who was also stationed at Fort Rucker, was able to obtain two tickets to the game. Crick's mother lived in Huntsville and had a connection in the Alabama athletic department. The men made their way to the game in search of postgame activities.

"We were both single and we thought that would be a great occasion to meet some college girls," Haines, now president and CEO of Raycom Sports in Charlotte, N.C., said. "We thought our best chance of getting invited to a party and meeting some girls would be to be on the winning team's side [of the stadium] at the end of the game. They would be the ones who felt like partying."

It was a logical plan, but one made more difficult to execute because of the play of Hunter and Manning and the constant lead changes, four in the final period alone.

"We didn't care who won, we just wanted to be on the right side of the stadium when the game ended," Haines said. "That last quarter, we kept going back and forth, from side to side. Not only did we end up on Ole Miss' side of the stadium at the end of the game, but we were so tired from constantly moving we didn't want to do anything after the game but sleep."

While moving from one side of the stadium to the other, Haines and Crick watched what was happening on the field. "That was probably one of the greatest college football games ever played," Haines said. "It was an offensive show that just lit up the scoreboard. . . . We would barely have found a place to sit when the other team scored and we moved again. I told Ed that the only people who may have covered more ground than Manning and Hunter was me and him. It was like we were back in boot camp."

Alabama's Donny Johnston kept the same seat throughout the game, probably because he was seated with royalty—Coach Bryant's wife, Mary Harmon. Based on his seat assignment he was afraid to move. A member of the Crimson Tide team, Johnston had a shoulder injury and wasn't able to play. Prior to the game, coach Sam Bailey gave Johnston a ticket so he could sit in the stands and watch the game. He glanced at the seat location marked on the ticket and as he found his seat he immediately noticed with whom he would be sharing time.

"Here I am, sitting with coach Bryant's wife at a football game and I was nervous, but was also watching every play. It was such a great football game. It was a game for the history books. I think if they were still playing today it would still be a one-point game, it was that good and that close. We were sitting there, and when it ended, I said [to Mrs. Bryant] that they'd be talking about that game for years to come."

• • •

These days, on any given Saturday, a college football fan can watch games from midmorning to, in some cases, well past midnight. That wasn't the case in 1969. On this particular October it wouldn't have mattered if other games were being televised. The action, drama, and talent exhibited in the rivalry, with Hunter and Manning leading the way, held the attention of the audience. From start to finish, the teams wrestled for control of the game.

Alabama took the opening kickoff and marched 76 yards in 15 plays for a touchdown, Johnny Musso getting the score on a 1-yard run. Ole Miss countered on the ensuing possession, driving 74 yards in 10 plays with Manning scoring on a 2-yard run for a 7-7 score. Ole Miss was on the move again on its next possession, but Riley Myers fumbled after catching a pass from Manning and being hit by Danny Gilbert at the Alabama 4-yard line. Paul Boschung recovered for the Crimson Tide, ending the threat.

Alabama then drove 96 yards in just seven plays—the key play being a 67-yard run by Ranager on a pitchout to the Rebels' 18. It was a play on which Ranager outran 10 members of the Rebels' defense, but couldn't distance himself from the last one making chase, safety Glenn Cannon.

"Cannon ran him down," Hunter said of the play. "I kidded him about it later and George said, 'I remember I never outran him in [high school] track meets, either.'"

Following Ranager's run and a 1-yard gain, Bubba Sawyer, on his only carry of the night, covered the remaining 17 yards for the touchdown. The Ole Miss offense took over again and pushed its way to the Alabama 9, but time ran out in the half.

The first half would simply be an appetizer for what was to come. And yet, Manning had already rushed for 57 yards and a touchdown and completed 17-of-22 passes for 154 yards. Hunter was more accurate in the first two periods, connecting on 9-of-10 throws for 90 yards.

Just when fans had caught their breath, the teams returned for the second half and picked up where they left off. Manning and the Rebels drove 65 yards in 11 plays for a touchdown, Manning hitting Franks with an 11-yard scoring pass to tie the game at 14-all. After the teams swapped punts, Alabama was back in form, Musso again scoring from a yard out. Manning was intercepted on the Rebels' next possession, but Alabama was forced to punt, setting up another Ole Miss scoring drive. This one covered 80 yards in a mere four plays. The second play was a 46-yard pass from Manning to tight end Jim Poole, followed by a 12-yard pass to Franks to the Alabama 17. Manning dropped back to pass again, couldn't find a receiver, and scrambled 17 yards for the touchdown, but the extra-point kick failed, a simple play that would prove to be a deciding factor.

Alabama punted to Ole Miss on the final play of the third period and set up one of the most exciting fourth quarters in SEC history. Trailing by a point, Ole Miss moved 86 yards in eight plays, the score coming on a 2-yard pass by Manning to Myers. A two-point conversion pass failed, leaving the Rebels in front 26-21. Alabama countered, covering 67 yards in 10 plays, Hunter getting the score on a 1-yard quarterback sneak. Alabama went for two, but was unable to successfully complete the play.

The third lead change of the quarter came on the next possession, Ole Miss requiring just three plays to go from its own 37-yard line to the end zone, Manning scoring on a quarterback sneak. Again the Rebels tried a two-point conversion and again they failed, taking a 32-27 lead. Alabama matched the score, going 80 yards in 11 plays. Using plays covering 9, 16, 15 and 13 yards, the Tide steadily moved down the field, but a sack cost it eight yards. Hunter bounced back with a 21-yard pass play to David Bailey to the Ole Miss 14, but the next three plays netted no forward progress, leaving the Tide facing a fourth down-and-10 situation.

Hunter took all 14 yards instead, throwing a pass to Ranager, who scored with 3:39 to play. "I remember Scott went over to the sidelines [during a time-out before the fourth-down play] and I went over too, and I think it was Jimmy Sharpe and Scott and coach Bryant. I remember coach Bryant saying, 'Just run the best play you've got,'" Ranager said.

Once again, a two-point play was attempted and once again it was fruitless, leaving Alabama in front 33-32. Beginning at its own 46, Ole Miss couldn't get anything going and was forced to punt, but the Rebels' defense stepped up and held the Crimson Tide, which was forced to punt the ball back to Ole Miss. But Ranager, who finished with four carries for 74 yards and three receptions for 68 yards and a touchdown, used his speed and sprinted downfield on punt coverage, downing the ball at the Rebels' 5.

With 1:48 to play, Manning and his team took its final shot at winning the game. Facing a fourth-and-12 play early in the drive, Manning hit Myers with a 15-yard pass for the first down. On another pass play, Alabama was called for a facemask penalty and the Rebels found themselves at their own 34. Yet another pass moved Ole Miss to the Alabama 49, but there was only eight seconds left to play. Manning threw to Franks, who picked up seven yards, but time expired, leaving Alabama as the winner.

"Every time I looked up in the third or fourth quarter, we were behind," Hunter said. "Every time we got the ball back, we knew we had to do something. We pretty much had the number of their defense, but Archie kept scoring points, too. I was just worried we weren't going to have the ball at the end. I thought the team that had the ball last was the team that was going to win. We didn't have the ball last, but we ended up winning. Archie put them in a position to win, it just didn't happen."

When it was all over, when all the points and yardage had been compiled and the game decided, the two quarterbacks met on the field, congratulating each other for a game well-played, but nothing was said.

"I watched him play some in the second half, but we were trying to figure out what we were going to do when we got the ball back most of the time," Hunter said. "Afterward, we shook hands. He had tears in his eyes. What could you say? Here's a guy who just played the greatest game any college football player ever had and his team had lost by a point. You didn't have to say anything."

Hunter, who had other big passing nights in his Alabama career, said the Crimson Tide defense wasn't to blame for Ole Miss collecting lots of yards and scores. Instead of his team's defense being criticized, he felt Manning should have been credited.

"I don't know if you could have put Lee Roy Jordan or the 1966 [Alabama] defense out there and shut Archie Manning down that night," he said. "No Alabama defense of any era would have slowed Archie down that night. It was just a matter of could we outscore them."

• • •

Even today, Ranager is asked about that 1969 game. It's a recurring story he enjoys retelling, again and again. A Mississippi kid—he was recruited heavily by Ole Miss and, in a state high school all-star game, caught three touchdown passes thrown by Manning—the game had special meaning for him.

"The game meant a lot to everybody because it was a rivalry, but it really meant a lot to me," Ranager said. "It was a real tough game. It was really, really intense and one of the hardest-hitting games I ever played in. Archie had a great game and so did Scott. . . . A few days after the game, people would say, 'Hey, I saw you on TV; that was a great game.'"

Not everyone who watched the game came away believing they had seen something special, though. "I always thought this was the most exciting game

I ever covered," former *Huntsville Times* sports editor John Pruett said. "A 33-32 game, Archie Manning vs. Scott Hunter, a nationally televised game delayed until an 8 PM kickoff because of the popularity of the *Lawrence Welk Show*. I remember telling coach Bryant a few years later, 'I think the 1969 Ole Miss game is the most exciting football game I have ever covered.' He stared at me and said, 'That's the *worst* football game I ever saw.' He thought it was disgraceful that an opposing player could account for 500-something yards in total offense and that his defense would allow 32 points."

• • •

It's impossible to ignore the numbers produced on that October night. As much as any other game played by either team, it is a game that *begs* that the statistics be quoted. Even by today's standards—games that feature spread offenses, five-receiver sets and athletes who are stronger, bigger, and faster—the yardage compiled by both teams stands up to comparisons.

The teams combined for 1,099 total yards (609 for Ole Miss, 490 for Alabama), 736 passing yards and 363 rushing yards. The teams even had 180 yards in kickoff, punt, and interception returns. The teams ran a whopping 80 offensive plays each and combined for 53 first downs.

Hunter and Manning threw passes to seven different receivers. Alabama's David Bailey had nine catches for 115 yards but no scores, while Ranager caught three passes for 68 yards and a score. For Ole Miss, Franks caught 13 passes for 191 yards and a touchdown, while wingback Vernon Studdard caught four passes for 122 yards. Alabama had seven players carry the football at least once.

The *other* numbers are just as impressive. Throwing a combined 81 passes, there was only one interception, which came in the first period. The referees called only seven penalties for a total of 73 yards, and although there were four fumbles, only one resulted in a turnover. Ole Miss punted only twice.

• • •

The reviews from a 15-year-old future college student assistant and head coach were much better. Based on his connections with the schools and particularly the Manning family, the game is recalled with great fondness.

"We've talked about it," Cutcliffe said of more than one discussion about the game with Manning. "It brought a smile to his face, even though they lost. It was just a classic football game. We talked about it and Peyton talked about watching film of it, and Eli too. . . . I am blessed. My association with the Mannings has been a blessing, not just from a football standpoint, but the Mannings as a family, too. I sure feel lucky.

"And I was lucky to be there that night. It was a great, great football game."

Apparently, if the guesswork by Hunter and Manning is accurate, another estimated 250,000 felt the same way.

CHAPTER FOUR

1971 USC

Alabama 17, USC 10
September 10, 1971
Los Angeles Coliseum
Los Angeles, California

The ability to keep a secret, of knowing when to share information and with whom, would play a key role in Alabama's visit to Los Angeles to play Southern Cal in 1971. It would be a pivotal game in Paul "Bear" Bryant's coaching career, a game that proved he could make changes and use those changes to the benefit of his team.

It was also a year in which he proved he could keep a secret and make sure everyone around him did so as well.

Opening the season against USC held great importance. Not just because of the significance of such a nonconference matchup. The previous season, the Trojans had traveled to Birmingham's Legion Field and convincingly whipped the Crimson Tide 42-24 on the strength of a powerful running attack, led by Sam "Bam" Cunningham, who scored USC's first two touchdowns and rushed for 135 yards.

The score indicates the game was closer than how it actually played out. The Trojans' offense produced a whopping 559 total yards, including 485 rushing yards. The USC defense was doing its part, too, allowing Alabama just 264 total yards, all but 32 of it gained with the passing game. The Crimson Tide threw 36 passes against Southern Cal. While it was productive in terms of yards, it didn't have the punch the Trojans' ground game carried.

"I was redshirted that year and watching that game was awful," John Croyle, whose first college football game would be the 1971 USC game in LA, said. "Southern Cal just completely dismantled us."

The loss left Alabama bruised and hurting, more in terms of ego than in black-and-blue marks. Southern Cal entered that game ranked No. 3 in the country, with Alabama ranked No. 12. When the Trojans finished with the Crimson Tide, Alabama fell out of the national polls and the Trojans remained among the nation's top-ranked teams. The loss, which came in the season-opener, sent Alabama's confidence into a tailspin. It would not win more than two games in a row all year and its final three games produced a win (Miami), loss (Auburn) and tie (Oklahoma in the Bluebonnet Bowl), the Crimson Tide finishing the year 6-5-1. Alabama had posted a 6-5 record in 1969 that included a 23-point loss to Auburn, a 27-point loss to Tennessee and a four-point loss to Vanderbilt.

Bryant knew it was time for a change. Some Alabama fans were whispering about the need for a change too.

"People in those days were grumbling, if you can believe it, that it might be time for Coach Bryant to go," Elliot Maisel, a longtime Alabama fan and supporter who attended the game at the Coliseum in 1971, said of preseason chatter. "Of course, we win that game and all of a sudden, coach Bryant is a genius again."

The win, which would be against a talented and No. 5-ranked USC team—Alabama started the season ranked No. 16 despite its disappointing records the previous two seasons, moving to No. 9 the following week— would jump-start the Crimson Tide to 11 straight wins.

The success started with being able to keep a secret.

• • •

In some moves that might have made the CIA envious, Bryant placed a call to then-Texas head coach Darrell Royal, whose team was running the wishbone offense, in the summer of 1971. He asked Royal if he would have a couple of days to talk. Royal said he would make time for his longtime friend, for him to just stop by his office. Bryant said he didn't want to visit him in his office, but preferred a place where the two men could talk privately and where they wouldn't be seen together.

As for the reason for the visit, Bryant told Royal he wanted some lessons on how to run the wishbone. Upon Bryant's arrival, the men, armed with game films and a projector, met at Royal's house and the lessons began. Three years earlier, recognizing his team's personnel was built for a run-oriented offense, not a passing attack, Royal charged offensive coordinator Emory Bellard, who would later serve as head coach at Mississippi State, with devising an offense that took advantage of its personnel. Bellard came up with the wishbone, a triple option offense.

The new offense had helped win a national championship for the Longhorns, who had finished no worse than No. 3 in the previous three season-ending national polls. After the visit with Royal in Austin, Bryant had another request of his friend. He wanted him to come to Tuscaloosa in a few weeks to speak at Alabama's annual high school coaching clinic, then he and Bryant would spend some time together playing golf while Bellard and the Longhorns' offensive line coach taught Crimson Tide offensive coordinator Mal Moore and others on the offensive staff how to run the wishbone. Royal agreed.

Alabama, having already gone through spring practice—its players had no idea of the behind-the-scenes work Bryant was undertaking—was about to become a wishbone offensive team, and quickly.

"We didn't have any idea what coach Bryant had planned," Moore said. "He didn't tell us until just before the coaching clinic what he had in mind. When he told us, he said, 'We're going to sink or swim with the wishbone.'"

In late July, just before preseason practice was about to begin, the Texas group arrived in Tuscaloosa and participated in the coaching clinic. Right after that, Moore, John David Crow, and Jimmy Sharpe went to a local hotel for three days and nights, watching film and working on a chalkboard as Bellard led classes on the wishbone, how it worked and how best to utilize its benefits. Bryant and Royal spent time in those sessions, too.

"We were at the Holiday Inn North and we just stayed in there," Moore said. "Emory stayed with us. He had cut up some film and showed us everything about the wishbone."

Before the Texas group headed back to Austin, Bryant, still a bit nervous about the switch but totally committed to it, extracted one more promise from Royal, aside from his secrecy. Could he call him any time he had questions? "Of course you can," Royal said.

Royal said he was surprised when Bryant first explained his idea. "They'd been throwing the ball a lot back then," Royal said.

He wasn't the only one surprised by the move. The Alabama players joined that list when they arrived on campus for preseason practice and were informed of the change in offensive philosophy at the team's first meeting. There was a rule attached with the switch: no one, absolutely no one, was to say a word about the change. The move was to be kept a secret and anyone who said a word about the change would have to explain himself to Bryant.

Practices were closed to the media and the fence that surrounded Alabama's practice field was covered so no one could stroll by and check out what was happening on the field. The SEC, which now hosts a three-day, football media event in Birmingham prior to each season that brings the coach and two or three players from each league team together for interviews, had a different approach in those days. It was called the SEC Skywriters Tour. The league chartered an airplane and a small group of writers would board the plane that visited at least two campuses a day, allowing the writers access to the coaches and players for preseason stories.

When the Skywriters arrived in Tuscaloosa and headed for Alabama's practice field, Bryant had his team run three or four plays from the previous season over and over again. When the writers left the field, the gates to the practice field were closed and once again the Crimson Tide returned to installing the wishbone.

"You couldn't do that now, not with the Internet and all the media coverage you have," Moore said of keeping the wishbone a secret. "You know in war, the element of surprise is a big factor. In that game, the element of surprise was a really big factor."

• • •

There was another story also developing at Alabama, and this one definitely was not a secret. It was a story that came about, at least in some measure, because of the 1970 Southern Cal game and the performance by USC's Cunningham and others. The racial lines for Alabama's football team hadn't yet been crossed in 1970, although those who worked with him and were close to him say Bryant had been talking of recruiting and signing African American players to the team in previous recent seasons. Wilbur Jackson of Ozark, who would join the 1971 team, was the first African American football player signed by Alabama. Mobile's John Mitchell, by way of a junior college in Arizona, would be the second African American signee, but would be the first to play for Alabama.

Ironically, USC head coach John McKay was responsible for Mitchell's arrival in Tuscaloosa, though he hadn't meant that to be the case. McKay and Bryant were close friends and during the summer, the two were playing golf together when McKay mentioned to Bryant he had signed a player from the state of Alabama whose name was John Mitchell. A few moments later, Bryant excused himself, found a phone, and called a member of his coaching staff, telling them to find John Mitchell and sign him. And that's what happened.

"I had signed to go to Southern Cal," Mitchell recalled. "I had played junior college ball in Arizona and a lot of guys I knew were at Southern Cal. When I went on my [recruiting] visit to Southern Cal, Sam Cunningham was my host when I was being recruited. To play at Southern Cal at that time, I was excited. I saw them on TV all the time and meeting John McKay was a thrill."

But the thrill and opportunity of playing at Alabama won out for Mitchell. "Growing up in Mobile, you knew about Alabama and you saw Alabama on TV a lot. You wanted to play at a place like that. I was an Alabama fan, but at that time, they weren't recruiting African American players. When they offered me a scholarship, I went there instead of Southern Cal because it gave my family a chance to see me play. I had played my first two years [of college ball] in Arizona, and my family couldn't see me play. I wanted them to see me play. That was important to me. I wanted to get a good education and make the team."

Mitchell would do a lot more than that. The 6-foot-3, 230-pound defensive end was a two-time All-SEC selection and in 1972 was an All-America selection. He was a starter in each of the 24 games he played for the Crimson Tide, Alabama winning two SEC crowns and posting a 21-3 mark in his time there. He was also named a defensive captain.

"It was going to be a difficult time for me, and for them too. It was a different exposure for me, but it was that way for them too," Mitchell said. "If people see you're a good guy, they take color out of it. We got along well. I was probably the first African American to attend a fraternity party [at Alabama]. The other guys made it easy just by being themselves. We were teammates and we were friends. We did a lot of things together, like going to parties and things like that."

And so USC lost a defensive end and Alabama gained an All-America player, who would make three tackles in the game, and a bit of history as well.

• • •

Another Alabama defensive end, John Croyle, was writing his own story. After a redshirt season he was going to be playing his first college game, and it was taking place in Los Angeles. The way he saw it, that was a pretty good start. "I distinctly remember three things about that game and that trip," said Croyle. "One, when we got to the Coliseum we watched that white stallion and the Trojan riding him and that was impressive and interesting too. Number two was noticing just how big Sam Cunningham was, and Lynn

Swann. All of [the USC players] really. They were huge, much bigger than us. Plus, you could tell they had guys on their team that were going to be pro players. And third, the night before the game we went to see a movie, like we usually did, and as we're about to go into the movie this big, black limo pulls up and two guys got out with an ocelot, and that was his pet. I knew right then we were in a different place. We weren't in Alabama anymore."

Croyle learned a few more things, too. He learned the USC players not only were bigger than he and his teammates but, "physically, they were just better than we were," he said. He also learned that tackling Cunningham was no picnic. "He was the first player I tackled in a college game." Croyle noted.

He also learned that Johnny Musso could really run with the football, the switch to the wishbone was a great idea and that there is a difference between being a good player and being a good player whose competitive spirit runs high.

"There was a play early when USC was on offense when one of their big ole guys caught (defensive end) Robin Parkhouse from the blindside and just wiped him out," Croyle recalled. "Robin was on his back right in front of me as I was standing on the sidelines. And when he stood up, his eyes were crossed. I'm looking at one of the toughest men I knew and he's cross-eyed. Coach Bryant told me to 'Get Parkhouse,' but Robin said, 'No you don't. I'm going back in there.'

"Coach Bryant jerked me back, and my feet went out from under me. I'm on the sidelines, on my seat. That was my introduction to college football. Think about that. I'm 19 years old. What a rush! Those memories are just great. It was a great experience. . . . Being that it was LA, the Coliseum, I was blown away and it was intimidating at first, but we were playing, and that took over. It was their yard, but how much fun is it to go into somebody else's yard and beat 'em? It was just great."

• • •

Alabama was anxious to show off its new offense, to finally pull away the veil of secrecy and let everyone in on the announcement. Especially Southern Cal. All those weeks of keeping quiet about the wishbone would come to an end on the game's first offensive possession. Alabama took the opening kickoff and Robert McKinney returned it 33 yards to the Crimson Tide 41, giving Alabama good field position to start its new offense.

Then the secret was out.

Terry Davis led the Crimson Tide offense out of the huddle to the line of scrimmage. Immediately, USC's defensive players noticed something was amiss, at least from all the game film of Alabama's previous season they had watched heading into the game. This wasn't a pro-style offensive alignment. This was different.

"When we lined up for that first play it was obvious they didn't know [the wishbone] was coming," Moore said.

Methodically, and with the Trojans' defense wondering just what the heck was going on, Alabama's offense moved down the field. The element of surprise worked perfectly. Johnny Musso took the first handoff up the middle of the Trojan defense for seven yards, then gained another yard off left tackle. That presented Alabama with a third-down play.

On that play, Davis picked up 19 yards, then he tried left tackle for three more. Quickly, Alabama had moved to the USC 29. A Davis pass to Jim Simmons netted 16 yards and a first down at the Trojans' 13, where Musso took a pitchout around right end for a touchdown.

Cunningham, who had inflicted so much damage on Alabama's defense the year before, took the field with his offensive teammates following the Crimson Tide's quick score. He was given the football on USC's first two plays, picking up a total of five yards. A pass play netted 12 yards for the Trojans and a first down, and Lou Harris followed with a 13-yard run. USC would run four more plays on the drive when the Alabama defense put a stop to things, Steve Wade intercepting a Jim Jones pass at the Alabama 10 and returning it 22 yards to the 32.

The wishbone was back at work. On the second play, Davis attempted his second pass, this one to Ellis Beck for nine yards. Musso, Beck, Davis and Joe LaBue took turns attacking the Southern Cal defense, pushing their way and eating up the clock toward another Alabama score. Alabama got as close at the USC 15, but a 9-yard loss on a play pushed the Tide back. It would get back as close as the 20, but the drive stalled there and Bill Davis, with Terry Davis holding, booted a 44-yard field goal for a 10-0 Alabama lead.

USC's offense had no better luck on its next possession, the Alabama defense limiting it to five plays, including a punt that was downed on the Alabama 9 on the final play of the first period. The Crimson Tide wishbone picked up where it had left off, but with some extra punch. On an 11-play drive, Alabama produced four first downs and four plays of 10 yards or more. USC's defense was still guessing, and Alabama's offense was clicking.

LeBue had runs of 13 and 18 yards, with Beck offering a 10-yarder and Davis completing a pass to David Bailey for 15 yards. With other smaller gains tossed in, Alabama found itself at the USC 20. From there, Beck produced back-to-back runs of 5 and 7 yards to the 8-yard line, where Musso took over, slamming off right guard for the remaining eight yards and a touchdown.

Not only was the wishbone working—Alabama had scored on its first three possessions—it was working well.

Moore was grinning broadly. "We scored the first three times we had the ball because they didn't know how to defend it," he said. "Their defense played pretty well, but they were reeling from the surprise factor. They didn't know what we were doing."

Although Alabama would grind out more yards on the afternoon, its scoring stopped with Musso's touchdown at the 14:54 mark of the second quarter. Southern Cal's was just beginning.

And it would begin soon.

A 22-yard kickoff return by Swann got things started, setting USC up on its 27. A third down-and-8 pass to Cunningham for 12 yards kept the drive alive and a couple of Harris runs, including a 16-yarder, helped move the Trojans to the Alabama 31. Four plays later, on second-and-goal from the 7, Jones tossed a scoring pass to Charles Young.

Alabama's offense followed the score by moving again, but just as it crossed over to USC's side of the field, a Davis pass, intended for Bailey, was intercepted by Bruce Dyer at the 35 and returned 20 yards to the Alabama 45 with only a few moments left in the half. Jones completed a pass to Mike Morgan for eight yards to the 37, and, with 17 seconds to play, found Swann for a first down to the Alabama 19. With two seconds left, Mike Rae was brought on to attempt a 36-yard field goal, which he made. The Trojans had closed the Alabama lead to 17-10.

USC received the kickoff to open the second half and quickly moved from its 21 to the Alabama 37. But there, on a Jones pass intended for Swann, the drive ended when Alabama's Steve Higginbotham intercepted the pass at the 19 and returned it five yards to the 24. Neither team could muster much offense the rest of the third period. USC had another possession halted by a turnover when Cunningham fumbled and Steve Williams recovered for the Crimson Tide at the Alabama 8.

The final quarter was much the same as the third. The teams opened by swapping punts and Alabama punted a second time, with Swann receiving the punt and using his speed and agility to produce a 57-yard return to the Alabama 28. But he may have been too fast for his own good.

"Swann was back for the punt and he broke it," McNair said. "We had David Bailey back and he was a great athlete, but the odds of him stopping Swann weren't good. Swann tripped up on his own feet."

The Tide defense stiffened. On a third-and-5 play the Trojans gained seven to the 16, but the play was disallowed because of a USC personal foul penalty. The follow-up third-down play produced an incomplete pass. On fourth-and 15 at the 33, USC decided to go for the first down. Rae, now at quarterback, scrambled, but came up four yards short and Alabama took over possession.

Alabama wasn't able to get much going offensively, but it did manage to erase more of the time left to play. So when Greg Gantt lofted a 44-yard punt and Swann lost a yard on the return, USC had only a few minutes left to play and a long way to go—the Trojans took over on their 6—to try and tie the game or possibly get a touchdown and two-point conversion for the win.

Alabama's defense, which played somewhat in the shadow of the new offense against USC, held its own once again. It also came up with another turnover. The Trojans had moved to the 43, but lost three yards on a running play. The next play ended with an incomplete pass and the follow-up play found Jones, back in at quarterback and back to pass, taking a big hit, causing a fumble that was recovered by Terry Rowell.

Alabama sent its wishbone offense back on the Coliseum field once more, this time to run out the remaining time, which it did. Davis, Beck, and Musso handled the ball-carrying chores, Musso picking up four yards on a fourth-and-2 play from the USC 28 and the Tide needing only two more plays to run out the clock.

• • •

It wasn't just any victory. The win not only avenged the pounding Alabama took from the Trojans in the previous year's season-opener at Birmingham's Legion Field, an unsatisfactory beginning to what would be a disappointing season. It marked Bryant's 200th career win, a significant milestone, and it came on his 58th birthday.

To honor the occasion, Finus Gaston, now a senior associate athletics director for the school and then the team's manager, wanted to make sure one thing took place after the game: that he secured the game ball. He did just that, scooping up the ball, which went to the winning team in those days, and heading up the tunnel toward Alabama's locker room. He sought out Musso, found the running back and handed him the football, explaining what it was and informing him of the milestone victory. Gaston suggested that Musso present the game ball to coach Bryant.

All of this was captured by a *Birmingham Post-Herald* photographer. In the *Post-Herald*'s next edition, on its front page, are two photos, one of Gaston in the tunnel, giving the football to Musso, and another of Bryant with the game ball after it had been presented to him by Musso.

Arriving back in Alabama the next day, when the plane landed, hundreds of Crimson Tide fans were there to greet the team. "There were so many fans you couldn't get from the plane to the buses," Gaston said.

Years later, Moore still marveled at the switch to the wishbone, when it was put into play and all that had to take place in order to make the change. Most of all, he remained in awe of his former boss.

"He always had the ability to change," Moore said. "He knew there needed to be a change and when he decided to make the change, he stuck with it. He decided with the quarterbacks we had we couldn't win throwing the football. . . . Think about it, that game was the start of a 10-year period in which we won 103 games. It was a great time to be at Alabama."

In the decade of the 1970s, Alabama would also win eight SEC championships and three national championships (1973, 1978, 1979), and the wishbone offense, buffered by some outstanding defensive units too, was at the heart of that success.

And that's no secret.

CHAPTER FIVE
1972 Tennessee

Alabama 17, Tennessee 10
October 21, 1972
Neyland Stadium
Knoxville, Tennessee

For Alabama and Tennessee fans alike, there is something special about the Third Saturday in October. There always has been.

Simply uttering the phrase evokes memories of a special rivalry, one that has produced its share of big moments and games for both schools. While both schools have other rivalries that carry more intensity or more meaning, especially in SEC play, that doesn't diminish the importance nor the intensity when the Vols and Crimson Tide get together for their annual game.

The matchup is rich in tradition and stories. The teams first met in 1928 with Tennessee claiming a 15-13 victory in Tuscaloosa. The closeness of that first game gave the series a perfect beginning and there have been many a closely contested game since that day, both teams laying claim to their share of victory celebrations and disappointing losses.

The players and coaches have done their respective parts in keeping the rivalry among the most anticipated in the Southeast. The fans more than do their part in stoking the fires of the rivalry. Because the rivalry is so well known and respected, fans of other teams often tune in to watch an Alabama-Tennessee game, fully expecting it to produce fireworks of some sort, generally wrapped around an exciting and well-played game.

The game between the two teams at Neyland Stadium in 1972 offered a perfect example as to the importance and competitiveness that is a constant part of the game played on the third Saturday in October.

There was plenty of buzz for the game. Tennessee fans were excited about their team, which was ranked No. 10 in the country and led by quarterback Condredge Holloway, a talented player with the ability to hurt defenses with his arm and his legs. The Crimson Tide entered the game ranked No. 3 in the country, a four-spot improvement from the No. 7 national ranking with which it began the season. The Alabama offense had its stars, and its defense was equally talented.

There was every reason to believe the stage was set for a typical, anything-can-happen, Alabama vs. Tennessee, Third-Saturday-in-October football game. It would prove to be that, and more.

Adding to the rivalry was Alabama head coach Paul "Bear" Bryant's emphasis on the Vols. Several former players have talked of the extra spring in Bryant's step and added volume in his voice, during the week of practice leading up to a Tennessee game. As a player, Bryant and his Alabama teammates were 3-0 against the Vols (1933-35). As a coach, his 25-year record at Alabama against Tennessee was 16-7-2, including a string of 11 consecutive wins (1971-1981) that began the year before the 1972 game and ended in his next-to-last season as Alabama's head coach. It also included a four-year string of Tennessee wins (1967-70).

Bryant's increased focus for games against the Vols is demonstrated in the stats. In his tenure at Alabama, the Crimson Tide held a 21-14 scoring average lead over Tennessee. During the 11-year winning streak the Crimson Tide was especially dominant, holding an average scoring edge of 28.4-12.2 over the Vols.

After victories over Tennessee, handing out cigars to players, coaches, and others in the Alabama locker room became customary. Various songs would also be sung. Again, the rivalry had its own measure, its own feel, its own identity. It doesn't come close to matching the Iron Bowl rivalry against Auburn, but then again no other Alabama opponent can ever attain that level of interest or competition for Alabama fans. But that doesn't mean the Tennessee game is just another SEC game, another league-scheduled opponent. There's a different texture to it, and winning that game (or losing it) means something to all concerned.

"I had heard a lot about [playing at] Tennessee, and at that time Tennessee and LSU had the biggest stadiums in the SEC," John Mitchell, an

All-America defensive player for the Crimson Tide who had played his first two seasons of college ball at a junior college in Arizona, said. "That was my first time there, seeing the boats come up the river bringing fans to the game. I will never forget that, just because it was so different . . . and because of the way the game played out."

• • •

All the scoring of the first half was wrapped up in one play, the last play of the half. Robert McKinney intercepted a Gary Valbuena pass and returned it 44 yards from the Alabama 34-yard line to the Tennessee 22. From there, Joe LaBue picked up five yards on a run and eight more on a second-down pass from quarterback Terry Davis. An illegal procedure penalty moved Alabama back five yards to the 14 and that's where Bill Davis took over, kicking a 31-yard field goal for a 3-0 Alabama lead as time expired in the half.

Prior to the field goal there was plenty of action and both teams played much the same. Alabama ended the half with seven first downs, 40 yards rushing, 102 yards passing, two turnovers, 27 return yards, 21 rushing plays, four pass completions and one penalty. The Vols had six first downs, 40 yards rushing, 89 yards passing, one turnover (a costly one), 21 return yards, 23 rushing plays, four pass completions and three penalties.

The score reflected the closeness of the game.

"Tennessee had a very good team and they had a good game plan," assistant coach Mal Moore, later to become the school's director of athletics, said. "They shut us down and we had a hard time moving the ball with any consistency."

Tennessee moved from its 21-yard line to its 44 on the game's first possession before punting the ball away. Alabama took over at its own 22 and four plays later, Wilbur Jackson fumbled the ball and the Vols recovered at the Tide 38. Tennessee moved close to the 27 before John Mitchell and Mike DuBose—who would team up for an even bigger play late in the game—tackled Holloway for a nine-yard loss. That led to a 52-yard field goal try two plays later by Rickey Townsend that sailed wide right.

The teams swapped punts before a pass by Alabama's Davis was picked off by Eddie Brown and returned 21 yards to the Alabama 46. But again, Tennessee's offense was stymied by a tough Crimson Tide defense, punting the ball back to Alabama. A fourth-and-2 play at its 45 failed to pick up a first down for Alabama, which turned the ball over on downs. The teams swapped punts once again, leading to the Vols' possession in which McKinney intercepted the Valbuena pass that led to Bill Davis's field goal and the half's only points.

Tennessee was quick to respond in the second half, using an Alabama turnover to take the lead. On the third play of the third quarter from the Crimson Tide 29, Paul Spivey fumbled and Tennessee recovered, also at the 29. Although a relatively short distance from the end zone, it took the Vols nine plays to score. The first eight plays were all runs by Haskel Stanback. He had runs of 1, 8, 1, 8, 0, 1, 8 and 0 yards to the Alabama 2, where Holloway took over, sliding around left end on a keeper for the touchdown.

The remainder of the third quarter was filled with punts and fumbles, both teams losing the grip on the football and the opponent claiming the loose football. Alabama was unable to parlay its find into points, but the Vols made use of its fumble recovery.

Quarterback Gary Rutledge fumbled on a second-down play at the Crimson Tide 37 and the Vols took over at the 28, giving them another close shot at a touchdown. But the Alabama defense did a good job of containing Tennessee's efforts and received some help when Holloway lost his footing on a keeper and lost eight yards. Looking at a fourth-and-12 situation from the 19, the Vols opted for a Townsend 36-yard field goal try, which he made, putting Tennessee in front 10-7 early in the final period.

Alabama's offense hit a lull. The Tide's next three possessions yielded only 10 plays (not counting punts), 13 yards and three punts. Time was running out for the Crimson Tide, which entered the game with a spotless 5-0 record and its lofty national ranking. If it was going to protect its unbeaten mark and maintain its Top 5 national ranking, it had to do something soon. Taking possession of the football at the Vols' 48 with only 2:39 to play after a 37-yard punt and 13-yard return by McKinney, Alabama set out to do just that.

• • •

It took just three plays for Alabama to tie the game. Davis tossed a 20-yard pass to split end Wayne Wheeler on first down, moving to the 28. The play was followed by a Steve Bisceglia run off right tackle for 26 yards to the 2. That's where Jackson took over, following behind the right tackle slot for two yards and a touchdown.

Bryant wanted to go for the two-point conversion and the win. Instead, he was convinced by assistant coach Pat Dye, who would later go head-to-head against Bryant in two Irons Bowls (1981, 1982) as head coach at

Auburn, to kick the extra point and tie the game and let the Alabama defense get the ball back to the offense.

"In a staff meeting that week, we talked that if a decision had to be made around the two-minute mark to kick an extra point to tie or try a two-point conversion for the win, we'd go for the win," Moore said. "And that's what it came down to. But we kicked the extra point. We reminded [Bryant] of what he said in the meeting, but [on the field, the decision was] to put the pressure on Tennessee and [Vols' head coach] Bill Battle to try and beat us."

Croyle was standing close to the coaches when the decision-making process was taking place. "I remember coach Dye looking at coach Bryant and saying, 'Coach, we'll get you the ball back.' To everyone's surprise, he went for the single point. We went for the tie and that blew everybody's mind."

Kicker Bill Davis trotted onto the field, kicked the extra point and tied the game at 10-all.

Now it was time for the defense to live up to Dye's expectations and Bryant's risk-taking by stopping the Vols and getting the football back in the hands of the Alabama offense for a shot at winning the game.

That is, of course, exactly what the defense did.

"Coach Bryant called everyone [on the defensive team] over to him and he told us, 'We need the ball; we need to get the ball back.' Obviously, the man was telling us to go out there and stop them and get the ball back. And that's what we did," Croyle said.

Tennessee flirted with doing the work for the Alabama defense on the ensuing kickoff. Stanback fielded the Greg Gantt kick and fumbled, the ball rolling out of bounds at the 17. Holloway and the Vols had visions of winning the game too, and he came out throwing. His pass on first down was overthrown. Stanback got a crack at generating some excitement and yardage, taking a pitchout and headed to the left side of the field, but he was stopped for an 8-yard loss back to the Vols' 11, the tackle made by the duo of Mitchell and DuBose. The Alabama defensive standouts would make a quick return to the spotlight.

On third-and-16 and Holloway with the football, DuBose—Alabama's head coach from 1997-2000, the fourth coach [second former Alabama player] to lead the Tide after Bryant—slammed into the Vols' quarterback, forcing a fumble. Mitchell, now assistant head coach of the NFL's Pittsburgh Steelers, was on top of the play too and recovered the loose football at the Tennessee 22.

"The most important thing about that game, of course, was with about 2:50 left we're down and we had to make a play, and we made a big play right there," Mitchell said.

The defense, as Dye had predicted, would get the football back to the offense. Now, it was the offensive unit's turn to do its part. Just as had been the case with the defense, the Alabama offense would make its contribution in speedy fashion.

Terry Davis took the snap, tucked the football under his arm, and ran 22 yards for the touchdown. The score came just that fast, produced in a rather matter-of-fact manner. Alabama added the extra point kick—no need for discussion this time—and the Crimson Tide, down 10-3 to start the final quarter and for most of the period, was on top 17-10.

Moore said the call was for the lead option and Davis took it from there. "We had a few [fans] who left the stadium with a little more than two minutes left in the game," he said. "I guess they wish they had stayed. . . . What a game."

Of course, by scoring so quickly, Alabama had done the Vols a favor of sorts. It had run a minimum amount of time off the clock, giving the ball back to Tennessee with 1:12 left in the game. That was enough time, with a little luck and a big play or two, to counter the Crimson Tide's touchdown.

Then again, the Vols would be facing the same defense that had just stopped them, created a turnover and given the Alabama offense great field position and an opportunity. As luck would have it for the Vols, the Alabama defense wasn't celebrating yet. There was more work to do.

Tennessee's last-ditch effort began at its 18, 82 yards from where it needed to be. Valbuena was at quarterback and his throw on first down was too long. On second down, Valbuena kept the football and was chased down and tackled by Mitchell all the way back at the Vols' 2-yard line, a loss of 16. Third down was no better and Valbuena's pass to Stanback resulted in no gain when Woodrow Lowe halted the play at the line of scrimmage.

Less than 30 seconds remained, but Tennessee conceded the ending; the Vols lined up to punt. Knowing it would not get the football back and trailing by a touchdown, Tennessee elected to punt. The kick was good for only 27 yards and Alabama took over, with 11 seconds to play, at the Vols' 29.

A keeper by Davis resulted in no gain, but there were offsetting penalties—Tennessee for personal foul, Alabama for holding—requiring the need for one more play. It was another keeper by Davis, but Alabama, having produced an exciting, come-from-behind victory against the Vols, had the biggest keeper of them all: another win over Tennessee.

• • •

At the end, as was the case at halftime, the stats indicated an incredibly close game. Almost a tie. Alabama had one more first down than the Vols and just 30 more total yards. Both teams had the same passing stat line—7-of-14 with one interception—but the Tide had 29 more yards.

Both teams had trouble holding the football, Alabama fumbling four times and losing three while Tennessee bobbled the ball three times, losing two. Both teams used two quarterbacks and had three receivers catch passes.

The scoreboard, and the reactions in the locker room after the game, told completely different stories, however.

"It's an understatement, of course, to say that I'm happy," Bryant said. "I'm awfully, awfully proud of them for having come back." And as if to add a little more salt in the rival's wound—those close to the program during Bryant's tenure are quick to note the legendary coach considered Tennessee the Tide's biggest rival next to Auburn and a team he felt would provide an accurate gauge of the strength of his own team—he added this: "It's one of the biggest victories we've ever had."

Although Tennessee lost the game that day in Knoxville, it would finish the year 10-2 overall, 4-2 in the SEC and ranked No. 8 nationally in the Associated Press' final poll. Alabama would also finish 10-2 overall, but would win the SEC crown and finish one spot ahead of the Vols in the final poll at No. 7, adding to the long list of close games, stats, and comparisons in the Third Saturday in October series.

CHAPTER SIX

1975 Sugar Bowl

Alabama 13, Penn State 6
December 31, 1975
Louisiana Superdome
New Orleans, Louisiana

Success, especially in the decade of the 1970s, was supersized at Alabama. The Crimson Tide, having switched to the wishbone offense, which was backed by a punishing and quick defense, posted 103 victories from 1970-79. But there was a problem—the Crimson Tide, at least at the start of the decade and for a few seasons before its start, had zero success winning its bowl games.

Many asked the simple question, how is that possible? There was no simple, easy answer, only the facts. Starting in 1967, Alabama played in a bowl game every year for eight straight years without a victory. Eight consecutive times it accepted a bowl invitation, arrived in the city hosting the game, then left without having added to head coach Paul "Bear" Bryant's all-time win total. As Alabama prepared to play Penn State on New Year's Eve of 1975, having posted an 0-7-1 record in its previous eight bowl appearances, the team had lost just one game all season in three of the previous four seasons. That one loss, each of those seasons, was in a bowl game.

"It wasn't like we had been playing badly in those [bowl] games," then-Alabama sports information director Kirk McNair said. "There were a lot of close games, but we hadn't been winning any of them." McNair cited a goofy officials' call in the 1973 Cotton Bowl (1972 season) as an example, as well as the two close games against the Fighting Irish of Notre Dame the previous two seasons that the Crimson Tide lost by a combined three points.

Still, the fact remained that Alabama hadn't been able to pick up a win in what was generally regarded as a reward for a good season—being invited to play in a postseason bowl game. The pressure was mounting.

"There were a number of bowl games in a row in which we didn't win and it was becoming an issue," defensive lineman Bob Baumhower, now a successful restaurateur, said. "And we had just lost two tough bowl games—maybe national championship games, though we won the UPI national championship in 1973—to Notre Dame the previous two seasons. I don't know that I would say we were under pressure, but I remember hearing a lot about it."

Pressure or not, everyone involved with the Alabama football program was aware of the streak of bowl games without a victory. When the Crimson Tide was invited to play in the 1975 Sugar Bowl—the first Sugar Bowl game to be played in the recently opened Louisiana Superdome—talk of that string of futility increased. It was time, Crimson Tide fans suggested, to put an end to it.

That wouldn't be a simple task. Standing in Alabama's way was Penn State, led by head coach Joe Paterno. The Nittany Lions had a strong team that featured a coming-right-at-you offense and a powerful defense. In truth, the teams and the programs had many things in common.

"I think Penn State was a program with a lot of similarities to our program and our fans," Baumhower said. "Their people, their fans, took a lot of pride in how they did things and how they supported their team, just like our fans, and there was a lot of respect for coach Paterno and how he ran his program."

The teams shared something else in common too: they both wanted, perhaps needed, to win the Sugar Bowl.

• • •

Regardless of the outcome, the game would be played on a grand stage. The recently opened Superdome was quite a change from Tulane Stadium, where previous Sugar Bowl games had been played. Located in downtown New Orleans, it was a huge facility, one that took a little getting used to when teams first entered the massive building.

Playing indoors would be different and it would take a little time to make visual adjustments to playing with a roof overhead and dealing with depth perception, but those adjustments were made fairly quickly. The biggest difference would be the noise in the building. Having nowhere to escape, when fans got behind their team in the Superdome, it not only was clearly heard, it was *felt*.

Baumhower said when the team first drove up to the building "it looked like this great big spaceship, but it was really neat."

Ozzie Newsome said it was that trip to the Sugar Bowl when he "fell in love with the city." He also earned a fondness for the Superdome. "It was kinda fun playing in there," he said. "I liked it."

· · ·

Richard Todd would lead the Alabama offense against Penn State. The senior had strongly considered signing with Auburn after a standout prep career in Mobile and had scholarship offers from a number of schools. The Tigers' offense, at the time led by Pat Sullivan, who would win the Heisman Trophy in 1971, was a passing offense, which best suited Todd's talents. "Auburn was throwing the ball a lot at that time, and I liked that," Todd said.

Alabama rarely gave much thought to throwing the football. The wishbone offense was in place and successful and the Crimson Tide used the pass more just to let opposing defenses know it was available than as a plan of attack. The triple-option running game was the main method of offensive travel, and the Crimson Tide got a lot of miles per gallon that way. Having narrowed his choices to Auburn and Alabama, one thought was persistent.

"I went to Alabama once," Todd said. "I really didn't like it that much, and the [wishbone] offense really didn't suit me. But Auburn told me I was going to be a running back if I went there, and Alabama was going to let me play quarterback. Still, the only reason I went to Alabama was to play for Coach Bryant. He was the best coach in the country, and I couldn't see playing for anybody else if I had the chance to play for him."

During a talk with Bryant in the coach's office during his recruitment, Todd asked if there was a chance the passing game might play more of a role in the wishbone in the future. "He was puffing on a cigarette, sitting behind his desk, and he said, 'No,'" Todd recalled. "He went on to tell me they had a great passer in Scott Hunter and they threw the ball when he was there, but the team hadn't done very well."

When he arrived at Alabama for his first practice, Todd discovered he wasn't the only quarterback who attracted the attention of Alabama recruiters. In fact, seven other quarterbacks had also been signed. Most of those players were moved to the secondary, to take advantage of their knowledge of the passing game and their athletic skills, but Todd remained at quarterback and earned the starting quarterback slot for Alabama's freshman team. Todd wasn't happy with the offense at first, but as time went on he adjusted to it and, with the team enjoying success, he came to appreciate it.

"Winning hides a multitude of sins," Todd said. "I felt kind of bad because it was not the type of offense I would like to have been playing, but at the same time, we were winning so much, I didn't care. Winning and being around Coach Bryant, I just felt like everything was right."

• • •

Alabama entered the season ranked No. 13 in the country and looking to win another national championship. The Crimson Tide boasted a good collection of talent including Todd, Baumhower, Woodrow Lowe, Callaway, Newsome, Steadman Shealy, Tony Nathan, Johnny Davis, Leroy Cook, George Pugh, Willie Shelby, Calvin Culliver and others. It was an experienced team led by a group of players used to winning. So when they started the season against No. 5-ranked Missouri at Birmingham's Legion Field, it seemed the perfect fit: a highly ranked opponent at home, a good jumpstart for the national title plans.

Missouri saw the game as a jumpstart to its season. And on that day, Missouri's vision of how the day would play out became the reality. Completely dominating the Crimson Tide from start to finish, the Tigers claimed a 20-7 win in the nationally televised game, scoring all 20 of its points in the first half—10 points each in the first and second quarters—while Alabama's lone score wouldn't come until the final period, with the game's outcome already decided.

Todd got his wish—he was allowed to throw more out of the wishbone in that game, but only out of the need to try and score quickly and catch up. He was 10-of-19 for 87 yards and a 14-yard touchdown pass to Newsome. Alabama, with just 118 yards of total offense, had only 31 yards rushing. James Taylor and Davis, with 13 yards each, were Alabama's leading rushers. Missouri didn't have trouble running with the football, picking up 206 of their 257 total yards on the ground.

One game, one loss.

"Winning the bowl game was a big, big deal," Baumhower said, "but I have to tell you, most of us couldn't forget that loss to Missouri. We couldn't get it out of our system. We never got the bad taste of that loss out of our mouths. We thought we had the best team in the country and we go and lose the first game of the year."

Newsome remembers the feelings he experienced after that game. "They just outplayed us," he said. "And that meant back-to-back losses [dating back to bowl loss at end of the previous season], which was unheard of at that time for Alabama football."

• • •

In an effort to shake his team from its unwanted bowl streak, Bryant decided to try a different approach for the 1975 Sugar Bowl. In recent seasons, the team had remained in Tuscaloosa, getting in practice sessions there, then arriving only two or three days before kickoff in the city that hosted the bowl game. For the game against Penn State, Bryant took the team to New Orleans eight days before kickoff, hoping to change things up a bit and give the players a chance to go out and enjoy the city in the first few days of their arrival before turning their total focus to the game against Penn State.

Moore said the change to an earlier arrival wasn't the only switch in what had been the norm for Alabama's bowl travel. The players, at least the first few nights, were allowed a little later curfew, too.

And that's where things got a tad interesting.

"One night, a lot of [players] were out late and they had bed check and some of us weren't in our rooms," Todd explained. "I was one of them. Coach Bryant got up the next morning [at a team meeting] and said there were 21 of us who were out late and missed curfew. A lot of the ones who were out late were starters. He wasn't happy. So he went around the room, saying something about each of the players who had missed curfew. He came to me and he said 'Here's Richard Todd, our newly elected captain, and he couldn't be found [after curfew].'

"Coach Bryant said he was going to send all of our names to our local newspapers and tell them that we had missed curfew, so that if we lost the game they wouldn't blame him. I talked with Mal Moore some time after that and he told me we didn't know how close we were to being sent home. He told me that Coach Bryant had already called for a bus and he was going to have all 21 of us put on that bus and sent back to Tuscaloosa. Mal said he and some of the other coaches said, 'Coach, you can't do that, you'll be giving away the game,' and they talked him out of it, but he wanted to send us all back."

Todd, who would earn Most Valuable Player honors in the game, almost missed his chance to play in the game before the team arrived in New Orleans. On a visit to close friend Baumhower's house, he was shown a souvenir Baumhower's parents had brought back from Jamaica—a long knife in a sheaf.

"He pulled the knife from its sheaf, and when he did so he had his fingers wrapped around the sheaf," Baumhower explained. "It was the type of sheaf that wasn't closed on both sides, so when he pulled the knife out, he cut his hand, his throwing hand. He didn't need stitches, but it was just a week before the game, just before we left, and I was stressed out like you wouldn't believe because it happened at my house. It was pretty tense for me, but everything worked out OK. He went on to win the MVP."

• • •

One of the players Alabama had always been able to count on was Woodrow Lowe. The Phenix City native, one of only two three-time, first-team All-America honorees in school history (joining Cornelius Bennett), was a steady force at linebacker, making play after play. It began with the first play he ever made for the Crimson Tide, on the first play he had as a member of the 1972 team. As a freshman in the Crimson Tide's first game that season against Duke, Lowe was on the kickoff coverage team to open the game. On the kick, he raced downfield, found the kick returner, and delivered an impressive tackle.

"That was a good start," he said. "I had never seen that many people in the same place in my life. It was a lot different than anything I had been used to. We got to the stadium about an hour and a half before kickoff, and we took our traditional walk around the field. Then we went into the locker room for about a half-hour to get ready before going on the field to warm up. When we came back out there, there were a lot of people already in the stadium. By the time the game started, it was full with about 75,000 people, I guess. I didn't know what to think."

But he did know what to do. Lining up for that opening kickoff coverage, Lowe did what he had been doing all his life on the football field: he made a tackle. "I think that's when Coach Bryant gained confidence in me," Lowe would say years later. "I think he knew then that I would be able to play."

Out of Central High School in Phenix City, where he is now the head football coach, Lowe had attracted attention from schools for his ability to find the football and make big plays, but he hadn't received many offers. In-state schools had contacted him, including Alabama and Auburn. He planned an official visit to Auburn before he traveled to Tuscaloosa, but plans changed. Located just 40 miles from the Auburn campus, Lowe and Central teammate Moses Hall had been invited for a Saturday afternoon game at Auburn. On the way to the game, Hall's car—"a beat-up, old car," as Lowe described it—suffered a flat tire, and there was no spare. What's more, the car suddenly developed other problems too. They were stranded (remember, this was before cell phones were commonplace) so they started hitch-hiking.

"By the time we got over there the game was over and we didn't talk with anybody," Lowe said. "We called our dads and they drove over and got us."

Auburn didn't call Lowe back. "They probably thought I wasn't interested," he said. "I guess it just wasn't meant for me to go to Auburn."

Alabama was still interested and the assistant coach in charge of recruiting Lowe, ironically, was Pat Dye, who would later become head coach at Auburn. "We've talked about that before," Lowe said. " . . . In our business, you never know where you'll end up."

Dye arranged for Lowe to make the trip to Tuscaloosa to meet with the staff, including Bryant. "Coach Bryant asked me if I wanted to play for the University of Alabama, and I said 'Yes.' I felt I had given my word, and that was as good as signing a sheet of paper. I didn't talk to any teams after that. . . . I'm not sure if I was the last person they offered a scholarship to, but I was pretty close if I wasn't the last."

As a sophomore in 1973, he would lead the team in tackles with 134 and also collect three interceptions. Lowe would later be named to Alabama's All-Decade team of the 1970s and he helped Alabama to a record of 43-5 in his time there.

On the day of the Sugar Bowl, Lowe was in the lobby of the team hotel, standing at the reservations desk where he had planned to pay for the incidental charges he had incurred during the stay. Out of the corner of his eye, he saw something move—the team bus.

"I threw down $10 on the counter—my bill probably wasn't three dollars—and started running, heading for the bus," Lowe said. "The bus took off before I could get to it. I know somebody on the bus saw me, probably Ozzie [Newsome] and Bob [Baumhower] too, so I started running after it, but I couldn't catch it."

Lowe's sprint was entertainment for the players and coaches on the bus, who watched as he would run down the street, almost catching the bus when it made a brief stop, only to fall behind again as the bus accelerated once more. "When Coach Bryant says 'Let's go,' the bus driver takes off, that's it," defensive coach Bill "Brother" Oliver said. "Here comes Woodrow through the hotel door, trying to catch the bus. Every time he got close, we'd pull away some more. He ran all the way to the dome, and that's a pretty good hop, skip and a jump. . . . We had motorcycle escorts to the dome, but we had to slow down every once in a while. Woodrow just kept running." Moore saw Lowe as well. "He was running along the side," he said. "I was pulling for him."

Nevertheless, Lowe found success that day. "I played one of the best games I've ever played that night. That last game of your senior year, if that doesn't get you motivated you don't belong in football."

Lowe belonged all right. He made 13 total tackles against Penn State, 10 of those being solo stops. "He played unbelievable," Oliver said. "He had about 40 or 50 bonus points (for defensive plays made). He just played a great game. Woodrow always played great." Crane agreed. "He just played the best game you've ever seen. He just played wonderfully."

He would have help, too.

• • •

Coach Bryant, sans his familiar Houndstooth hat— he was told by his mother when he was growing up not to wear a hat indoors—led the Crimson Tide out onto the Superdome floor to try and halt Alabama's streak of winless Bowl games. He had said in the days leading up to the game that would not be an easy task because the Nittany Lions were a solid and talented football team.

It was time to find out which team would be better on this New Year's Eve.

Penn State opened the game on offense and converted on two third-down situations, but the third, requiring 11 yards for a first down, came up four yards short at Alabama's 48 yard line. Instead of punting, Paterno sent place-kicker Chris Bahr out to attempt a 62-yard field goal, perhaps figuring there would be no wind with which to contend. It was an interesting decision, but an unsurprising result: the kick fell short.

Alabama took over at its 20 with Todd at the offensive controls. The Crimson Tide put points on the scoreboard on its first drive. The biggest play came on the third play, the Tide facing a third-and-4 situation. Todd found Joe Dale Harris on a 54-yard pass play that placed Alabama at the Nittany Lions' 20. A 9-yard pass to Newsome followed, putting the Tide at the Penn State 11 and it would eventually get as close as the 3 before the drive stalled. From there, on a fourth-and-goal situation, Alabama opted to attempt a field goal. Danny Ridgeway kicked a 25-yarder (after a five-yard penalty against Alabama moved the ball back to the 8) for a 3-0 lead.

That would complete the first-half scoring. Neither offense could get anything going the remainder of the half and didn't produce any real threats of a score. The teams combined for 242 yards of offense and had just six first downs each. Penn State played the first half without committing a penalty.

The one thing that stood out was Alabama's offensive switch, allowing Todd the opportunity to throw the football more than he had been allowed in the regular season, though the numbers still were anything but staggering. He was 5-of-7 for 108 yards, all but 42 of the Crimson Tide's first-half yardage. His throw to Harris on the first series had accounted for almost half of those yards and set up the field goal.

The teams returned to swapping punts at the start of the second half, the end result of the first three offensive possessions. Penn State started its second possession at its 31 and worked toward changing that trend. A John Andress scramble resulted in a 24-yard gain on a third-and-8 play to the Nittany Lions' 49. Another third-down play produced an 18-yard pass to Woody Petchel to the Alabama 33. The next third-down play left Penn State two yards short of a first down at the Alabama 25, which led to Bahr's return. His 42-yard field goal was good, tying the game 3-3 with less than five minutes to play in the third quarter.

Alabama responded right away, and again a big pass play would be the key.

Willie Shelby gained seven yards on first down from the Crimson Tide 20, and after a one-yard gain on the next run, Mike Stock picked up six and a first down at the Alabama 34. From there, Todd and Newsome hooked up again, this time for 55 yards down the right sideline down to the Penn State 11.

Todd was hit and fumbled on the next play. Though he recovered the ball, the play lost three yards. It wouldn't matter. Todd pitched to Stock, who took off around the left side and didn't stop until he had covered 14 yards and found the end zone for what would be the game's only touchdown. Ridgeway's extra point put Alabama back in front 10-3 with 1:42 left in the third quarter.

Penn State answered Alabama's score. Steve Geise took a pitchout from Andress on first down from the Penn State 20, slipped down the right sideline and picked up 29 yards and a first down at the 49. Consecutive running plays netted Penn State 4, 3 and 8 yards to finish off the third quarter and place the Nittany Lions at the Alabama 40.

Andress started the final period by tossing a 9-yard pass to Mickey Shuler, followed two plays later by a 4-yard run by Geise and another first down at the Alabama 27. Three running plays netted the Nittany Lions just eight yards and staring at a fourth-and-2 play at the 20. They opted to attempt a field goal. Bahr was good on his try again, this time from 37 yards out.

Back came Alabama.

Tony Nathan had returned the kickoff 22 yards to the Alabama 27, and Todd ran around right end for eight yards to start off the series. Stock failed to gain any yards on the next play but picked up three when two were needed for the first down. Willie Shelby gained four and Calvin Culliver had back-to-back runs of 5 and 8 to give Alabama a first down at the Penn State 45.

After a keeper by Todd failed to make a gain, the quarterback went back to the pass, finding Stock for a 20-yard gain to the 25. A follow-up pass to Newsome picked up seven more yards before Todd was tackled for a five-yard loss back to the 23, creating a third-and-8 play. Going to the pass again, Todd hit Jerry Brown for a 15-yard gain and a first down at the Penn State 8. But three plays found the Crimson Tide three yards back at the 11, and Ridgeway was called on for another field goal try. He hit this one, too, from 28 yards out. Alabama held a 13-6 advantage with 3:19 to play.

Penn State's next possession covered just 25 yards—from the Nittany Lions' 14 to their 39—before it ended on a fourth-and-1 play in which Rick Mauti failed to pick up the needed yard to keep the drive alive. Conley Duncan and the entire Alabama defensive line closed off Mauti's path.

Alabama took over with 1:15 to play close enough to mount another scoring drive. Instead, the Crimson Tide merely used running plays to pick up a first down—that coming on a Johnny Davis carry for four yards on a third-and-4 play that ensured the victory. Todd handed off to Stock on first down, then dropped to one knee on two consecutive plays, running out the remaining time.

Todd completed 10-of-12 passes for 210 yards. "I think we had to know they were going to be a tough team to run on, so they let me throw a little bit more," he said. "I only threw 12 passes, which isn't a lot, but we were only throwing the ball about five or six times a game before that, so it seemed like a lot. I was just a slow fullback, really, in that offense. The main thing is we threw on first down more than we had to try and change things up."

Todd carried his Sugar Bowl success home to the Senior Bowl in Mobile. It was there he really grabbed the attention of NFL scouts and vastly improved his NFL draft stock. That's because, now operating out of a pro-style offense, he threw for 332 yards and two touchdowns.

Todd was the sixth overall pick in the first round by the New York Jets, where former Alabama standout Joe Namath had led the team to a Super Bowl title. "I think Joe had a lot to do with me being picked by the Jets," he said. "The Senior Bowl was probably the biggest thing to happen to me in my career."

• • •

Alabama would win its next five bowl games—including the 1979 Sugar Bowl featuring the famous goal-line stand that gave the Crimson Tide the 1978 national championship—before losing to Texas 14-12 in the 1982 Cotton Bowl at the end of the 1981 season. Bryant would coach the team only one more season after 1981, his players closing out his storied career with a 21-15 win over Illinois in the 1982 Liberty Bowl, his 323rd all-time win as a head coach. A month later, Bryant died of a heart attack.

Following Bryant's tenure, Alabama continued to win Bowl games, winning four straight after the Liberty Bowl before losing to Michigan in the Hall of Fame Bowl. In the 1993 Sugar Bowl, led by Gene Stallings, who played for Bryant at Texas A&M, Alabama would return to the Sugar Bowl for another important win, beating Miami 34-13 to win the 1992 national championship.

But it was the 1975 team in the first Sugar Bowl in the Superdome that ended the Crimson Tide's string of Bowl disappointments, a win that still carries significance today.

CHAPTER SEVEN
1977 USC

Alabama 21, USC 20
October 8, 1977
Los Angeles Coliseum
Los Angeles, California

When Alabama traveled to Los Angeles to play Southern Cal in 1977, it wasn't just a terrific midseason, nonconference matchup of college football powers. It was an all-star game.

An NFL-all-stars-to-be all-star game.

Although it wasn't in use at the time, the NFL could have held its annual Combine right there at the Coliseum. Or one of its Pro Day workouts. It would have been appropriate. The Trojan and Crimson Tide rosters were filled with future NFL players. More than 50 to be exact. That's how many players on the two rosters would later be selected in the NFL draft or signed to free agent contracts.

That's not just a couple of good teams, that's a pair of franchises.

And that's what made this particular game special and why, many believe, it played out the way it did.

USC, coached by John Robinson, had a roster that included 35 players who would go on to play in the NFL. Included among that number were future Pro Football Hall of Fame inductees Anthony Munoz and Ronnie Lott, as well as Rob Hertel, Clay Matthews, Paul McDonald, Jeff Fisher, Mosi Tatupu, Dennis Thurman, Charles White, and Mike McDonald.

The Alabama roster, led by Paul "Bear" Bryant, had 16 future NFL players, including Ozzie Newsome and Dwight Stephenson, who would later join Lott and Munoz in the Pro Football Hall of Fame. Other future pros from the Crimson Tide roster included Barry Krauss, Marty Lyons, E. J. Junior, Tony Nathan, Rich Wingo, Jeff Rutledge, Bob Cryder, Johnny Davis, Don McNeal, Byron Braggs, and Billy Jackson.

"There had to be between 30 and 40 [NFL] draft picks in that game. It was just unbelievable," Newsome, now the general manager of the Baltimore Ravens, said in recalling all the players who participated in the game. "There were so many pro players who played in that game, it was just incredible. You can't believe how many guys who were in the stadium that night went on to the NFL. I don't think there's ever been that many on the same field for a [regular season] college game since."

At that time, the rivalry was strong and the games important. It was a matchup that always drew national attention. That was especially true in 1977. Consider the matchups: Bryant vs. Robinson, Lott vs. Newsome, Braggs vs. Munoz, White vs. Krauss; and not the least of which was Deep South powerhouse against West Coast powerhouse.

All that was necessary was to line off the field, assign some officials, turn on the scoreboard, throw a football on the field, and stand back.

You might also want to hold on.

• • •

Southern Cal student Laz Denes was excited about the Alabama game, and not necessarily because the Crimson Tide roster, like the Trojans', included several pro prospects. He wanted to get a good look at another part of the Alabama team: the girls of Alabama. He was not disappointed.

"It was my freshman year at USC, and that was the day I decided I was going to find me a Bama girl to marry before the day I die," Denes says, at least partially joking, though he would indeed later marry an Alabama girl, Kathy Rooks, who graduated from the university. The couple met while working at the *Palm Beach Post* newspaper in West Palm Beach, Fla.

"I was a 17-year-old freshman, shirtless and in shorts, yelling my head off from the last row on the west goal line with my fellow *Daily Trojan* newspaper mates who weren't working the game either," Denes said of the '77 game.

"We were No. 1 so, as things always went in those days, we just figured we were going to pull this one out in classic USC style. Turns out, that wasn't so. Those Bama guys in their white, tear-a-way jerseys were the scrappiest bunch I'd ever seen, full of energy all day long on a sweltering hot September afternoon. By late in the second half, I was so tired of seeing that big, white No. 22 jersey of Tony Nathan's cutting back and forth all over the field, picking up yards, killing valuable clock time."

As if his introduction to Alabama football and Nathan in particular wasn't enough, Denes would also be introduced to another aspect of Alabama football: its fan base. "I'd guess about 30,000 of them, all dressed in their crimson, were just loving it all," Denes said. "They were the loudest visiting bunch I'd ever heard in the Coliseum."

After the game, he and others who worked on the *Daily Trojan* staff heard his editor had snared a bunch of t-shirts and other Alabama gear from someone with the university. The group met at the University Hilton across the street and picked out an Alabama item or two to wear.

"I got a crimson No. 12 t-shirt jersey and quickly put it on," Denes said. "We saw in one of the banquet rooms at the Hilton that some Bama folks were celebrating big-time after beating the No. 1 team in the nation 2,000 miles from home. We walked in, got ourselves some beers, and tried to blend in with the Tiders. For some stupid reason, since we were wearing our new Bama shirts, we decided to pretend we flew out for the game from 'back home in Bama.'

"That's the day this USC boy fell in love with the Bama Nation. I love these people."

• • •

Assistant coach Paul Crane was in charge of scouting USC and putting together Alabama's game plan for the Trojans. It wasn't unusual. Bryant always assigned his coaches specific games each season in which they would be in charge of watching film on the opponent, scouting their strengths and weaknesses and putting together their ideas for the best plan of attack against that opponent.

Crane not only came up with a plan, he provided a demonstration.

Kathy Rooks Denes and Laz Denes (left, center) celebrate an Alabama bowl victory with friends Ed and Marianne Thiede. California native Laz made himself a promise he would marry an Alabama girl one day — he did when he married Kathy. (Photo courtesy of Kathy Rooks Denes.)

Mark Meadows, then a senior manager with the team who is now the executive director of the BBVA Compass Bowl in Birmingham, said he remembers Crane's speech and demonstration quite clearly. He said the theme of Crane's talk, given on Wednesday night the week of the game, centered on perceptions. One of the perceptions, Meadows recalled, was from Crane's days in the NFL playing for the New York Jets. "He said when he was with the Jets the perception [by others] of people from Alabama was that they were barefooted hicks in overalls," Meadows said.

The perception surrounding the Alabama-USC game was that the Trojans were too big and too talented for Alabama to handle. Crane didn't see it that way. "They were very talented and they had great size and athletes on their team," Crane admitted. "But when I was in the pro game, Lou Michaels had always said that you could take a little Coke bottle and hit a big Coke bottle and the little Coke bottle would smash the big Coke bottle."

So as Crane was speaking about USC and its tendencies, at the same time mixing in his theme of perceptions, he wrapped a small, 8-ounce Coke bottle in a towel. He then did the same with a larger, 12-ounce Coke bottle as players and the other coaches looked on, wondering what Crane had planned.

As he was driving home his point, telling the Lou Michaels story, Crane took the small Coke bottle and slammed it down on the bigger Coke bottle. "The little Coke bottle just shattered the big Coke bottle," Meadows recalled. "Then he told them the team that hits the hardest would win the game. . . . He got everybody's attention."

The message had been delivered.

"I have to tell you," Crane admitted more than 30 years later, "I practiced that deal with the Coke bottles. But when I did it [for the team], it worked. I think it was pretty effective. When I did it, there was just absolute silence. Afterwards, Coach Bryant gave me a compliment about that, telling me it was very motivational."

The small Coke bottle has a place of honor in the Crane's home today. His wife Heike had a small trophy, with the Coke bottle as the centerpiece, made for her husband. "It's really neat," he said.

• • •

Alabama's first offensive series was quick and none too productive. The Trojans' defense delivered a statement: this isn't going to be easy. Quarterback Jeff Rutledge received the message.

"On the first play from scrimmage, Jeff Rutledge and one of their big, ole tackles and a running back were all laid out on the field," offensive coordinator Mal Moore, now the school's director of athletics, said. "It looked like somebody shot a gun down through there. Jeff took stitches across his lip. It looked frightening."

It was going to be that kind of day.

A punt and 15-yard penalty for interference against Alabama after that initial possession set the Trojans up at their own 46-yard line. The first three plays, all rushes, picked up 20 yards. After a one-yard loss on the next run, White slipped off the left tackle for a dozen yards, putting USC at the Alabama 23. Four plays later, Mike Carey kicked a 32-yard field goal from the 15 for a 3-0 USC lead.

Less than seven minutes into the game, the Trojans' field goal would account for the only points of the first half. Not that the teams didn't try. On the next three combined possessions, neither team found its way to the opponent's side of the field, though Alabama got close at the 50. A Hertel pass on the first play of a USC drive was intercepted by Davis Dewey Mitchell, giving the Crimson Tide the ball at the Alabama 40 with 50 seconds left in the first period. The Tide offense made short gains, but nothing substantial and after nine plays punted back to USC.

When the Trojans' offense misfired too, they punted. Newsome took the punt at the Alabama 20 and returned it 47 yards, but a clipping penalty moved the Tide all the way back to its 14. The teams swapped punts again and Alabama put together some offensive action. Nathan picked up seven yards on a pitchout around right end, followed by a 10-yard Lou Ikner run around left end. Rutledge gained four yards on a keeper, and another trip around left end led to seven yards for Ikner, plus 15 yards for a facemask penalty against USC. The ball now rested on the USC 21.

On a third down-and-6 play from the 17, Rutledge pitched to Ikner, who threw a pass to Newsome in the end zone, but the pass fell incomplete. Roger Chapman entered the game to attempt a 34-yard field goal to tie the score, but the kick was blocked by Larry Braziel and recovered by Thurman.

USC ran a few plays and punted, leaving just a few seconds in the half. Rutledge took the snap at the Alabama 18 and downed the ball as both teams headed to their respective locker rooms.

Those expecting a close, tightly contested game had received just that in the first 30 minutes of play. Those who were expecting an offensive display did not get their wish. Alabama had produced just eight passing yards, one yard less than USC. But that would be all of Alabama's passing yards for the day, while USC would dramatically improve its numbers in that area.

A 21-yard punt return by Newsome, after the Alabama defense had held USC to open the second half, put the Crimson Tide offense to work at its

49. Rutledge picked up nine yards on a keeper on the first play, followed by a 3-yard Davis run and an additional 15 yards for a facemask penalty to the Trojans' 43. Davis then carried for 13. Nathan picked up six to the USC 5. It was all Davis from there as he gained two, then one and, on the drive's seventh play, a 2-yard touchdown run. Just that quickly, Alabama had claimed the lead, 7-3.

Ball control would be the Trojans' calling card on its next possession. Starting at their own 20, the Trojans used a pair of short-gain running plays before Hertel connected with Randy Simmrin for 23 yards. A no-gain running play was followed by yet another 23-yard Hertel-to-Simmrin pass play. An illegal procedure penalty backed USC up five yards and a 4-yard running play got most of that back before Hertel decided it was time to look for Simmrin again, connecting with him on a 20-yard pass.

Now at the Alabama 24, the Trojans produced a series of nine short running plays. Along with a facemask penalty against Alabama, USC had moved to the Alabama 1 before a 5-yard loss pushed the Trojans back to the 6, where they faced fourth-and-goal. Robinson chose to kick a field goal and Frank Jordan did just that, making a 23-yarder and trimming Alabama's lead to 7-6.

With only 1:26 left in the third period, fans were about to get their money's worth. The expectations of what the matchup of the two teams could produce was about to be met.

Alabama took possession at its 23 and used a 12-yard Rutledge run and yet another facemask penalty against USC following a 3-yard gain on the first play to quickly move to the USC 47. Davis picked up three yards and Nathan took a pitchout to the right for 12 more yards to the 32 on the final play of the third period. After Rutledge picked up a yard, Major Ogilvie claimed 12 to the 19. Three plays later, Nathan slammed into the end zone from a yard out.

Alabama's offense would be back on the field in just a few moments after a Hertel pass on the second play of the ensuing drive was batted by John Mauro and intercepted by Travis McGriff. The play, which started with USC owning the football at its 20, ended with Alabama controlling the ball at the Trojans' 8. After a five-yard illegal motion penalty against the Tide moved the ball back to the 13, Nathan ran around right end on a pitchout for 13 yards and a touchdown. As quickly as fans could say "Did you see that?" Alabama was in front 21-6.

The teams swapped three-and-out offensive series and punts, and USC reclaimed the ball at its 9 with 9:34 to go. Hertel's first pass was too long, and Lynn Cain followed with a 6-yard run. That's when the pass became the first option. Hertel hit Cain, Simmrin, and Howard Studdard all for back-to-back-to-back 12-yard pass plays to the Alabama 49. After a 2-yard run, Hertel started throwing again, this time for 28 to Simmrin and 14 to Calvin Sweeney to the 5 for a first-and-goal situation. A first-down pass fell incomplete and after a delay of game penalty that led the Trojans back to the 10, Hertel found Sweeney on a touchdown pass.

The Trojans went for the two-point conversion, making it on a Hertel-to-Tatupu pass play, putting the score at 21-14 with less than six minutes to play.

Alabama's offense ran six plays before having to punt the ball away. The kick was downed on the USC 21 with 3:08 remaining. Hertel threw for 4, then 13, followed by completions for 9 and 14 to the Alabama 39. Two incomplete tosses led to a 22-yarder to Sweeney and another first down at the 17. Hertel connected with William Gay for 8, and a pass in the end zone to Sweeney was broken up by Ricky Tucker. On third down, a pass intended for Simmrin in the end zone was flagged for defensive pass interference, giving USC a first-and-goal at the 1. A pitchout to Cain covered the remaining yard, and the Trojans had a touchdown.

They also had a decision to make, with only 34 seconds left to be played. Would they kick the extra point to tie the game? Or would they go for the two-point conversion and the win? Robinson chose the latter.

"No, we didn't think about that [kicking the extra point]," Robinson said later. "I couldn't come in [to the USC locker room] and look at my team in the face after going for a tie. There's just no way. It's impossible. You play to win the game. That's the only way. The kids played too hard out there, and they don't play to tie."

So the Trojans lined up for the two-point conversion.

McNeal said Alabama's defensive huddle prior to USC's two-point conversion try was businesslike. The players understood what was at stake. "What would happen, we didn't know, but we knew we could stop them," he said. "We just kept saying, 'Everybody do your job. If everybody does his job, we'll be OK.' That's exactly what happened. We said, 'Get your head up and don't be down [because of the Trojans' touchdown]. We need to do our job and get this done.'

"The offense has all the advantages on those kinds of plays. They know what they're about to do. We have to try to figure that out and stop it. They had the advantage, but hopefully they have seen some swagger from us and they see that we have confidence, and that they're going to have to earn it. I believe that's what happened. We did our jobs."

Southern Cal had its play ready. Hertel prepared to throw a pass, but Wayne Hamilton put a quick and big rush on him, deflecting Hertel's pass. The ball found its way into the hands of Alabama linebacker Barry Krauss for an interception, and the two-point try was thwarted.

Alabama 21, USC 20.

"Wayne Hamilton, on that two-point conversion, he just comes in like he knows what's happening, like he knows the play," then-Alabama Sports Information Director Kirk McNair said. "Krauss got the interception, but the play was made by Wayne Hamilton and his pass rush."

USC made the decision to go for the win; Alabama made the winning play.

"I kept trying to decide, am I going to watch or not going to watch," Newsome, who decided to watch, said. "We all call Wayne Hamilton 21-20, even today," he said of the nickname his former teammate earned that day in LA. Newsome said he came away from the game with a lifelong memory. "That might have been the most excited I have ever been in a football game," he said. "That win kept us in the national championship hunt."

Meadows said he didn't just trust his eyes as to the result of the two-point conversion attempt. He looked for a clearer sign.

"There's a great picture of me standing next to Coach Bryant and some others, looking up at the scoreboard to make sure the score didn't change," Meadows said. " . . . I remember there were 35 seconds left on the clock when the quarterback dropped back, and Hamilton rushed in and deflected the pass and Krauss intercepted the ball. Calvin Hannah called me about two weeks later and told me about the picture. He had to have taken it as soon as Krauss made the interception."

Afterward, Callaway could see the effect the win had on his head coach. "You could tell it meant a lot to Coach Bryant," he said. "It meant a lot to everybody, but it really meant a lot to Coach Bryant."

The Coke bottle-smashing Crane said he was proud to be associated with the game. "Even though we were smaller, we came out on top," he said. "The team just played well and the coaches did a great job. Bill Oliver did a great job with the secondary. . . . It was a huge game for us, and our guys just outplayed them. That was a great group of players, and it was a real exciting game."

• • •

A 31-24 loss at Nebraska in the second game of the season, even more so than the win over then-No. 1-ranked Southern Cal, was enough to keep the Tide out of the national championship hunt to which Newsome referred, in part because the Crimson Tide was ranked No. 4 in the country at the time and the Cornhuskers were unranked. Alabama, which won its remaining seven games of the year, including a 35-6 waxing of Ohio State in the Sugar Bowl, was ranked No. 2 in the final Associated Press poll with an 11-1 record.

"That game is relived to this day," Newsome said of the win over the Trojans. "I think that's what's special about college football."

Sports writer Phillip Marshall said Alabama's focus, from the start of spring practice following the 1976 season to the final play of the Sugar Bowl win over the Buckeyes, was on just one thing—winning the national championship. The Crimson Tide came close, but fell just short of its goal. "That team, like other teams from time to time, you just thought they were going to win [the national title], but they didn't," he said. "They won it the next two years and that season helped in that way, but they didn't win it. Those teams—the '77, '78 and '79 teams—those were Bryant's last great teams at Alabama."

Sylvester Croom, a former Alabama player, said the '77 season "started a great stretch for us [with the back-to-back national championships that followed]. We had a lot of great guys, a lot of great players."

• • •

Beating Southern Cal, especially that particular Southern Cal team, made quite a statement and impression. Newsome remembers the joy he and his teammates felt after the game, knowing they had stood toe-to-toe with a true powerhouse and won the fight.

"We didn't get caught up in all the being-in-Hollywood stuff," Newsome said. "That whole game, we were fighting for our lives. We got the running game cranked up in the game and that set the tone."

• • •

There was another person who had hoped to play pro football after his college career had ended, another player who had hoped to play against USC and compete against the talent that was on the field that day. Alabama quarterback Jack O'Rear had shared starting duties with Rutledge the season before, but a knee injury in late August had forced him to spend the first part of the 1977 season trying to get his tender left knee healthy again. It appeared he might be able to make a return to action for the USC game, but on the Tuesday before the game he re-injured the knee, forcing him to end his college career prematurely.

Two days later, he was undergoing surgery to repair the damage. Having already used his redshirt year, the senior's career came to an end without getting the opportunity to play his senior season.

"We gave it a good shot," O'Rear was quoted as saying in a story on him in *Tidal Waves*, an Alabama athletic department publication of the time. "Heck, I mean, with the help of the doctors and Coach [Jim] Goostree [head trainer]—who was just super the way he worked and worked with me—we gave it a good shot. For seven weeks in a row I was right in there, in the training room, and I mean I really did some work with those weights and all, trying to get the knee right again.

"I really hate that I can't play, especially since this is my last year. It happens to more people than me, though; but I never, ever thought it would happen to me."

Understanding how hard O'Rear had worked to get back in the lineup, his Alabama teammates voted to give him the game ball from the 21-20 win over No. 1-ranked USC.

It was almost like a Hollywood script.

CHAPTER EIGHT

1979 Sugar Bowl

Alabama 14, Penn State 7
January 1, 1979
Louisiana Superdome
New Orleans, Louisiana

Without fail, whether he is covering a college or NFL game, whenever Paul Kennedy finds himself in the Mercedes-Benz Superdome in New Orleans for a game, he always makes his way to the 1-yard line. He stands there, looks around the Superdome and its expanse, takes in the short distance from the 1-yard line—actually, less than a yard away—to the end zone, and tries to imagine what the moment must have been like back on Jan. 1, 1979.

He wasn't there. To be honest, he can't remember exactly where he was when Alabama's famous goal-line stand against Penn State in the Sugar Bowl took place, nor where he watched it. His memory of the play, which he watched on TV, has also been sketched for him by replays of the game over the years. Still, the play is as clear to him today as though he had been there, as though he had been standing on the Superdome sidelines or providing the play-by-play call from the press box.

To this day, he still marvels at the play itself and the will and determination needed to make the play a success. He marvels at the timelessness of the game, at how quickly fans will share their memories and thoughts about the play. He said he remains constantly amazed at the level of emotion evoked in the sharing of those memories several years after the fact.

"Every time I've been to the Superdome for a game, any game, I go to that spot," Kennedy, who was the football play-by-play announcer for Alabama's radio broadcasts in the mid-1980s, said. "I consider it holy land. You still feel it right there."

Penn State entered the game unbeaten and holding the nation's top ranking. Alabama, with one loss, was seeking to claim the national championship for itself, and it had the team to make that happen—a strong defense with some offensive punch and good all-around play.

Alabama had something else, too. It had chemistry. The 1978 team was one of confidence and talent and the right combination of the two ingredients, mixed within the framework of players who despite the team's national ranking played as though they had something to prove. They would indeed prove themselves that night.

• • •

The Sugar Bowl had become an almost annual trip for Renee Busby and three of her friends. Going to New Orleans to watch Alabama play football was a no-brainer. Busby had attended the two previous Sugar Bowls Alabama had played (1975, 1978), and this one was expected to be the best of them all. It pitted No. 1 Penn State against No. 2 Alabama with national championship implications. Getting tickets to the games at previous Sugar Bowls hadn't posed a problem. This one would be different. Of the four women, including Sue Bell Cobb, who served as Chief Justice of the Alabama Supreme Court from 2007-11, only two would end up with tickets. Two, including Busby, would decide the asking price was too high, so they retreated to their French Quarter hotel room to watch the game on TV.

It was a suite, so it wasn't all bad, but it certainly wasn't the same as being inside. "To be that close—to be in the same city as the game and not be in there—that was hard," Busby said. "Even though I got chill bumps watching the game, it wasn't the same as being in there. I would have loved to have been in there. Not being able to see all the things you could have seen if you had been in there—'Bear' and Joe Pa [Penn State head coach Joe Paterno] on the sidelines—knowing everyone else was in there having a great time in the Superdome, that was frustrating."

Doug Knoll was inside. He had his tickets and arrived early, as ready for the game to begin as any of the Alabama fans in attendance. He had been eagerly awaiting the game, feeling it would be a great matchup and that Alabama had a good chance to stop the Nittany Lions and win the national title. Knoll had pledged Sigma Chi, and his fraternity brother, Tommy Praytor, had gotten tickets for the game by way of his dad. "It was one of the most incredible experiences of my life, along with the 1993 Sugar Bowl [in which Alabama defeated No. 1-ranked Miami and won the national championship]," Knoll said. "We had a great day and a great night there. It was unbelievable.

"With all the Alabama fans there, it was so loud. We expected to win, so you just waited for it to be over so you could celebrate. Joe Pa and Bear Bryant, it doesn't get any better than that."

Knoll would later tell Busby all about his experiences. The two would meet a few years later, start dating and eventually marry. Almost eleven years into the marriage, the couple decided to adopt and were blessed with a little girl they named Caroline Bryant Knoll. Yes, Caroline's middle name is in honor of the former Alabama football coach.

"A couple of years after we married, we were in Tuscaloosa for a game and we were at the Bear Bryant Museum during a Bear Bryant Namesake Reunion," Busby recalled. "At the time, we didn't know what it was and when we found out it was for kids named after Coach Bryant we decided that if we ever had a son his middle name would by Bryant. That same year, *People* magazine had a story on the reunion, and we thought that was cool."

When the couple found out it would be adopting a little girl, the debate as to Caroline's middle name began. "It was between Rebecca, my mom's middle name, and Bryant," Busby said. "We ended up with Bryant after a coin toss, which was [tossed] by our friend Kristen Campbell. The coin kept landing on Rebecca and I kept telling Kristen to keep flipping. In the end, we decided on Bryant."

Almost every football season, Caroline and her parents make it to Tuscaloosa for the annual Bryant Namesake Reunion, as well as every other Alabama home game they can fit into their schedules.

For sure, Renee's and Doug's was a marriage made in Crimson Tide heaven. "I kind of developed it on my own," Knoll

Doug Knoll, daughter Caroline Knoll (second from left), Caroline's friend Kaelyn Horn and Renee Busby pose in front of the statue of Alabama head coach Nick Saban that is located in front of Bryant-Denny Stadium. (Photo courtesy of Renee Knoll.)

said of his interest in Alabama football. "Growing up in the '70s, how could you not be an Alabama football fan? Then I met Renee. I thought I was a big Alabama fan until I met her. She was an even bigger fan than I was."

So of course, the Sugar Bowl would be a factor in the couple's marriage. The 1990 Sugar Bowl—ironically, pitting the Crimson Tide against Miami; the Hurricanes winning this one, 33-25—was the first Alabama game they attended together, less than a year after getting married.

• • •

A year before, on Jan. 2, 1978, Alabama had dismantled Ohio State 35-6 in the Sugar Bowl. The win gave the Crimson Tide an 11-1 record, the only loss coming to Nebraska, 31-24, in Lincoln the second week of the season. "We wanted to be national champions," defensive back Murray Legg said, "and Coach Bryant said if we won [the Sugar Bowl] convincingly that everything would take care of itself. Driving back home the day after that game—we probably had a group of about seven cars following each other, a bunch of us and our girlfriends—we heard [on the radio] that Notre Dame had jumped over us to No. 1. We had to pull the cars off the road. We were devastated. After a while, we got back in our cars and continued the drive back. But I tell you, that was huge motivation for us for the next year. Huge motivation."

It wasn't as if Legg needed extra motivation. He grew up loving Alabama football, listening to John Forney call the games on the radio and watching the "Bear Bryant Show," the coach's Sunday highlight show with Charlie Thornton—must-see TV for Alabama fans—every week. His love of the team was started by his grandfather, Lee Legg.

Legg, then nine years old, and his grandfather were standing just outside the stadium. After a couple of moments, the elder Legg grabbed his grandson's shoulder and turned him to face another direction to see the Alabama head coach.

"He looked at me and said, 'Hello young man.' I said, 'Hello, hello,'" Murray Legg recalls. "My grandfather told Coach Bryant, 'He's going to play quarterback for you one day, coach.' And Coach Bryant said, 'That's great. I look forward to that.' Right then, I knew I was going to play football at Alabama. I was going to do everything I could to play football at Alabama."

As the team's quarterback, Legg helped lead Homewood to the 1974 Alabama Class 4A state championship. His grandfather saw every game they played. In fact, Lee Legg never missed one of his grandson's games, from the third grade until college. "I played a lot of sports growing up—football, basketball, baseball, ran some track, played some tennis—and he was at every single event," the grandson said of his grandfather. "I never knew until years later that when he would go to some of my games he would have to go back to work, sometimes until ten or eleven o'clock at night, to make up the time he missed while watching me play."

Lee Legg died after his grandson's sophomore year at Alabama. "He didn't get to see us win [the national championship], but he got to see me wear that crimson jersey, and that was great for him and me. He was something else."

Before his death, Lee Legg would attend many of Alabama's practices, and after practice, when talking with his grandson he would always offer the same advice. "You keep your nose clean, even if you have to use both sleeves," Murray Legg said. "He was my biggest fan."

• • •

There wouldn't be a lot of scoring, but there would be more than a few mistakes. The teams would combine for six interceptions, 20 punts, four fumbles (only one was lost, that one setting up what would become Alabama's famous goal-line stand) and 19 penalties for a loss of 126 yards. That's not exactly stellar play, yet the goal-line stand and several other team and individual plays made the game a classic.

Alabama would start the game at its own 20-yard line and push its way to the 39 before punting the ball to Penn State. The Nittany Lions' offense managed just three plays before punting the ball back to Bama, which took over at its 44. After a short loss on a run, a Gary Rutledge-to-Steve Whitman screen pass on second down picked up 11 yards, and a pitchout to Tony Nathan on the next play was eventually fumbled out of bounds, but not before he picked up eight yards and a first down. Rutledge and Major Ogilvie offered back-to-back 3-yard gains, but a pass to Whitman was dropped, leaving Alabama with a fourth-and-3 play at the Penn State 33. Alan McElroy was called on to attempt a 51-yard field goal, but it was short and wide to the right.

Chuck Fusina completed a pass good for 18 yards on first down, but two downs later, trying another pass, Fusina was intercepted by Legg and Alabama took over at its 34. The possession would advance only to the Nittany Lions' 43, where Alabama punted once again. Another Penn State punt followed and Alabama's Rutledge, on the final play of the first period, a third-and-10 play, fumbled but recovered his own mistake, losing three yards and setting up a punt on the first play of the second period.

The second period brought even less offensive success at the beginning, the teams combining on four consecutive three-and-out series. Penn State took over for the third time in the quarter at its 20 and moved to its 35 before Byron Braggs sacked Fusina for a loss of 21 yards to the 14. Fusina fumbled the ball but a teammate recovered, avoiding giving Alabama great field position. The next play produced only a yard, and the Nittany Lions punted again.

Rutledge would have success passing on the ensuing possession, at least at first. Starting at the Alabama 47, Rutledge threw a screen to Bruce Bolton for 16 yards, then tossed a screen pass to Whitman for another 16-yard pickup to the Penn State 21. After a 3-yard run by Whitman, Alabama and Rutledge went back to the pass but this time the throw ended up in the wrong hands. Rich Milot intercepted the throw at the 8 and returned it to the Alabama 37, seeming for a moment that he would return it 92 yards for a touchdown. Ogilvie managed to get to Milot and make the tackle.

"People ask me about the biggest plays I made at Alabama," Ogilvie would say years later. "One of them was in this game. We had driven the ball down to around their 20 and they intercepted one of our passes. They were gone [it seemed], and I was the only player left who could stop [Milot], and I made the tackle. It's funny, the two biggest plays I made at Alabama were defensive plays.

"The other came against Auburn on special teams. I was playing safety on the kickoff team and James Brooks had broken through and was on his way to scoring a touchdown, but I was able to make the tackle. Coach Bryant always said the game was divided into three parts—the kicking game was most important, with the defense a close second. Offense was a distant third."

Alabama's defense was being called on to stop the Nittany Lions, which it did. Once again, Braggs broke through the Penn State offensive line and got to Fusina, sacking him for a 15-yard loss back to the Penn State 48 on a third-and-10 play that followed a run for no gain and an incomplete pass.

With 1:11 left in the half, Alabama got the ball again, starting at its 20. The offense would be heard from this time. Ogilvie gained three on a run and Penn State called a time-out. A Rutledge-to-Nathan screen pass picked up five more and Penn State called another time-out, hoping to make a third-down stop and have one last offensive opportunity before the end of the half. Whitman picked up the first down with a 5-yard run, then Nathan was handed the ball and he slipped away for a 30-yard gain to the Penn State 37. Now, it was Alabama calling a time-out to conserve time. A pitchout to Nathan accounted for seven more yards, and Alabama called its second time-out with 15 seconds left. At the Penn State 30, Rutledge fired a pass to Bolton in the back of the end zone for a touchdown with only eight seconds remaining. The extra-point kick gave Alabama a 7-0 lead.

Penn State threw an incomplete pass on the half's final play. While Alabama had a staggering lead on the stat sheet, the Crimson Tide had just seven points. The Alabama defense, which would gain much glory in the closing minutes of the game, had been stout in the first half, limiting Penn State to three first downs and only 28 yards passing. The Nittany Lions were charged with minus-7 yards rushing on 17 carries. Alabama's offense had produced nine first downs and 214 total yards (129 rushing, 85 passing).

There wasn't any celebrating going on in the Alabama locker room. In fact, some of the Crimson Tide players were feeling ill, including Ogilvie. "The Sugar Bowl people had set up something for the two teams the night before the game at an oyster and shrimp bar, and several of us ate too many," Ogilvie explained. "I was one of them. I hadn't really slept well the night before, and after getting your bell rung a couple of times in the game, you really felt it, and there were some moments when you didn't feel too great."

Alabama did feel good about its six-play, 80-yard scoring drive near the end of the half that gave it a little breathing room. It would prove to be an important drive.

Ogilvie said Alabama's coaches decided to use fewer audible calls in the second half because the crowd noise in the Superdome was so loud it made communicating a play-change difficult.

Penn State would have to deal with the crowd noise first, and the noise was amped up a bit by Alabama fans feeling good about the Crimson Tide's seven-point lead and the way its defense was playing. Fusina and company again failed to move against the Tide defense, forcing another three-and-out series. Alabama matched the three-and-out offense on its ensuing possession and Penn State had the ball again at its 20. On first down, Fusina dropped back to pass, but his attempt was picked off by Jim Bob Harris, who was run out of bounds by Mike Guman after a 22-yard return, setting up the Crimson Tide at the Nittany Lions' 33.

The Tide started with a 1-yard gain by Nathan and picked up five more yards on an offsides penalty by Penn State. Nathan gained two more, with Whitman adding a 4-yard run, followed by a 2-yard run. Rutledge was sacked for a loss of two yards, and a screen pass to Lou Ikner lost two more yards, giving Alabama a fourth-and-12 situation from the Penn State 23. McElroy got the call again, this time from 40 yards away, but he pushed the kick wide right.

After a Penn State punt, Alabama took over at its 29. On a third-and-10 play, trying to make something happen, Rutledge's pass, intended for Tim Clark, was intercepted by the Nittany Lions' Pete Harris at the Alabama 48. A third-and-6 play found Fusina completing a 25-yard pass play to Guman to the Alabama 19. After a 2-yard pickup by Guman, Fusina threw a 17-yard touchdown pass to Scott Fitzkee, and Matt Bahr tied the game with his extra-point kick.

Ikner would give Alabama's offense a charge after a pair of short offensive series by both teams. Penn State boomed a 50-yard punt after its failed possession. Ikner received the punt and returned it 62 yards to the Penn State 11. Alabama was penalized five yards on the first play for illegal motion. Rutledge then gained a yard before Nathan gained seven yards on a pitchout around the right side. From the 8, Ogilvie got the call on the same play—pitchout to the right—and covered the remaining distance for the touchdown, capping a three-play, 11-yard drive. Only 21 seconds remained in the third period. Just four minutes after Penn State had tied the game, Alabama had reclaimed the lead.

That set the stage for the final period and a fourth-down play that will live forever in Alabama football lore.

• • •

The two offensive units started the fourth quarter in a pattern that had been repeated often throughout the game—back-to-back punts. At the 12:21 mark, Penn State took possession and mounted a scoring threat. From their 31, the Nittany Lions steadily moved downfield, getting runs of 6, 5, 5 and 3 yards before a Fusina pass to Guman collected 9 more. Fusina completed another pass, this one to Brad Schovill for 19 yards, and suddenly Penn State was at the Alabama 28. But E. J. Junior tackled a Penn State player for a 5-yard loss on the next play, and Fusina, trying to get the touchdown on the following play, was intercepted by Don McNeal in the end zone.

Alabama opened the door for Penn State moments later. On a third-down play, Rutledge rolled left and fumbled on a lateral. Penn State recovered the ball at the Alabama 19, and the Nittany Lions' offense was in business again.

Instead of scoring a touchdown that would tie the game, though, Penn State would find itself on the wrong side of history, the wrong side of one of college football's biggest moments.

Matt Suhey got the drive started in a big way, smashing up the middle for 11 yards and a first down at the 8. Guman got the call on the next play, picking up two yards on a pitchout to the left. On second-and-goal from the 6, the play that lives on in the shadow of the goal-line stand took place. It is a play that, if it had not been made, would have erased any chance of a goal-line stand.

"Every time we're at a function together, [former Alabama basketball coach] Wimp Sanderson will say, 'If you had covered your man there never would have been a goal-line stand,'" Legg says of the good-natured jab Sanderson offers. He is referring to McNeal's outstanding tackle of Fitzkee, keeping him out of the end zone two plays prior to the goal-line stand. Legg was supposed to cover Fitzkee.

Legg said he had studied reels and reels of game film on Penn State prior to the Sugar Bowl and noticed there were only two times when the Nittany Lions lined up as a tight end. He knew Penn State's approach in both cases. So when Fitzkee lined up at tight end on second down, Legg, who was responsible for signaling defensive coverages for the secondary once the opposing offense lined up, was certain he knew what was coming, and certain how the play would end.

"I knew where he was going and what play they were going to run," he said. "I was certain of it. I remember thinking, *he's going to go to this spot and I'm going to read the play, step in front of him and intercept the pass and return it 98 yards for a touchdown.* I really believed that. But they threw in a new wrinkle, and when I saw what was happening, there was no way I could get to him, no matter how fast I could have run."

But McNeal could. Legg said a Penn State player tried to push McNeal into the end zone and away from the play, but McNeal fought off the block, got to Fitzkee and made "a great, great play."

McNeal, who had intercepted the Fusina pass in the end zone earlier, sprinted to catch up to Fitzkee along the right sideline, and when he did, delivered a strike that kept the Penn State player out of the end zone, driving him out of bounds a foot away from a touchdown.

"I just was in the right place and doing things I was supposed to do," McNeal explained of his touchdown-saving tackle. "I was covering a guy out of the backfield and I saw what was happening and got over there and made the perfect tackle and drove him out of bounds. . . . I had to take care of my responsibilities first and then help out. I was just reacting, really. But it was the perfect tackle, otherwise he scores. I remember Curtis McGriff running over to me and saying, 'Great tackle, Don.'

"I will always remember that second-down play. I had my man and I saw everything that was happening like there was no one else there. It had to be a perfect tackle because we couldn't let him fall down [forward]. That's not something you really practice, it was just instinct."

Sylvester Croom said the McNeal play was the "greatest single-effort play I think I've ever seen. That was a great, great play. He was doing his job and comes out of the end zone and makes a great tackle. That wasn't a good play, it was a great play. When you watch that play, it looks like an easy touchdown."

Former Alabama Sports Information Director Kirk McNair credits McNeal's play as being just as important as the fourth-down play. "The second-down play is the one that counts," he said. Fitzkee caught the ball running parallel to the end zone. McNeal hit Fitzkee and drove him straight out of bounds, or there wouldn't have been a goal-line stand."

"I told him, 'Don, that play was incredible,'" Legg said of his words to McNeal after the play. "I told him if we won the game I would kiss him. . . . Don was such a talented player. He had skills the rest of us wish we'd had."

Two more great plays, perhaps perfect tackles, would have to be made. Penn State was on the one-foot line and looking to tie the game. It had the offensive line and backfield to easily score from a foot away, but it would be matched against a defense that had steadily gained confidence with its play throughout the game and now, based on McNeal's outstanding tackle, had gained a little more.

On third-and-goal, Suhey got the call, charging up the middle but gaining nothing. Paterno called a time-out as the Nittany Lions' staff mulled over what play to call next. As the officials spotted the football one foot line away from the end zone before Penn State took the time-out, Alabama's Marty Lyons watched Fusina, who was looking to see where the ball would be placed. As he stepped away and the players caught each other's attention, Lyons offered some play-calling advice.

"You better pass," Lyons said.

It was, as the moment has often been referred to over the years, "gut-check time."

"In the huddle, all the young guys were looking at Marty, me, Rich [Wingo], all the seniors," Legg recalled. "A bunch of us seniors spoke up. We said that no one in the country had worked harder than we had for four years and that it all came down to this. We gambled that Coach Paterno was not going to get tricky, that he would come right at us because he believed his team was good enough to gain one yard. Sure enough, they did; they came right at us. If they had faked a handoff up the middle and gone around end they probably would have scored because all 11 of us went to the middle."

Fusina perhaps should have taken Lyons' advice to heart. Instead, on fourth-and-goal and the football one foot away from the end zone, with the national championship hopes of both teams in the balance, the Nittany Lions decided to run the football. Fusina handed the ball to Guman, who tried to leap over the Alabama defensive line. He picked the wrong spot. Waiting for him in midair was linebacker Barry Krauss, who delivered a powerful, helmet-to-helmet tackle. The blow stopped Guman in his tracks, in the air, and ended Penn State's drive right there. Legg had offered help, as had McNeal, who made a strong move at the line to bottle up movement and was able to get to Guman just before he made his leap. Defensive lineman David Hannah had built a human dam of sorts at the line of scrimmage, plugging a direct route to the end zone. Lyons, Braggs, and Wingo were there too, as were others. In reality, there was a sea of crimson jerseys, and Guman could not part it.

The Superdome erupted into cheers, almost loud enough for Busby to hear in her hotel suite.

ABC-TV's Keith Jackson, known to many as the voice of college football, especially during that time, was providing the play-by-play for the Sugar Bowl. Here is how he called the goal-line stand:

> *"The yard marker in the Sugar Bowl shows a half-a-yard to go for the touchdown and the possibility of tying or going ahead for Penn State. Nineteen-game win streak, only undefeated team in the country, ranked No. 1 in the nation; Alabama ranked No. 2. Everything could be hanging on fourth-and-goal and a half-a-yard. . . . Guman . . . He didn't make it! . . . Tremendous goal-line effort by Alabama turns Penn State away from half-a-yard."*

Back in her hotel suite, Renee Busby was as happy as anyone who didn't have a ticket to the game could be. "That was probably the most fantastic game, especially the goal-line stand," she said. "We were going crazy in the room. The whole time, I just remember wishing I was there. Even though we were going crazy and Alabama was winning, I wished I was there. I remember asking my friends later what the goal-line stand was like in there, and they just gloated and said, 'You should have been there.'"

Knoll was, and he was thrilled. "I wasn't sure if [Penn State] scored or not [on the fourth-down play], we couldn't tell. We didn't think they had, but you couldn't be sure until the defense ran off the field," Knoll said. "I don't remember much after the goal-line stand. It was just crazy."

• • •

Krauss was a talented high school football player in Pompano Beach, Fla., a player who would take his talents to Tuscaloosa where he would become the central figure in the 1979 Sugar Bowl's goal-line stand, a player who would go on to have a successful NFL career too. Yet no matter the other plays in his prep, college and pro careers, it is the goal-line stand for which he is best known, and it is the play—the moment—he most embraces.

In 2006, Krauss cowrote a book, *Ain't Nothin' But a Winner: Bear Bryant, the Goal-Line Stand, and a Chance of a Lifetime,* with Joe M. Moore. And while artist Daniel Moore's painting, *Goal-Line Stand,* is one of the most popular of the many memorable Alabama football moments Moore has depicted in his talented, successful style, Krauss too has painted his version of the play that has also been sold as prints across the Southeast.

But to Alabama fans, even though he offered sideline reports during the 2007 football season for the team's radio broadcasts, Krauss will always be the player in the middle of Moore's *Goal-Line Stand* painting and prints; ole No. 77; the linebacker who tackled Guman head-on and helped the Crimson Tide win the 1978 national championship.

"I actually broke my helmet, and I had a pinched nerve, so when I hit him, my whole left side was paralyzed," Krauss told the *Sporting News* in an interview years later. "I had repeated problems with it, but it went totally numb and I was in excruciating pain. When I hit him, it took everything out of me. It just seemed like everything slowed down.

"I remember Murray Legg came over and pushed us back, and I believe without him they would have scored. I was able to stop them at the top long enough for Murray to push us back. I remember, I was laying there in pain, thinking, *My God, that freaking hurt.* I couldn't get up. I remember the crowd was deafening, and Marty Lyons picked me up and I said, 'Did we stop them?' And he goes, 'Yes, we stopped them.' And I didn't realize that we did it."

In Richard Scott's book, *Legends of Alabama Football,* Krauss told Scott he is often reminded of that play and often thinks of that game. "It lives in my heart," Krauss is quoted in the book as saying.

Krauss was named the game's Most Valuable Player, the first lineman to be so honored since Walt Yowarsky, a tackle for Kentucky, earned the award in 1951. Yowarsky's head coach? Paul "Bear" Bryant.

"It's a great feeling to be named the Most Valuable Player of the Sugar Bowl," Krauss said after the game. "On the fourth-down play, we just lined up and hit them head-to-head. . . . It's a great privilege to play for Coach Bear Bryant and the University of Alabama. It takes a team to put it all together and we put it all together today. Coach Bryant is the secret because he kept us loose throughout the game, and that includes during the halftime. He is the difference."

• • •

The game wasn't over. Not yet. In fact, there was still plenty of time for a lot of things to happen. Though most who recall the game and the goal-line stand usually think of the fourth-down "gut-check" play as taking place late in the game, in truth there was still 6:39 left to play.

"It wasn't over, but the momentum had shifted dramatically," Croom, who showed video highlights of the game to his Mississippi State team before its game in the 2007 Liberty Bowl, said. "Our confidence was so good, they just knew somebody was going to make a play."

And now Alabama had a reversal of fortune of sorts. The defense having just stopped Penn State from scoring now turned the football over to the offense, which found itself only a few inches removed from the end zone. They now had to find a way to push the ball away from the end zone and not commit a turnover, lest a mistake such as a fumble erase what was accomplished by the defensive stand.

"I remember going out on the field and looking at where the football was and thinking what a dangerous place it was in," Ogilvie said. "It was just a few inches from the goal line, and we were going to have to get it out of there. That was a treacherous spot. They could have gotten a safety on us very easily, and we would have had to kick the ball back to them. We were able to hold on to the ball and get a little working room. I'll tell you though, like Yogi Berra would say, that game wasn't over until it was over."

Nathan took a handoff on first down and punched the ball out four yards to the 5. Ogilvie gained a yard on second down and Nathan gained three, leaving Alabama facing fourth-and-2 and an obvious punting situation. The punt was terrible, going out of bounds at the Crimson Tide 20, which would have put Penn State in excellent field position again. But the Nittany Lions, in a perhaps game-changing mistake, was penalized five yards for having 12 players on the field. The Crimson Tide ran off six more plays before having to punt the ball away again, this time punting to the Penn State 21 where the Nittany Lions would take over with 2:42 left.

Penn State made another mistake right away, committing a 5-yard delay of game penalty, pushing the ball back to the 16. Fusina got it back, throwing a 16-yard pass to Fitzkee for a first down. The next play was a 5-yard pass to Guman. Krauss knocked down a pass on second down before a screen pass to Guman accounted for six yards and another first down. Fusina went back to Guman, the duo combining on a 14-yard pass play, with Scovill catching a pass for just two yards. The Nittany Lions were now on the Alabama 41 and the Crimson Tide coaching staff called a time-out.

Fusina's next throw on third down was to the end zone, but it was incomplete. With less than 90 seconds to play, the Nittany Lions had to try and pick up the first down or a touchdown on fourth-and-8, but Legg broke up the pass and the football went back to Alabama with 1:16 to play.

Alabama ran plays and Penn State called a time-out. Eventually, the Crimson Tide, on a fourth-and-6 play, punted back to Penn State. Fusina's pass on first down was intercepted by Mike Clements, Alabama's fourth interception of the game, and one more play—a 4-yard run by Nathan—was all that was required to erase the remaining seconds and secure Alabama's victory, not to mention its impending national championship.

"It was a sure-enough football game that old-timers could appreciate, and those of us who played in it were glad to be a part of," Ogilvie said. "I was proud to be a part of it and glad when it was over. That was a tough, tough football game. I don't know how many times trainer Jim Goostree went out on the field to look after somebody, but it was a lot. It was the hardest-hitting game I ever played in, and there wasn't a close second."

• • •

The next day, Murray Legg once again found himself in a caravan of cars, heading back home after a Sugar Bowl game. This time, the news was much better. "We heard someone say on the radio that Alabama was expected to be named the national champions," he said. "We pulled off the road again, this time to celebrate."

After the disappointment of the previous year, Legg wasn't taking anything for granted. He decided he needed to see it in print. He wouldn't believe the talk until he saw it in print. If the story in the next day's newspaper told of Alabama winning the national championship, then he'd really celebrate. "That night before I went to bed, I set my alarm clock for four or five o'clock in the morning," Legg said. "When it went off, I jumped up and went to the 7-Eleven and bought a paper. When I saw it, I went to my girlfriend's apartment and woke her up. I was so happy. I went straight to her stereo and played 'We Are the Champions' by Queen, turned it up loud. I played it over and over again for probably thirty minutes. I don't think [the neighbors] minded."

CHAPTER NINE
1979 Auburn

Alabama 25, Auburn 18
December 1, 1979
Legion Field
Birmingham, Alabama

If ever there was a player destined to play for the Alabama Crimson Tide, a player who seemed natural wearing the team's crimson jersey and running onto the field with his teammates, it was Steadman Shealy.

The fact that he played quarterback—perhaps the most notable position in the program's long and storied history, a position filled before him by players such as Joe Namath, Ken Stabler, Pat Trammel, Richard Todd, Bart Starr, and Steve Sloan—only enhanced the association.

Shealy grew up in Dothan following Alabama football along with the other members of his family. There was no question where his loyalties were placed for the Iron Bowl each season, or for any other Alabama game. Because of Alabama's success during the 1970s, Crimson Tide games were televised a lot, giving Shealy and his family several opportunities to watch their favorite team on TV.

In high school, Shealy developed into a fine quarterback. As such, he caught the eye of many college recruiters. He helped lead Dothan High School to the Class 4A—at that time, the largest classification in the Alabama High School Athletic Association—state championship game his junior and senior seasons. That only attracted more attention for Shealy, who had several schools, especially SEC schools, seeking his signature on an athletic scholarship.

The attention was so intense that one night he had one-fifth of the SEC's head coaches at his house. Doug Barfield, who in 1976 was heading into his first season as head coach at Auburn, having replaced legendary Ralph "Shug" Jordan, had made his way to the Shealy family's living room to try and convince the young quarterback to forego his childhood loyalties and play football for the Tigers.

While Barfield was making his pitch, Georgia head coach Vince Dooley, who grew up in Mobile, played at Auburn and was now one of the game's most respected coaches in leading the Bulldogs, was sitting in a car in the Shealy's driveway, awaiting his opportunity to talk with the young quarterback and his parents.

Barfield and Dooley had competition. Many other head coaches for schools across the Southeast had phoned the Shealy residence to talk with young Steadman and try to persuade him to join their football team. As Barfield was making that same pitch in person, Shealy's mother stepped into the living room, offered an "Excuse me" to the group and told her son he had a phone call.

Alabama head coach Paul "Bear" Bryant was on the line.

Shealy took the call.

The youngster said, "Hello," and the unmistakable growl of a voice on the other end, skipping all the how-are-you? pleasantries and other conversation-openers, got right to the point. "What color jersey have you always wanted to wear?" Bryant, obviously aware of Shealy's boyhood loyalties and the fact competition was in the Shealy house, asked.

"Crimson," Shealy said.

"What's the problem then?" Bryant responded.

And with that, the recruitment of Steadman Shealy officially ended, even with Auburn's head coach in his living room and Georgia's head coach sitting in a car in the family's driveway.

"It was tremendous," Shealy said of the phone call. "When I signed, it was carried live on radio in Dothan, and all anyone could talk about was that Coach Bryant was coming to town to sign Steadman Shealy."

That moment would play an important role in the events of Dec. 1, 1979, the date of the annual Iron Bowl game that season. Barfield, the man in the living room whose recruiting pitch was ended by a phone call taken in another room, would lead a tough and talented Auburn team against Bryant's Alabama team, its offense led by Shealy, the player who said "Yes" to Bryant and "No" to everyone else who sought his talents.

Shealy would be the trigger of an 82-yard, game-winning drive in which he scored the winning touchdown, leaving Barfield and perhaps others who kept tabs on the Tigers' recruiting efforts in 1976 to ask themselves some what-if? questions.

They shouldn't have wasted their time. Even if Bryant had visited the Shealy house on another night or made his phone call at a different time, the result would have been the same—Shealy was born to play at Alabama, and if Bryant made a scholarship offer, it was going to be accepted.

It was a natural fit.

• • •

Alabama, which had won the 1978 national championship, was in position to repeat the task the following season. In '78, Alabama started the year No. 1, fell to No. 7 after a loss to Southern Cal in the third game of the year, and moved to No. 8 the next week after beating Vanderbilt. The Crimson Tide slowly climbed back into the upper echelon of the rankings the remainder of that regular season, rising to No. 2 after a win over Auburn and setting up a faceoff with No. 1-ranked Penn State in the 1979 Sugar Bowl. That, of course, would become one of the most famous games in Alabama's football history; the goal-line stand against the Nittany Lions late in the game helped the Crimson Tide to a 14-7 win and the national championship.

The 1979 season began with Alabama at No. 2, where it remained until it moved into the top spot the week of its sixth game of the year, when it defeated Tennessee 27-17, allowing the Vols the most points by an opponent that season heading into the Auburn game. The Alabama defense played a big role in fashioning the record and national standing, having produced five shutouts (Baylor, Wichita State, Florida, LSU and Miami). The Crimson Tide carried its No. 1 ranking into the Iron Bowl showdown with Auburn. Alabama's offense was averaging 33.4 points a game and the defense was allowing an average of just four points a game.

But with so much at stake, along with the Iron Bowl mystique, this game had a completely different feel. This one wouldn't go as easily as many of the Crimson Tide's previous 10 games.

• • •

One glance at Tommy Wilcox is all it would take anyone, even the most casual of fans, to come up with the perfect description of him: football player. He was indeed that. He not only played the game, he lived the game. He loved the essence of football; its subtlety and its nuances, as well as its pace and its undeniable smashmouth appeal. He loved the game and loved playing the game. He even loved practice. And yet, having grown up with the game, there was an aspect of it he had yet to experience, a subtlety of sorts he did not yet know but of which he was about to be introduced.

Tommy Wilcox of Harahan, La., was about to play in his first Iron Bowl. It would be an experience he would learn to treasure.

"I was a freshman that year," he said of the 1979 Alabama-Auburn game. "It was the first time I had played in the Iron Bowl. Being from Louisiana, I knew what it meant to me to beat LSU and prove that I made the right decision [on where to play football]. Most of our guys knew the [Auburn] guys. They had played against each other or with each other in high school. And they wanted to win the Iron Bowl and prove they had made the right decision on where to play too.

"It's different. It's just a different game. And if anybody tells you it's just another game they don't have their head screwed on right. . . . It was for bragging rights and owning the state. And on top of that, we're trying to stay undefeated and win the SEC championship and have a chance to play for the national championship. It's not like the game wasn't big enough in the first place."

The game was plenty big, as Wilcox quickly learned and as Alabama and Auburn fans already knew. This one would test the boundaries of the big definition, with all that was riding on the game for the Crimson Tide and simply because, as Wilcox pointed out, it was the Iron Bowl, which to many, especially in the state of Alabama, is the greatest rivalry in college football.

The Crimson Tide player in Wilcox—the one who twice earned All-America honors, the SEC's 1979 Freshman of the Year, the Alabama Decade of the 1980s and Team of the Century selection, and the two-time All-SEC pick—understood the meaning of the game and why it was important; the football player in Wilcox recognized its symbolism, its tradition, and its fan-crazy, 24-7/365 importance.

Both sides of Wilcox's personality couldn't wait for the game to get started.

• • •

The 1975 Auburn game was a great night for wide receiver Kevin Pugh and his Alabama teammates, one that lives on today through DVDs and video tape. "That game has been getting a lot of play lately on Crimson Classics," Pugh said of a series of great games in the program's history. "It's fun to watch those games again and to be able to relive them with your family."

This one would be deserving of the title of "classic."

• • •

Auburn would have enjoyed nothing more than to upset Alabama's national championship hopes and the opportunity was at hand. Carrying an 8-2 record with just one SEC loss going into the game, the Tigers, who would finish the year ranked No. 16 in the Associated Press' final Top 25 poll, were capable of accomplishing the feat.

Yet Alabama's biggest opponent on this particular day, at times, was itself.

Time after time, the Crimson Tide made a mistake or produced a turnover, the kind of miscues that kept Auburn in the game.

For its part, Auburn had trouble holding on to the football as well, especially in the early stages of the game. Alabama kicked off to the Tigers to start the Iron Bowl, the kick taken in and fumbled by James Brooks at the Auburn 23-yard line. It was recovered by Alabama's Randy Scott at the 23. Instead of putting together a quick score, Alabama ended up losing eight yards back to the Auburn 31 and chose to punt.

Auburn's fumble troubles continued when the Tigers fumbled twice on the series following the Alabama punt, though they recovered both drops. Then Alabama got into a habit of making mistakes. On its second offensive possession at its own 34-yard line, Alabama received a second down, 19-yard run by Major Ogilvie and several other shorter, yet effective running plays before Billy Jackson fumbled on the 10th play of the drive at the Auburn 6. He recovered his mistake but lost 10 yards. A Utah pass to Ogilvie produced just four yards and forced an Alan McElroy field goal attempt of 30 yards that missed the mark.

Auburn started the ensuing drive from its 20 and marched methodically downfield toward a score. Like Alabama, the Tigers took advantage of a strong running game, pounding out short runs until Joe Cribbs broke loose for a 35-yard gain to the Alabama 23 that ended up moving the ball to the 12 when an Alabama penalty was added to the play. A third down-and-11 play from the 13 led to an offensive pass interference call against the Tigers, pushing the ball back to the 30. Jorge Portela kicked a 47-yard field goal from there to give Auburn a 3-0 lead with 44 seconds left in the first quarter.

The Crimson Tide responded. A Don Jacobs-to-Pugh pass on the second play of the ensuing possession produced 16 yards. After six running plays and an incomplete pass, followed by another running play, Alabama was at the Auburn 28. That's when Shealy, back in the game, connected with Pugh for a touchdown pass that put Alabama in the lead.

Alabama's next offensive drive would have a similar look and produced similar results. Starting at its 35, the Crimson Tide ran eight running plays and one pass play—a 13-yarder from Shealy to Pugh—that put it at the Auburn 1. From there, Shealy pushed his way into the end zone for the score.

Less than three minutes remained in the half, and although both teams would get another offensive possession, neither mounted a threat. Alabama had a 14-3 lead and 183 yards. Auburn, with just seven passing yards and four fumbles, though it lost only one, had little to show for its play in the first two periods.

Auburn's trouble holding on to the football would transfer to the Alabama sideline in the second half, and it would be noticed right away. On the first play of the third period, Shealy lost his grip on the football after a 3-yard gain, and Ken Hardy recovered for the Tigers at the Alabama 21. The mistake wouldn't hurt the Tide. On a third-and-13 play from the 24, Auburn was tagged with a 15-yard personal foul penalty that moved it back to the 35, where the Tigers punted into the end zone.

Two plays into Alabama's next drive, Edmund Nelson hit Ogilvie to induce a fumble, and Freddie Smith recovered for the Tigers at the Tide 28. The Auburn offense struggled again, but managed a 39-yard Portela field goal for a 14-6 score.

Once more, Alabama couldn't hold on to the football as Steve Whitman dropped the ball on the Tide's first play of its next offensive possession, but he managed to fall on the loose ball himself. But two plays later Alabama lacked the yards for a first down and punted.

Three possessions, three fumbles, two lost fumbles, one punt, 20 total yards.

"We had our backs to the wall a couple of times because of turnovers, but we were able to overcome those," Wilcox said. "Really, I thought it was two great teams, both playing hard and both hitting hard."

Looking to improve on its second-half performance, Alabama's offense started its fourth possession of the third quarter at its own 28. Whitman gained three yards before Shealy slipped around left end for 27 to the Auburn 42. After Billy Jackson gained three yards, Whitman picked up 17 to the Auburn 22, followed by a 10-yard pass from Shealy to Pugh and another first down at the Auburn 12. Poised to produce another touchdown, Alabama let the opportunity slip through its fingers. Literally. Shealy fumbled the ball, and Auburn's Harris Rabren recovered at the Tigers' 16.

But the Tigers would return the favor. Two plays later, Cribbs lost the handle and E. J. Junior recovered for the Tide at the Auburn 22. Whitman had runs of 8 and 3 yards to gain a first down at the Auburn 11. Shealy picked up a yard, Ogilvie was stopped for no gain and Whitman picked up 5 to the 5-yard line, where a fourth-and-4 play awaited. Not taking any chances, Bryant opted for the field goal and McElroy was true on his 23-yard kick. Despite its troubles holding on to the football and other mistakes, Alabama had a 17-6 lead.

Auburn's offense couldn't move against the Alabama defense and punted the ball back to the Crimson Tide, but—yes, once again—Wilcox fumbled the punt. Dan Dickerson fell on the football for Auburn, which had the ball at the Alabama 37. After a 1-yard gain and an incomplete pass, Charlie Trotman tossed a 36-yard strike to Cribbs for a touchdown. A two-point conversion attempt failed, but just like that, the Tigers were back in the game at 17-12 with eight seconds to play in the third period.

Alabama's offense had a three-and-out experience and punted back to the Tigers, who were gaining confidence and momentum. Starting at their 33, the Tigers were hit with an encroachment penalty to start the drive, but on second down Trotman and Byron Franklin connected on a 55-yard pass play to the Alabama 14. Don McNeal made the tackle that kept the play from going for a touchdown. After Cribbs picked up three on a run and Trotman threw an incomplete pass, Trotman looked to throw again, finding Mark Robbins for 11 yards, a touchdown and the lead at 18-17, after another two-point try failed.

If he hadn't already discovered it, Wilcox was finding out in an all-too-real way that the Iron Bowl was special. "It was one of those games like I've never seen before," he said. "That game was unlike any game I've ever played in in my life."

• • •

The time had come for Alabama to make something happen. It did, but not before another fumble, though it managed to maintain possession. Ogilvie, on the first play following Auburn's Trotman-to-Robbins score, lost the handle on the football, but Shealy was there to recover it and pick up four yards in the process. Shealy then produced runs of 9 and 15 yards before Ogilvie collected two yards to the Alabama 48. Shealy found Pugh for a 9-yard strike and Auburn was assessed a 15-yard penalty on the play, moving the Crimson Tide to the Auburn 27. Whitman stormed off right guard for a big 20-yard gain, and Shealy, reading the defense on the option, slipped through the Tigers' defense for the remaining eight yards and a touchdown. He then tacked on a run off right end for the two-point conversion to put Alabama back in front, 25-18.

"That was a matter of confidence," assistant coach Sylvester Croom said of the game-winning drive. "Those guys had been in a lot of football games at Alabama. They'd been there before. Those were special people. They had a lot of seniors, and they were experienced seniors, experienced people. They were not arrogant, but they were confident."

Pugh said that confidence, that we've-been-here-before knowledge was recognizable in the huddle, and Shealy was the leader. "Steadman was the field general, he was in charge of that huddle, just like he always was," Pugh said. "There were a lot of seniors, a lot of good, experienced players in that huddle, but Steadman was definitely in charge. He was the one talking. He pulled us together and he told us, 'OK guys, this is it; we've got to take it 80 yards and score. This is what we've been practicing for, this is why we ran all those drills, this is what all that work has been for, for something like this.'"

Recalling that drive a few years later, Shealy said, "We knew what we needed to do, what we had to do. That's what made our team special. It wasn't just that we *wanted* to go down and score, we knew we *had* to go down and score. We had to win that game. One, it was Auburn, and that was enough. Two, we had an undefeated season and we didn't want to give that up. And three, we were No. 1 and we wanted to stay No. 1 and win the national championship. When you look back on that season and what we wanted, that was our goal, to be national champions. We knew we had to win the game to make that happen, which meant we had to score on that drive."

The rest of the offense joined its quarterback and, while it had its troubles throughout the game, on that drive—driven, no doubt, by the fact it was the Iron Bowl, not to mention the national championship implications that existed—it pushed forward as it had so many other times. With its back against the wall, with the team's season and how it would be defined in the balance, Alabama drove 82 yards in seven plays for the game-winning score.

"Steadman and the guys on the [offensive] line just took that game over," Croom said. "It was a great season, a national championship season, but I think all that came down to that drive. It's all about execution. You're on the spot. Every down counts, every play counts. And on that drive, everybody did their jobs. . . . They had a will to win. They took the ball and moved down the field. I remember thinking, *If we don't cross the 50-yard line, if we don't keep moving the ball, we might lose this game.* They kept moving the ball."

There was still 8:17 left to play and plenty of time, as had been proven in the previous 51:43 of the game, remained for another switch in the game's momentum and lead. As it turned out, Auburn almost needed only a few seconds.

Brooks received the kickoff at the Auburn 5 and almost atoned for his fumble of the game's opening kickoff in a big way. He darted past, through, and around Alabama defenders and appeared headed for a sure touchdown when a streaking Jeremiah Castille, who in the official game stats is not credited with a tackle nor an assist, caught Brooks from behind by the shoulder pads and finally wrestled him to the ground, along with the help of McNeal, after a 64-yard return.

"Senior managers get a national championship ring if the team wins one," Colin Macguire, known to Alabama fans as "Big C," said. "And I saw my national championship ring maybe getting away. . . . We did what you call a safe kick, kicking it in a corner, but James Brooks grabs it and takes off. He starts cutting across the field and I'm standing there watching, saying, 'Oh, God!' . . . Then Jeremiah Castille caught him from behind on the 31-yard line. I'll always be forever grateful to Jeremiah for catching up to Brooks. He's always going to be one of my favorite players of all time."

Still, the Tigers had great field position at the Alabama 31.

It wouldn't be close enough.

Auburn's offense would have three possessions before time ran out, including the one set up by Brooks' return [and Castille's and McNeal's saving tackle], but managed to gain just 19 yards. On a fourth-and-2 play on the first series, a Trotman pass to Mike Locklear fell incomplete. The same was true of a Trotman-to-Rusty Byrd pass on a fourth-and-10 play on the second series and of the game's two final plays that accounted for the third series after Alabama's go-ahead score.

When it was over, Alabama had fumbled seven times, losing four, all four lost fumbles coming in the third period, when the Tide lost the handle on the football five times. Auburn fumbled six times but lost just two of the mistakes.

Despite its struggles and its many attempts to give the Tigers scoring opportunities, Alabama managed to hold Auburn to 249 total yards and 18 points. Despite itself, Alabama's offense rolled up 394 total yards, with Shealy managing 99 yards rushing and two touchdowns and another 64 yards passing and another score. Whitman rushed for 107 yards, and Ogilvie had 65. Pugh caught five passes for 76 yards.

Just as importantly, several Alabama streaks remained intact with the win, which was the Tide's 20th consecutive win (the nation's longest such streak at the time), the 23rd straight SEC win (then a league record) and— the most important stat within the state's borders—the seventh straight win over Auburn.

Equally as important, Alabama remained unbeaten and in the race for the national championship, which it would claim with a 24-9 win over Arkansas in the Sugar Bowl, giving Bryant and the Tide back-to-back national titles for the first time since the 1964 and 1965 seasons.

Colin 'Big C' Macguire and his friend Joe Henley get ready for another Alabama football game. (Photo courtesy of Colin Macguire.)

"I was definitely very proud of the team for winning," Bryant said afterward. "I was particularly proud of them for coming from behind. The drive for the winning touchdown was one of the finest I have ever seen. We had to have it. Shealy was at the throttle, but there were 10 other people who had a lot to do with it.

"Even though [Auburn] scored a lot of points, our defense played spectacularly. And the offense played well enough to win. The statistics might not be impressive, but the licks passed were impressive by both sides. . . . This was one of the greatest wins we've had. It was one we needed badly. We had to have it to keep those streaks alive and to keep our hand in the [national] championship."

Bryant was asked if he felt his team would still be ranked No. 1 in the country when the next polls were released. "I don't know, but I guess we're going to find out," he said. "I'm going to vote for us."

The Crimson Tide did not hold on to its No. 1 ranking, falling to the No. 2 slot in the Associated Press poll, Ohio State taking over the No. 1 position. But after Alabama topped Arkansas 24-9 in the Sugar Bowl on New Year's Day and Ohio State lost, the Tide claimed its second consecutive national championship, receiving 46 of the 67 first-place votes in the final poll. Southern Cal, which finished No. 2, received the remaining 21 first-place votes.

How talented was the 1979 Alabama team? This talented: the Associated Press and United Press International selected All-SEC teams each season and that year, there were 11 Alabama players—Steadman Shealy, Major Ogilvie, Byron Braggs, E. J. Junior, Dwight Stephenson, Don McNeal, Jim Bunch, Mike Brock, David Hannah, Thomas Boyd and Jim Bob Harris—named to the combined first teams. Five more—Tommy Wilcox, Steve Whitman, Wayne Hamilton, Rick Tucker, and Buddy Aydelette—earned combined second-team honors. That's a total of 16 (of 22 starters) making first- or second-team All-SEC. Stephenson won the Jacobs Trophy, Bryant was the SEC Coach of the Year pick by the AP and UPI, and Shealy finished 10th in the Heisman Trophy balloting.

The Sugar Bowl win would close out the ultra-successful decade of the 1970s in proper fashion—with an undefeated season and the national title. Alabama won 103 games in the '70s, including some impressive, still-popular wins. High on the list of such wins during that decade is the one the Crimson Tide produced at Legion Field in the final Iron Bowl of the '70s.

In Shealy's Dothan law office, there is a large reminder of that win and of that day, that game, that touchdown, that moment—a large print of artist Daniel Moore's painting *All on the Line*, which depicts Shealy stepping between two Auburn defenders, their grasp around his ankles, into the end zone for the game-winning touchdown. The print is displayed in a spot where everyone who enters his office will see it.

The only thing that would have made the painting and the story perfect is if Alabama had been wearing its home crimson jerseys, the one Shealy had told Bryant he always dreamed of wearing, instead of the visiting white jerseys the Tide wore that game. No matter. In his heart—"I love Alabama football and I love the university," Shealy said—it's the only color he ever wore.

CHAPTER TEN
1981 Auburn

Alabama 28, Auburn 17
November 29, 1981
Legion Field
Birmingham, Alabama

History, some Iron Bowl fans will quickly suggest, is made each time Alabama and Auburn meet in a football game. Records are of no concern. Playing for a national championship or conference crown? That only raises the stakes a bit. No matter the type of season that has been enjoyed or survived to that point, how the season is measured can sometimes come down to simply winning the Iron Bowl. It is the ultimate measuring stick of a season at Alabama and Auburn.

All that is necessary to make an Iron Bowl game important is a field, a football, and a scoreboard. The teams, and their respective fan bases, will take it from there.

Yet at times, true historic significance—the type recognized beyond the loyalties of the state, beyond the state's borders and beyond the opposing sidelines—has been attached to the playing of the Iron Bowl. That was certainly true of the 1981 game. That was the game in which Alabama head coach Paul "Bear" Bryant would attempt to become the winningest major college coach of all time at that time in the game's history.

Standing in his way was Auburn, his school's most intense rival, led by one of Bryant's former assistant coaches, Pat Dye, who was in his first season at the helm of the Tigers' program.

The 1981 Iron Bowl didn't just provide historical ramifications, but it was also loaded with all the drama and emotion available from one football game.

Auburn head coach Pat Dye (left) and Alabama head coach Paul "Bear" Bryant chat prior to kickoff of the 1981 Iron Bowl. (Photo by Mike Foley, courtesy of Mike Foley.)

This would be the first chance Bryant had to claim his 315th career victory, which would lift him above Amos Alonzo Stagg, whom he tied for the all-time major college wins mark with 314 two weeks earlier at Penn State, when the Crimson Tide beat the Nittany Lions 31-16.

Bryant would only need one shot at breaking the record.

"We had all that pressure on our shoulders (to win Bryant's 315th game), and it was the Iron Bowl," All-America defensive back Tommy Wilcox said. "But if you're a football player, you want to play in those kinds of games because if you can win those kinds of games you can win any kind of game. If you can win a game like that, you can win a championship."

Playing under pressure was as commonplace for the 1981 Crimson Tide team as starting a game with a kickoff. The countdown to 315 wasn't limited to that season. Once Bryant had tucked away his 300th victory in a 45-0 win over Kentucky at Legion Field on Oct. 4 the previous year, Alabama fans started calculating when Bryant would break the record. Those calculations hadn't figured in a 6-3 loss to Mississippi State in 1980, nor the 24-21 loss to Georgia Tech in the second game of the '81 season. Nor did they figure in the 13-13 tie with Southern Miss, which came between convincing wins over Ole Miss and Tennessee.

It may have come a little later than expected, but when the chance to win No. 315 fell on the Iron Bowl game, it seemed as though other forces were in play. To many Alabama fans, Bryant getting his first chance at win No. 315 against archrival Auburn was the perfect setting.

• • •

Before the stage could be set in Legion Field against Auburn and Dye, the Crimson Tide had to go to State College, Pa., and win there, which was certainly a strong test. In fact, that game was historic too; it would be the game in which Bryant tied Stagg's record of 314 wins against a coach, Joe Paterno. And it came with the same pressures, the same determination, the same everybody's-watching atmosphere.

Because of the game's significance, Mike Tankersley wanted a front row seat for the game at Penn State. He just didn't know how to go about obtaining that seat. As sports editor of the *Crimson White*, Alabama's student newspaper, he felt it was important to be there. Regardless of that standing, he *wanted* to be there. But the cost of such a trip was more than he could afford.

He tried to come up with a plan, a way to get to the game at minimal cost, but none of his ideas were workable. He had enrolled in grad school specifically so he could be the *Crimson White* sports editor and have the opportunity to cover Bryant's quest to break Stagg's record. One of the friends he mulled ideas over with was Bill Lumpkin III, the son of then-*Birmingham Post-Herald* sports columnist Bill Lumpkin Jr. It was the younger Lumpkin, based on a suggestion from his father, who provided Tankersley with a plan that had merit.

The plan was simple: call Coach Bryant, explain his situation and ask if there might be an extra seat available on the team plane for the sports editor of the student newspaper. Tankersley, willing to give anything a try, did just that. A few days before the game, Tankersley received a telephone call. The woman making the call asked, "Is this Mike Tankersley?" A bit groggy from being awakened by the ringing of the phone, Tankersley said, "Yes, it is." The woman replied, "Please hold for Coach Bryant."

"I was awake now," Tankersley said.

Bryant told him there would be a seat reserved for him on the team plane. Other plans were also put in motion that took care of his other needs—hotel room, credentials, and meals. He took his seat on the team plane for the flight to State College and recognized for the first time what he already knew but, for some reason, hadn't considered: some of the players were in a class he was teaching as part of his graduate school requirement. Yet he was more surprised at seeing Mary Harmon Bryant, Coach Bryant's wife, walk up and down the plane handing out chewing gum to all the players. And, of course, he was surprised by the presence of the man who made the trip possible, the reason for the trip as it were: Coach Bryant himself.

When the plane landed and the team bused to its hotel about thirty miles outside State College, Tankersley was struck by how Bryant took charge. "It was a different scene with his players than you saw on Saturdays," he

Mike Tankersley (center) was provided a seat on the Alabama team plane and a hotel room to cover the Penn State game in 1981, when Paul "Bear" Bryant tied Amos Alonzo Stagg's record of 314 career wins. Tankersley is seated between players Al Blue (left) and Anthony Smiley. (Photo courtesy of Mike Tankersley)

remembered. "He was directing players to their rooms and such and there was a different interaction. It was interesting."

Tankersley caught a ride with the state troopers who accompanied the team to the hotel room that had been provided for him in State College. When he arrived, he noticed three Alabama fans sleeping on a couch in the hotel lobby. Understanding others had offered him a helping hand to get him there, he came up with his version of pay it forward, offering to let the Tide fans stay in his room. The trio gladly accepted, and they all tailgated together the next day before the game.

Having taken photos from the sidelines in the first half, Tankersley moved to the press box for most of the second half before returning to the sidelines near the end of the game. As the final seconds ticked away in the Alabama victory, he ran onto the field to take more photos, finding the mob scene that surrounded Bryant. As players lifted their coach on their shoulders, Tankersley lifted his camera above his head and clicked off some shots. "On the TV the next day, showing a replay of the game, I saw myself taking those pictures," Tankersley said.

Then he watched as the Penn State fans—"a very classy group, very classy" Tankersley said—applauded as Bryant walked off the field. "It was so loud and so sincere, it just brought chill bumps to me," he said.

"On the bus [to catch the plane for the flight home], Coach Bryant was sitting in the front and I got a good, close look at him. The man looked like he had aged 1,000 years that season. He had allowed me to interview him before the season started and now, he looked so tired. I thought to myself, *this is the most successful football coach in the history of the game and look what it's doing to him.*"

• • •

Split end Joey Jones, now head football coach at South Alabama, understood the importance of the Penn State game, too. It was a game that meant a lot to him and the other players, a gift they wanted to present to Bryant if for no other reason than to end the wait *for him* as quickly as possible. The sooner win No. 314 was in hand, the sooner the opportunity to win No. 315 would arrive.

"I remember going into the locker room after the game. I walked in right behind Coach Bryant and I remember thinking what it meant to me and to the program. Usually after a game, after a win like that, players would be hugging and high-fiving. That game, everybody was looking at him. During the game, I was trying to feel what he was feeling at that time, at that moment. Every chance I got, I would stand close enough to him to see if I could figure out what he was thinking or hear what he was saying. I truly believe he didn't like putting that burden on us, the pressure of tying the record. He thought of us more than he thought of himself, and you could feel that."

More pressure, for Bryant and his players, was on the way. The 31-16 Penn State win would only serve as a hint of what their lives would be like for the next two weeks. The off week between the Penn State and Auburn games seemed perfectly sandwiched in a long season at the start of the year. Now, it seemed an eternity away.

"We didn't want to lose it; one, because it was Auburn, and two, because it was 315," Jones said. "We didn't want it to hold over to the next game, whenever that might be."

• • •

From the start, it was easy to see that this would be another classic Iron Bowl battle. As the stands quickly filled, fans arriving early in anticipation of the game and the moment at hand, a steady buzz began to hum throughout Legion Field, only more intense than usual. Even those who wouldn't play a down were nervously waiting for the start.

"The place was on fire," Legg said. "You could feel it everywhere. The Iron Bowl will never again be what it was then, what it used to be, when the stadium was half Alabama and half red, and half Auburn and half blue. I know it's important to have games on campus now, and that's good, but back then, when it was half-and-half, it was just incredible, just really incredible. And I got to play in three of those, and," Legg added, pausing for effect, "I never lost to Auburn."

Auburn drew the first hit, holding Alabama's first offensive possession to a three-and-out series. Chuck Clanton returned the punt that followed

55 yards to the Alabama 13. The Crimson Tide's defense returned the favor, allowing the Tigers to advance only five yards, setting up a 25-yard field goal try by Al Del Greco that missed the mark.

And that was just the start.

Taking over at its 20, Alabama struck quickly. Kenny Simon lost three yards on the first play, but quarterback Alan Gray quickly made up for the loss by slipping around left end for 63 yards to the Auburn 21. From there, Alabama used its running game to pound its way closer to the end zone, Gray getting the score on a quarterback sneak on a third down-and goal play from the 1.

Little else was accomplished offensively in the middle of the quarter, but Auburn made a late drive toward a score, only to have the opportunity taken away. Auburn drove from its 30 to the Alabama 8 where it had a first-and-goal situation, but Auburn quarterback Ken Hobby's pass was picked off at the 1 by Wilcox, ending the threat on the quarter's next-to-last play.

After an Alabama punt, Auburn's offense started another drive. Beginning on its 49, thanks to a 37-yard punt return by Clanton, the Tigers needed just three plays to reach the Crimson Tide's 31. From there, the yards were harder to come by, and Del Greco was called on to try another field goal, this one from 43 yards out. It too missed the mark, leaving Alabama in front 7-0 with 10:29 remaining in the first half.

Two offensive possessions later, Auburn's offense finally cashed in. A fair catch of an Alabama punt placed the Tigers at their own 37. From there, fullback George Peoples slammed off left tackle and kept going for 63 yards and a touchdown. Just that quickly, the game was tied.

On Alabama's ensuing possession, Gray fumbled on the first play and Auburn's Zac Hardy recovered at the Alabama 10, giving the Tigers a chance to produce another quick score. Three plays and just six yards later, Auburn lined up for another field goal try, and it turned out like the previous two—without points. A bad exchange on the snap led to no field goal try, giving Alabama the ball at its 26.

Once again, Alabama tried to open the door of opportunity for the Tigers. Quarterback Walter Lewis's deep pass to Joey Jones was intercepted by Mark Dorminey on the Auburn 23 with 1:20 left in the half. Gaining 24 yards on the first three plays, the Tigers closed out the half on four consecutive incomplete pass attempts. Through all the craziness of the first 30 minutes of play, the teams were tied.

The second half would prove to be interesting and closely played, too.

On its first crack at things offensively, Alabama was on the move. A facemask penalty on a third-down play in which the Crimson Tide had come up short of making a first down kept the drive alive at the start and moved Alabama from the 50 to the Auburn 31. A fourth-and-2 play garnered two yards by fullback Ricky Moore and once again, the drive continued, this time from the Auburn 21. After an incomplete pass and a five-yard penalty against the Tide for illegal motion, quarterback Ken Coley flipped a Utah pass to receiver Jesse Bendross who slipped away from the defense for 26 yards and a touchdown.

Auburn countered the score. Having failed to pick up a first down, the Tigers punted to Alabama. Jones fumbled the punt, which was recovered by Auburn's Clanton at the Alabama 2. Two plays later, Lionel "Little Train" James slid around right end for the touchdown and a tie game. Again.

The rest of the third period was dominated by turnovers. Benny Perrin picked off a Hobby pass at the Alabama 17 and returned it 18 yards to the 35, but four plays later, Alabama gave the ball back to the Tigers when running back Mickey Guinyard, after picking up 10 yards to the Auburn 33, fumbled, and Tim Drinkard recovered for Auburn. A three-and-out offensive series led to another Auburn punt . . . and another Alabama fumble. Once again, Jones couldn't get the handle on the punt and Auburn recovered.

Auburn was finally able to take advantage of a turnover. And finally, Del Greco would provide the points. Starting at the Alabama 33, a holding penalty moved the Tigers back to the 42, and three plays later, a clipping penalty pushed them back to the 39 after having reached the 23. They closed out the third quarter facing second-and-19 at the 33.

On the first play of the fourth quarter, Auburn became the beneficiary of a penalty that moved the Tigers all the way to the Alabama 13. Auburn punched and pushed its way to the 2, but facing a fourth-and-goal situation there, Dye chose to take the safer route, sending Del Greco in to attempt a 19-yard field goal. This time, he made the kick and Auburn had a 17-14 lead, its first lead of the game. As it would turn out, it would be the Tigers' only lead of the game.

The Crimson Tide retook the lead and control of the game on its following possession. Jones provided a 20-yard kickoff return to the Alabama 25 and on a third-and-6 play, Lewis connected with Bendross on a 12-yard pass that moved the Crimson Tide to the 41. Another Auburn penalty, this one a holding call, aided Alabama on the team's next third-down play and moved the Tide to the Auburn 38. That's where Lewis and Bendross hooked up again, and where Alabama reclaimed the game for good. Bendross's second touchdown, this one a 38-yard reception, gave the Crimson Tide and Bryant a 21-17 lead, but there was still 10:07 left to play.

Alabama would use that time to pad its advantage.

The Crimson Tide defense limited the Tigers to a three-and-out series, and an Auburn punt placed the Crimson Tide at the Auburn 49. Linnie Patrick put his stamp on the historic game. The running back, who would get only four carries in the game, made the most of two of them. On first down, he went off right end for 32 yards to the 17. Jeff Fagan picked up two yards on the next play before Patrick finished off the drive, scooting 15 yards off right end, this time for the score.

Watching the game at his home on TV, Keith Dunnavant, author of the books *The Missing Ring and Coach* said, "The thing that stands out to me was Linnie Patrick, and the fourth quarter he had. He had been a highly regarded recruit and he had said he was going to win three Heisman Trophys and contend for a fourth one his freshman year. That got under Coach Bryant's skin right off the bat. . . . He was suspended a couple of times and had been in and out of Coach Bryant's doghouse.

"The 1981 season had been a disappointment and now here was the game to win No. 315 and who's in there in the fourth quarter but Linnie Patrick, a guy who had his guts checked so many times, a guy who was seen by some as the antithesis to the program in so many ways, is the guy who is one of the heroes of the game. Of *that* game. It said a lot about his character. He just kept coming back."

There was only 7:06 left to play, only 426 seconds until Bryant became the all-time winningest major college football coach.

Auburn's final offensive possession ended when Perrin intercepted a Hobby pass and returned it 37 yards to the Alabama 44, leaving 23 seconds of game time. Lewis took the snap, dropped to one knee and Bryant was on top of the coaching mountain alone.

There was even a game plan for just such an ending.

"I was right there next to Coach Bryant," Legg said of the game's final seconds. "We had talked about it with the team, that if we won there were going to be a lot of people coming on the field and we needed to protect Coach Bryant, so we wanted the players to come to where he was and form a wedge so he would be able to move behind us. Myself, Sylvester Croom, Jeff Rouzie and some others, we're yelling at the players to come up [toward Bryant]. But they're a little confused. Some are caught up in the moment and celebrating and some others forgot, but we finally get enough players over there. . . . It was just an amazing, amazing scene with all those people and all those cameras following him everywhere."

Joey Jones remembers the scene, too. "All the media there, you just felt for Coach Bryant," he said. "Most of all, though, you were proud for him. That game wasn't about us, it was about Coach Bryant and what he had accomplished. We were just grateful to be the team that won that game for him. We had come out and played pretty good in the fourth quarter. I thought we played the better game."

What Alabama had done was follow Bryant's advice. "Coach Bryant always said big games will be won on five or six plays, and we had to make those five or six plays," Wilcox said.

The celebration and congratulations shared on the field were nothing compared to the celebrations taking place in the stands, outside Legion Field and all across the state by Alabama fans. It was the Iron Bowl, which meant 365 days of bragging rights for the Bama Nation, but it was also the game in which their coach earned the title they had given him long ago: the best (and winningest) coach in the land.

"To me, Alabama fans are the greatest fans in the country," Wilcox said. "They'll recall stuff to me that I had completely forgotten about. They remember plays that you made and they want to tell you about them when they get a chance to meet you. They're the greatest fans in the country because they don't like to lose, they'll follow you anywhere you go and they'll celebrate when you win."

They were certainly celebrating now.

• • •

The two coaches—the teacher and the student; the friends—met at midfield after the game. Dye, in his first Iron Bowl as Auburn's head coach, had prepared his team well, but it was Bryant, chasing history, and his team that had made the plays that counted most, those five or six plays he always preached to his team it needed to make to win the game.

"Looking at Coach Dye and Coach Bryant talking, it was a special moment," Scott Hunter, then working as a sports anchor for WKRG-TV in Mobile, said. "Auburn was ready, and Coach Dye had them ready to play. They didn't have as much talent [as Alabama], but he had them ready to play and an upset was a possibility. To be there and to see that, to see Coach Bryant win his 315th game and to see the coaches meet at midfield, that was just a thrill for me."

It was special indeed for all concerned.

"I had grown up as an Alabama fan, a fan of Coach Bryant's," Dunnavant said. "That was my third year as a sportswriter and I was still stuck on that divide, and still a kid. This was history. This was special. And I'm not sure in those days that we knew it wouldn't be that way forever."

• • •

The Alabama locker room was a madhouse, and the phone was ringing.

A special phone had been set up for Bryant to receive congratulatory phone calls, a couple in particular. Number one on that list, a call from President Ronald Reagan. "I was highly flattered and the squad was too," Bryant later said of President Reagan's phone call. "He congratulated the team and the coaches. He remembered that he attended one of our practices in a tuxedo a few years ago. I reminded him that when he was a cub reporter I met him at the Rose Bowl [as a player for Alabama]. . . . Ex-President [Jimmy] Carter also called, and I appreciated that too. I told him that we had two great teams here in the South. Senator Jeremiah Denton called, and I appreciated that. I couldn't hear him too well because it was getting pretty noisy by then."

Tankersley was in the Alabama locker room when Bryant received some of the calls, and when the phone was no longer being used, he admits he had an illegal thought. "I thought about stealing it," he said of the phone, "but I didn't think I could get away with it."

CHAPTER ELEVEN

1982 Liberty Bowl

Alabama 21, Illinois 15
December 29, 1982
Liberty Bowl Memorial Stadium
Memphis, Tennessee

The end of the most successful coaching era in Alabama's long football history came quietly and with only a hint of celebration. For Crimson Tide fans, Paul "Bear" Bryant's decision to retire after 25 seasons at the school was a somber moment, even though he made his exit in victory.

The win was significant, and not because it placed his all-time victory total at 323, at that time more games than any other major college coach had ever won. There was perhaps more pressure on the members of the 1982 team in that game than had been experienced by any other team in Bryant's days at Alabama. The reason was simple: it "wouldn't be right," players and others have said many times since that night, for Bryant to leave the game on a losing note.

It seemed everyone who followed and loved college football, with the exception of the Illinois team, its coaching staff, and its fans, wanted Bryant to win his final game. Accomplishing that feat wouldn't be a simple task.

• • •

The announcement caught everyone by surprise. While those recruiting against Bryant repeatedly told prospects he was close to retirement for years, Alabama fans didn't want to think about that possibility, and for the most part, recruiting prospects weren't swayed by the talk. When Bryant announced the 1982 Liberty Bowl would be his final game as the team's coach—he made the announcement just two weeks before the game was played—the task for the Crimson Tide, and the motto for the game, was clear:

This one would be for The Bear.

The 1982 season hadn't played out as many had hoped, including for Bryant himself. The Tide had lost its final three games of the regular season to LSU, Southern Miss, and Auburn, carrying a 7-4 record into the Liberty Bowl. In 1981, when Bryant broke Amos Alonzo Stagg's all-time win mark with his 315th victory (against archrival Auburn, no less), it was the highlight of a year that found the Tide posting a 9-2-1 mark and claiming the SEC crown.

From 1971 to 1980, Bryant's Alabama teams won at least 10 games every season but one (finishing 9-3 in 1976) and picked up eight SEC championships and three national championships—1973 (United Press International), 1978 (Associated Press), and 1979 (AP and UPI). So the '82 season didn't meet the standards Bryant himself had established for the program. Though he certainly wasn't being asked to step down—to make such a suggestion would have been career suicide for anyone—Bryant was experiencing some health problems and had begun giving some thought to the day when he would step aside.

On the heels of the tough finish to the '82 regular season, Bryant decided that time had arrived. On Dec. 15, with many of the state's top sports writers in Orlando, Fla., set to cover Auburn's scheduled Dec. 18 game against Doug Flutie and Boston College in the Tangerine Bowl, Bryant let the world in on his little secret.

"This is my school, my alma mater," he said at the press conference announcing his decision. "I love it and I love my players. But in my opinion, they deserve better coaching than they have been getting from me this year."

With his decision, Bryant transformed the Liberty Bowl from just one of the pre-New Year's Day bowl games into *the* bowl game of the year. The Liberty Bowl suddenly carried the same weight as the Rose Bowl and Orange Bowl in terms of interest and, quite suddenly, ticket demand and media credential requests.

The city of Memphis would play host to Bryant's last game. The Liberty Bowl, at least that year, went from "other bowl" designation to a historic event. Ardent Alabama fans bought every ticket they could find, as did others who simply wanted to be there for Bryant's final game as Alabama's head coach. That was the approach, too, of sports writers and broadcasters, not only in Alabama but across the country . . . and beyond.

"The thing about that game that stands out the most to me was all the press, the international press," All-America defensive back Tommy Wilcox said. "It wasn't just writers from Alabama and across the country, but from all over the world, wanting to cover Coach Bryant's last game."

As such, Memphis became the center of the college football universe.

"For Memphis, this was special," said Harold Graeter, now Associate Executive Director of the Liberty Bowl. In 1982, Graeter was a 20-year-old college student who helped the bowl by taking on various jobs. "Memphis is a great football town and there are a lot of Alabama fans in Memphis. To be the game Coach Bryant hand-picked for his last game was special."

It was especially exciting for Graeter, who was given the task of tape recording Bryant's comments each day after practice for a local radio station. The memories of those practices are still strong today. "I would stand next to him, a 20-year-old kid in a room with seasoned newspaper guys, and ask questions," he said. "One of those days, I stuck the mic right under his chin. I must have gotten it really close because he said, 'Boy, do you want me to eat that thing?' It was special being a part of all that in a peripheral way."

• • •

Linebacker Eddie Lowe of Phenix City—the brother of All-America linebacker Woodrow Lowe and father of former Alabama running back/kick returner Jonathan Lowe—would have a standout performance in the game. But it's not the tackles and the interception he had that he remembers most. He remembers the incentive.

"That whole week was emotional," he said. "We did not want to lose that game. We weren't going to lose that game. Can you imagine if we had lost that game? We wouldn't have been allowed back in [the state of] Alabama."

Perhaps no one understood the significance of the game more than Mal Moore, who had spent several seasons on the sidelines alongside Bryant, most as offensive coordinator. Bryant's influence on Moore's career and life is unmistakable, and life as Moore knew it at that time was about to change in a big way.

"That game and everything was very, very hard for me personally," Moore, former Alabama Director of Athletics, said. "I'm sure it was hard for him. . . . I knew I was leaving Alabama. I had been [on staff] a long time. I hated to see a great thing come to an end, so it was very hard for me. I was thankful we won it so he could go out with a win."

The day before the game, Bryant met with members of the media in his hotel suite as he had always done at previous bowl games. Immediately everyone involved recognized this meeting wouldn't be like any of the other such gatherings.

"That meeting was quite reflective," *Huntsville Times* former sports editor John Pruett said. "I think he had a pretty good idea how sick he was. Usually, those meetings lasted about 15 minutes, but this one lasted at least an hour."

Someone suggested a photograph be taken of Bryant with all the reporters at that meeting. Many writers in the state, who have held on to their copy of the photo, keep it where it can easily be found.

Phillip Marshall, who at that time was sports editor of the *Montgomery Advertiser*, was among those at the meeting. For him, it was another chance to speak and spend time with Bryant, whom he had known since he was a youngster. Marshall is the son of the late Benny Marshall, the former *Birmingham News* sports editor and Alabama Sports Writers Association Hall of Fame member, who had been a close friend to Bryant.

"Those were different times," Marshall said. "Back then, there was more warmth between reporters and the people they covered." That was certainly true of the elder Marshall and Bryant. Once, Benny Marshall took Phillip and his brother along with him on a trip to Tuscaloosa to cover a Bryant press conference. The boys stayed outside and played while their father attended the press conference.

"I was probably 10 or 11 at the time," Marshall said. "Me and my brother were standing around and we looked up, and there was Coach Bryant. He had seen us outside and he asked my daddy, 'Are those your boys?' My daddy said, 'Yes,' and he stopped to come outside and see us."

• • •

Kathy Rooks was an editor of the *Crimson White*, Alabama's student newspaper, that year, but she had already graduated. Other staff members invited Rooks, a longtime Alabama football fan, to go with them to the Liberty

Bowl and help cover Bryant's final game. She didn't hesitate in accepting the invitation.

In 1976 as a junior high school student in Pisgah, Rooks and some of her junior high classmates served iced tea to Bryant and others who attended a "Ray Maxwell Day" program to honor the Crimson Tide player. "He made all us little girls feel special. He was so sweet," Rooks, now Kathy Rooks-Denes, said. She already believed Bryant was special, but his appearance in the small town and his kindness to her and her friends only enhanced Bryant's stature with Rooks, who still has her copy of the Ray McDonald Day program that features autographs by Alabama players McDonald, James Taylor, Johnny Davis and Danny Ridgeway, who were also present. Right above McDonald's photo on the program is the coach's signature, "Bear Bryant."

"It was special having him there," Rooks said.

Six years later, she found herself on the sidelines of Liberty Bowl Memorial Stadium, wearing one-inch-heeled cowboy boots and no gloves on one of the coldest nights she had ever experienced, especially for a football game.

• • •

The memory of Bryant's last game and Bryant in that game is one that is still etched clearly in the mind's eye of Alabama football fans of the time. They remember Bryant wearing a huge, heavy, long weather coat with a fur collar on the icy-cold evening. Instead of his trademark houndstooth hat, Bryant wore a baseball cap. He looked to many to be older than they had remembered him looking before.

On the other sideline, head coach Mike White and his Illini knew they were the underdogs, that most everyone across the country was pulling for Alabama—pulling for Bryant—to win the game. Quarterback Tony Eason, who would later play in the NFL, directed a potent Illinois offense.

After turning the ball over to the Illini on a fumble on the game's first possession, Alabama avoided letting Illinois take a quick lead when Randy Edwards blocked a 34-yard field goal attempt. The Crimson Tide then covered 76 yards in just four plays—the big play coming on a 50-yard pass from quarterback Walter Lewis to Joey Jones—with Ricky Moore scoring on a 4-yard run.

Jeremiah Castille claimed the first of his three interceptions in the game on Illinois' next possession, ending another scoring threat, and after Alabama gave the ball back to the Illini on a fumble, Castille delivered a monster hit on Dwight Beverly near the goal line. Beverly fumbled and Alabama recovered, ending yet another scoring threat. Illinois' next possession ended with another Castille interception. After an Alabama punt, the Crimson Tide came up with another interception, this one by Johnny Elias, also at the goal line.

But Illinois returned the favor, picking off Lewis on the ensuing play and taking over at the Alabama 15-yard line. With 1:03 left in the half, Joe Curtis scored on a 1-yard run, but the extra point attempt failed, leaving Alabama in front 7-6. The score stood for the first half.

Eason had thrown 32 passes in the first half, rolling up 247 passing yards but no scores. He had also been picked off four times while the Illini rushing attack had provided only 18 yards on 13 carries. Alabama had 190 yards of total offense and had thrown only six passes, three finding the mark and two being intercepted, with one incompletion.

Just in case Alabama's players had forgotten his pregame message, Castille offered it again. "Jeremiah really spoke up during halftime," Lowe said. "He has great leadership skills and he just motivated everybody."

The motivation would be needed. Eason had a lot more passes to throw, and Alabama had a one-point lead to try and protect.

Illinois punted following its first two possessions. A 53-yard field goal try by Peter Kim fell short of the mark on Alabama's first possession of the second half. The next time Alabama got the ball, it made the possession count. Driving 50 yards in 10 plays, the Tide used some razzle-dazzle, with receiver Jesse Bendross running a reverse around the left end for eight yards, untouched, for the score. Kim's kick put Alabama in front 14-6 with 5:07 left in the third quarter.

Illinois bounced back. With Eason continuing to throw, the Illini drove 68 yards on 13 plays to score another touchdown, the points coming on a 2-yard pass on a fourth down-and-goal play from Eason to Oliver Williams. The two tried to connect again on the two-point conversion, but Castille was there, batting the pass away from Williams's grasp. There was 11:53 remaining in the game.

Alabama answered the Illinois score on its ensuing possession. It was a methodical drive, using a good balance of the run and pass. Moore and Linnie Patrick produced 12-yard runs, a pass to Jones was good for 10 yards, a Lewis keeper accounted for nine, and other smaller plays helped Alabama move toward the end zone. A 2-yard gain by Craig Turner from the Illinois 3 gave Alabama a first-and-goal opportunity at the 1. The next play, Turner covered the remaining yard for the touchdown, and Kim's kick made it 21-12.

Beverly fielded the ensuing kickoff and returned it to the Alabama 44, and Eason hit Mike Martin for a 32-yard pass play on first down, moving to the Bama 12. Gaining just six yards on the next three plays, Illinois settled for a 23-yard field goal, trimming the Crimson Tide lead to 21-15 with 6:12 left. Alabama fumbled on its follow-up possession, and Illinois took over at the Crimson Tide 24. The situation was ripe for Illinois to score a late touchdown and take the lead.

Eason was hit on a sack and had to leave the game for a while, with the Illini at the Alabama 22 facing a fourth-and-8 situation. Backup quarterback Kris Jenner entered the game, his second appearance of the night, and repeated the play of his first appearance: he threw an interception, this one picked off by Lowe. After Alabama punted with 1:45 to play, Illinois and Eason charged again. Starting at its own 19, Illinois produced a 23-yard pass on its first play, then 13 on the second play. Eason scrambled for five yards, then passed for 10 more. The Illini were at Alabama's 30 and looking to steal the win.

"Illinois was driving and it didn't look like we could stop them," Croom remembers of those final moments. "I remember when they crossed the 50-yard line thinking, *If they score, it's over.*"

Even the sports writers were pulling for Alabama to make a play. "That's the first time—and the last time—I remember sports writers openly pulling for a team to win," Pruett said. "Not in the press box, but on the field later. A bunch of us were standing in the end zone at the end. No one wanted to see [Bryant] lose that last game."

Marshall remembers sharing the same sentiment. "I remember thinking Illinois was going to win," he said. "There haven't been many games where I've had a real rooting interest in who wins, but in terms of thinking, *I really would like him to win,* I really did."

Eason prepared to throw another pass, but Alabama defensive end Russ Wood, charging untouched from the right side, blindsided Eason with a crunching tackle. Eason held on to the ball on the 10-yard loss but had to leave the game. That brought Jenner back on the field, and he kept his streak alive—his pass was intercepted by Robbie Jones, sealing the Alabama victory. Paul Fields, Alabama's backup quarterback, came on the field, took the snap and took a knee twice to run out the remaining seconds.

Castille—who had three interceptions, eight tackles and a pass breakup—and the rest of the Alabama team had kept their promise, sending Bryant into retirement with a victory in his final game as the Crimson Tide's head coach. The Alabama defense, despite surrendering 423 passing yards on 58 attempts and 35 completions by Illinois (Jenner was 0-for-3 with three interceptions), offset those numbers with some strong stats of its own: seven interceptions (three by Castille and one each by Wilcox, Lowe, Jones, and Elias), one fumble recovery, four sacks, two tackles for a loss, and three pass breakups.

"It could have gone either way in the fourth quarter, but luckily we pulled it out," Wilcox said of the result. "It was more a relief than anything else. . . . We had played just like the script was written the first part of the season. And although the last part of the season may not have been by the script, that last game was."

• • •

The victory was cause for celebration, a big celebration, but that's not how it felt. Alabama had won the game for its coach, presented him with a victory to close out his career. But the prevailing mood was of sadness, not happiness; of loss, not of victory. Alabama won the game but was losing its beloved head coach.

A tent had been set up to handle all the media who wanted a chance to hear Bryant make his postgame comments. Rooks, still frozen by the elements but warmed by the result, found a place right in front of the podium where Bryant sat, camera in hand, ready to record history. "At the press conference, you couldn't tell from Bear's demeanor that we had won the game," she said. "He looked so tired, so ready to not be doing that anymore. I snapped off a couple of pictures, then just sat and watched him. I couldn't help but cry."

McNair remembers the scene with a clarity that still surprises him. "There was just a great sadness that he wasn't going to be coaching Alabama anymore," he said. "Coach started talking about an analysis of the game, just like he would have for any other game. He tried to make it not about him, but it was about him."

Bryant then joined his team in the dressing room. The mood was no better there.

"Coach Bryant went around and patted the head or helmet of every player," Hale said. "There was just this realization of what was happening. There was almost absolute silence. I think the silence was out of respect. . . . I'll tell you, I just felt fortunate to be part of that, very fortunate. . . . In the annals of college football, [that game] has to be one of the most historic moments in the game."

The emotion that had gripped Sylvester Croom, former assistant coach on Bryant's staff, all week now had a stranglehold on him. "That was the most depressing locker room I've ever been in," Croom said. "It was like a mausoleum in there. It was over. There was just sadness and quiet. . . . There was no jubilation. There was relief we had won, but there wasn't a sound. Guys—coaches and players—were crying."

Keith Dunnavant, who would later write *Coach*, a Bryant biography, as well as *The Missing Ring*, about Alabama's unbeaten, untied, uncrowned 1966 season, had watched the drama unfold on TV. "I remember how old Coach Bryant looked that night," Dunnavant said. "The whole game was just so sad. It was a good game, but it was sad. It didn't seem quite real. We thought Coach Bryant would live forever."

That, of course, wasn't true, as Alabama fans—all college football fans— would learn much too soon. A month later, having suffered a massive heart attack, Bryant was dead. The man who had once said if he wasn't coaching football "I'd croak in a month," had indeed died just a month after coaching his final game.

His funeral drew live TV coverage, almost unheard of at that time, and thousands arrived in Tuscaloosa just to stand outside the church where the funeral service took place. After the service, his casket was placed in a hearse, driven past Bryant-Denny Stadium, then on to Birmingham for the burial service. The line of cars following the hearse stretched for almost two miles. Standing on every overpass along the interstate to Birmingham, people gathered just to get a glimpse of the hearse carrying Bryant's body.

• • •

Returning to the Liberty Bowl in 2007, Croom had a great feeling of familiarity. It felt right. "The Liberty Bowl is important to me," he said a day before his team defeated Central Florida, capping an eight-win season for the Bulldogs. The 25th anniversary of Bryant's final game was recognized prior to kickoff and was a focus throughout the week leading up to the game. "It's where I coached my first bowl game, as a graduate assistant [at Alabama] for the game in 1976, and I was here for Coach Bryant's last game in 1982. Now, my first bowl game as a head coach is here. It's a little strange, to be honest with you, but it's something I'm very thankful for."

Croom said that once he started walking around the stadium, his first trip back since the 1982 game, things and areas became familiar again. The emotions did, too. Observers have suggested that Croom takes many of his coaching ideas and approaches from Bryant, and Croom is quick to agree. On the eve of the '07 Liberty Bowl, Croom said he knew what his former coach would expect.

"I know what Coach Bryant would want me to do," he said. "He'd want me to win the game."

Some things never change.

CHAPTER TWELVE
1985 Georgia

Alabama 20, Georgia 16
September 2, 1985
Sanford Stadium
Athens, Georgia

Everyone was watching. Having produced a 5-6 record the previous season, the first losing season by an Alabama team since the 1957 season, Alabama fans were concerned. No one wanted to go through that again. So when the 1985 season-opener against SEC foe Georgia was scheduled for a national television broadcast on Labor Day night, college football fans across the country, especially those in the state of Alabama, tuned in to see what would happen.

Truth be told, there were concerns. But at the same time, the Alabama team was developing a bit of confidence, having prepared to prove itself and prove to be a team that could accomplish a lot of goals. It was, the Crimson Tide players felt certain, not a team that was going to produce a second-straight losing season.

Mike Shula had established himself as Alabama's starting quarterback, and he had help, including some newcomers, who were expected to provide some offensive punch. Defensively, Alabama was led by Cornelius Bennett, Curt Jarvis, Randy Rockwell, Brent Sowell, Jon Hand and others, a group that figured to be among the best in the SEC.

What remained unknown was how Alabama would react if its back was against the wall; if the Crimson Tide had to make a play on either side of the football, to win the game. The previous season, Alabama opened the year by losing four of its first five games, including a nine-point loss to Vanderbilt in Tuscaloosa and a 10-point loss to Georgia, the team against which it was opening the 1985 season on the road. The Tide played better down the stretch in 1984, beating rival Auburn by two, and its two late-season losses were by a combined three points, but the question marks remained. Would the ineffectiveness of the previous season roll over into the 1985 season, or had the Crimson Tide learned from the disappointment?

Alabama fans wouldn't have to wait long for the answer.

"The importance of the game against Georgia was magnified because of what had happened the year before," Paul Kennedy, then Alabama's radio play-by-play announcer, said in describing the anticipation that greeted Alabama in its season-opener. "There were a lot of questions. What Alabama team would show up? What are they going to do? It was a classic confrontation and a game that offered a lot of things: Alabama versus Georgia, Labor Day evening, taking on Vince Dooley's team, national television."

There was a lot of pressure placed on Shula's performance. Would he be able to generate more production from the offense with his passing, as well as his understanding of Alabama's offense and what head coach Ray Perkins and his staff wanted—what it needed—from that offense? Kennedy, who said Perkins once told him that Shula broke down game film better than some NFL players, believed Shula was the right player to lead the Crimson Tide, and that he was ready to do so.

"I remember the day his mother dropped [Shula] off at Bryant Hall [then the athletic dorm] as a freshman," Kennedy said. "I was living in Bryant Hall at the time. She had to bring Mike because his dad [then Miami Dolphins head coach Don Shula] was involved with his own team. I remember being impressed by him. He exuded class. That his mother brought him to campus said a lot, I thought, about their family. He was quiet, but you could tell there was a confidence about him. I think that came out in the Georgia game and that entire 1985 season." It presented itself the next season as well.

"Any time a quarterback arrives at Alabama, there's a curiosity," Kennedy said. "Any time you're asked to play quarterback at Alabama, you're not looked at as among the rank and file. You're different."

Because of his father's success and his own recruitment, that factor was magnified for Shula. The 1985 season was his junior year. He had picked up some playing experience the year before, demonstrating he had the ability to lead the offense. But he hadn't given anyone a glimpse, at least not in a game situation, of the calm demeanor and big-play ability he would employ against Georgia.

• • •

The first quarter of play produced five punts and an interception. A Shula pass was picked off with Alabama at the Georgia 22-yard line. Georgia gained just 10 yards in the period. Another of the night's long line of newcomers, Alabama wide receiver Al Bell, also a junior college transfer, introduced himself to Alabama fans in a big way early in the second period. He hauled in a Shula pass just two plays into the quarter and completed a 50-yard drive with a 16-yard scoring catch. After the teams swapped a pair of punts, Georgia mounted its best drive of the first half, moving from its own 30 to the Alabama 21, where the Bulldogs kicked a 38-yard field goal with 76 seconds left. Alabama carried a 7-3 lead to the locker room at the half.

Van Tiffin matched Georgia's field goal with a 48-yarder in the third quarter to give Alabama a 10-3 edge heading into the final period. He missed a 47-yard attempt in the fourth quarter, and after Alabama recovered a Georgia fumble moments later, returned to kick a 41-yarder that was true with 8:31 to play. The Bulldogs responded to the turnover and field goal by driving 73 yards in nine plays for a touchdown on an 11-yard pass, but a two-point conversion try failed, leaving Georgia trailing 13-9.

With 4:21 remaining, Alabama's offense took possession and came close to running out the remaining time, but the drive stalled at the Crimson Tide 33 and, facing a fourth down-and-9 situation, Chris Mohr was called on to punt. The game then took a dramatic swing. Mohr's punt was blocked and, after the football had been batted by players from both teams, it was recovered in the end zone for a Georgia touchdown by Calvin Ruff—yes, a Georgia Bulldogs player named Ruff.

Suddenly, Alabama, which hadn't previously trailed the Dawgs that evening, was behind. And there was only 50 seconds remaining in the game. Sanford Stadium, loud much of the game but missing that spark, was now alive, and Georgia fans had plenty of spark. It appeared the Crimson Tide would open the season in a disappointing and frustrating fashion.

One sportswriter who was seated in the stands that night, the *Atlanta Journal-Constitution*'s Tony Barnhart, took in all the action and the sudden change in momentum. Then the AJC's assistant sports editor, Barnhart recalled, "I was working that night; for two years I didn't write. They were the two most miserable years of my life, but I learned a lot," he said. Now the author of CBS Sports.com's "Mr. College Football" column, Barnhart took in the game from a fan's perspective. "Come to find out later, that was a [tip] drill they had actually worked on, to get the ball moving forward," Barnhart said. "I was thinking at the time, *Alabama's outplayed Georgia all night long and Georgia's found a way to win this game.*"

But those remaining 50 seconds, as it turned out, would be more than enough time for Shula and the Alabama offense to reverse the momentum and reclaim the lead.

Facing first-and-10 from his own 29, Shula's first pass was long and overthrown. He then connected with Greg Richardson for 16 yards to the 45, and then found Bell again, this time for 30 yards to the Georgia 30. Another pass to Richardson was good for 13 yards to the 17, and that's where Shula and Bell combined once more, this time for a touchdown—a game-winning, quick-as-lightning, did-you-see-that? touchdown, with 16 seconds to spare.

"Coach Perkins called the first play, and I think I called the next one," Shula said of the game-winning drive. "With each one, something opened up for us. On the touchdown play, Coach Perkins anticipated they would blitz, and sure enough, they blitzed. Al Bell was open, and I was able to get the pass to him and we scored on a 17-yard pass play."

Simple as that.

Apparently, Alabama had some drills it had been working on, too.

"Believe it or not, that was something we had worked on all week—the two-minute offense," then-assistant coach Jim Fuller said. "You hear coaches talking about practicing and being ready. Well, that was one of the things we had worked on. We knew exactly what we were going to do. There was a definite sense with everybody on the team that we were going to do it. We were going to score."

When Bell caught the pass from Shula and raced into the end zone, Barnhart turned his attention to the Alabama sideline. "I remember looking down on the field and watching Ray Perkins jump out of his shoes," said Barnhart, who would later write a book with Dooley on the Georgia coach's years as the Bulldogs' head coach. "I was impressed with how methodical the drive was. They knew what they wanted to do and where they wanted to go. Georgia was usually very good in those situations."

Shula's mother had been seated with the other Alabama fans in the stadium, but the pressure of the game got to her and she left her seat, too nervous to sit still and watch. But she listened. "She told me later she got so nervous she had to quit watching," Shula explained. "She left her seat and walked away. She was standing at a place where she couldn't see the field because of a wall. She told me she saw the touchdown pass in the air, but that she couldn't see, and then she heard our fans start cheering and she knew what had happened."

Shula, who in 2003 was named Alabama's head coach, mentioned the detail paid to the two-minute offense during practices the week of the game and said the work obviously paid off. It was also important, he said, because when called upon, the offense felt it was ready to make those plays that it had prepared for that moment and that opportunity.

"In the huddle for that last series, it was very businesslike," he said. "We got in there close together. We had to squeeze in there because it was so loud, especially after they had blocked the punt for the touchdown to take the lead. The Georgia fans were really loud, but no one [in the huddle] seemed nervous. I think you're actually more nervous watching a game like that than when you're playing in it. All of us were just so excited, especially after we scored.

"It felt great. Standing on the sideline, all you could hear was our fans in their little corner of the stadium, cheering. It had been so loud after they had scored their touchdown, and now, it was quiet except for our fans. That's a great sound for a visiting team."

Alabama's offense collected 307 total yards, and Shula was 9-of-13 passing for 136 yards, two touchdowns and an interception. Georgia managed just 210 total yards. Bell, in his Alabama debut, caught four passes for 77 yards and two touchdowns. "He gave an unbelievable performance," Kennedy said of Bell.

It sparked a 4-0 start to the season, a win streak that ended with a 19-17 loss at Penn State, followed by a 16-14 loss to Tennessee in Birmingham. But the Crimson Tide wouldn't lose again, although it played to a 14-14 tie at LSU, and finished with a 9-2-1 record. The confidence gained from the game-winning drive against Georgia would be called on again, when Alabama drove late to beat archrival Auburn in the Iron Bowl, 25-23, on a last-second, 52-yard Tiffin field goal.

Having made their way from the upper deck of the stadium to the sidelines, the game's energy intensified for the *Dothan Eagle's* Jon Johnson and Ken Rogers. "I remember being impressed with how composed Shula was," Johnson said of his close-up view of the quarterback. "In that way, he was a lot like Ray Perkins—showing little emotion, very businesslike. When he threaded the needle over the middle to Al Bell and how the Georgia fans went silent, that was impressive. For the first game I covered [professionally], it was amazing. It's still so clear to me today. I had been to a lot of football games before, [but] there was something special about that one."

Johnson's job was to gather quotes and information for a follow-up story in Wednesday's edition of the *Eagle*. Rogers assigned himself the deadline pressure of getting in the game story for the next day's Tuesday paper. Because of the late start and the game's sudden shifts in the final moments, that proved to be a challenging task.

"Because of the way it played out, I was making notes and writing the story as it went along, but I kept changing it, so I'd scratch out what I had to change and just keep going," Rogers said. "How could you not get caught up in a game like that? We knew it was a very big game for Alabama, and a big game for Georgia and their fans too. [Georgia] made a play to take the lead, but then Alabama made a late drive to win. It was crazy."

What was, perhaps, crazier was getting the story to the newspaper office before deadline. Because of the limitations on their coverage, Rogers decided the best way to get the story in would be to write it out on a pad and dictate it to someone back in the newspaper's office in Dothan. So when they had collected all the information and comments after the game, Rogers took his pages of notes, even those that had been scratched out, and grabbed the first phone available in the back of Georgia's press box, ready to play the sportswriters' version of *Beat the Clock*.

"Once I got that phone, I knew I was going to be on it for a while," Rogers said. "I was just out of school and I didn't realize it was going to be so hard. I would hate to have to write and send in a story that way now."

• • •

Perhaps the greatest compliment paid to Shula and Alabama and its come-from-behind victory would come in a quiet way. Years later, after Shula had completed his playing days and was working as an assistant coach in the NFL, he was told a story that still brings a slight smile to his face today.

"Bill Lewis, who was on Georgia's [coaching] staff that year, told me that after that game every time Georgia practiced its hurry-up offense, Coach Vince Dooley would put the ball on the 29-yard line and put 50 seconds on the clock."

It seems Alabama fans aren't the only ones who have a clear memory of what happened at Sanford Stadium that night.

CHAPTER THIRTEEN

1985 Auburn

Alabama 25, Auburn 23
November 30, 1985
Legion Field
Birmingham, Alabama

I n what college football fans in the state of Alabama believe is the game's
most intense rivalry—a view shared by some outside the state's borders as
well—Alabama and Auburn fans hang on every play, every movement, every
breath of the Iron Bowl. When the teams face off in their annual end-of-the-
regular-season game, the matchup is analyzed from every conceivable angle.
Players and coaches too.

It is said—one would assume, in jest—that in explaining the intensity
and importance of the game to "outsiders," there is a simple rule of thumb:
the Iron Bowl isn't life or death; it's more important than that.

Yes, it's a tongue-in-cheek phrase, but there are those who would suggest
the saying isn't too far off the mark.

In truth, the Iron Bowl can't be described as much as it has to be
experienced. Perhaps it is similar to someone who has experienced skydiving
trying to explain to someone who has yet to give it a try how it feels to leap
from the airplane into the open skies, soar toward the ground below, then
pull the ripcord of the parachute and descend safely back to earth.

Of course, the good-natured Alabama or Auburn fan, in a sort of built-
in one-upsmanship when it comes to their favorite game of the year, would
probably shrug off someone's tale of a skydiving adventure and suggest
jumping out of an airplane is a lot safer than playing in the Iron Bowl.

In a way, that's an off-handed explanation of the game. It's equal parts legend, exaggeration, tradition, athleticism, passion, craziness, seriousness, luck, preparation, intensity, and heart. At any one moment, all those factors could be in play, or just one could be the determining factor in the game's outcome.

So one can understand the plight facing *Dothan Eagle* sports writer Ken Rogers, born in Cincinnati and raised in Indianapolis, attempting to explain the Iron Bowl to family members who view it as just another football game in a season filled with football games.

"I'm not from the South, and I tried to tell my family about the Iron Bowl," he said. "I tried to tell them that you can really *feel* how important the game is to everybody in the state. And not just the football fans, but to everybody. I tried to tell them you really can *feel* it. It's unmistakable."

The 1985 Iron Bowl marked the first time Rogers covered an Alabama vs. Auburn game. He said he really did feel the difference in the game compared to all the others he had covered that year. He would recognize definitively just how different the game is from all others the two teams play and why the difference is so obvious.

For Rogers to draw the 1985 game as his first Iron Bowl ever would be something indeed. Although there have been great, close, back-and-forth Iron Bowls since, the 1985 game is considered as perhaps the best of all time (at least by Alabama fans who don't enjoy reliving the "Punt, Bama Punt" 1972 game in which Auburn blocked a pair of Alabama punts and returned both for a touchdown in the famous 17-16 game).

Some Auburn fans might even begrudgingly tab the 1985 game as the best ever.

Rogers, on this particular November night in Birmingham, had no other Iron Bowl experiences for comparison. Since that night, all other Iron Bowl games, at least for him, have to be compared to the '85 game. And it's going to take a helluva game to top his first Iron Bowl.

"Some of my cousins went to Ohio State. You try to tell them to imagine the Ohio State-Michigan game for comparison, but that's not right either," Rogers said. "There's passion in that game. But not like here, not like for the Iron Bowl. So you tell them that football here is important, more important than they know. It divides everything, but it also unites everything. When that game is played, it is the only thing people care about."

To be honest, Rogers himself had to be convinced of what he would later try to explain to family members. He didn't understand the connection, the sheer focus the game demanded. But he quickly gained the knowledge.

"In the press box before the game—and I had never had this happen to me at any sporting event before, ever—the Alabama and Auburn fans were trying to out-yell each other," Rogers said. "During this, before the kickoff, the hair literally stood up on my neck. It was like an involuntary shot of adrenaline. It was like somebody was telling me to pay attention.

"I've only had that happen to me a couple of other times before, but I remember it so clearly. And I paid attention."

How could one not pay attention? The usual 50-50 split of tickets for the game was in force and the crowd was electric. Again. Pat Dye had his Tigers playing well, and the same was true of Ray Perkins's Alabama team. Once again, how the season would be viewed by its fans, its measure of success, would depend on the outcome of the game.

Paul Kennedy, then the radio play-by-play voice of Alabama football, felt the same things Rogers was feeling, and he mentioned it to a friend. "I remember saying, 'It may not be this way anywhere else.' I was driving to the stadium and I remember thinking the outcome of the game would determine the quality of our life for the next year," Kennedy said.

Joe Kines, then Alabama's defensive coordinator, said Perkins, a former player under head coach Paul "Bear" Bryant, understood the rivalry as well as anyone, and part of his preparation for the game in the days leading up to the game was to make sure he did everything he could to make his players understand the game's history and impact.

"Coach Perkins had some ex-players come in and talk to the team that week," Kines said. "The players that came in, they all told the players that they would remember this game for the rest of their lives. They were right."

The Alabama players wouldn't be the only ones who will forever recall the events of that game, that night.

• • •

Both offenses started slowly. Auburn's first two possessions produced just 23 yards and a pair of punts. Alabama's first possession garnered only four yards. Midway through the period, Alabama changed all that. Backed up against the end zone, starting from its own 6-yard line, quarterback Mike Shula and the Crimson Tide offense seized the momentum. A pass to Al Bell on a second-down-and-12 play picked up 19 yards. On the next play the duo connected again, this time for 18 yards. A Shula-to-Chandler pass gained nine more. On a third-and-10 play, the Tide gained 14 on a pass to Craig Turner, and they found themselves at Auburn's 14. Later, a third-and-2 play was good for five yards to the Auburn 1, which was followed by a Turner one-yard touchdown run. Alabama had traveled 94 yards on 13 plays for a score, and the Alabama fans filled Legion Field with sound.

It would get a little louder. On Auburn's second play from scrimmage on the ensuing possession, Jon Hand forced quarterback Pat Washington to fumble, and Alabama recovered at the Tigers' 13. The Auburn defense held, and Alabama settled for a 26-yard Van Tiffin field goal and a 10-0, first-quarter lead.

Two plays into the second period, Auburn punted to Alabama. Greg Richardson fielded the punt and returned it 50 yards to the Auburn 13, but once again Alabama's offense struggled to take advantage of the field position and came away with another Tiffin field goal, this one covering 32 yards. It was beginning to look like the game might be a rout for Alabama. That wouldn't be the case.

A Trey Gainous punt return of 37 yards put Auburn at Alabama's 47. Washington hit Freddy Weygand with a pass for a 44-yard gain to the Alabama 9. After a 2-yard gain, Bo Jackson, who would later win the Heisman Trophy and become the star of Nike's "Bo knows" commercials and print ads—and who also headlined the "Bo Bikes Bama" campaign that raised thousands of dollars for tornado victims, many of whom lived in the Tuscaloosa area— scored a touchdown on a seven-yard run.

Alabama fashioned one more score before the half. Taking over with less than four minutes left in the second period, Alabama and Shula worked its way downfield. A fumble was recovered by Shula, keeping the drive alive early. The Crimson Tide inched its way to the Auburn 25, where the drive stalled. Tiffin ran back on the field, booting his third field goal of the half to give Alabama a 16-7 lead.

But that's not how the half ended. Instead, Auburn's passing game came alive, quickly moving the Tigers to the Alabama 31, where Chris Johnson booted a 49-yard field goal, cutting the Crimson Tide's halftime advantage to 16-10.

The second half provided few offensive fireworks, but it also produced something that would prove interesting after the fact. It would be a play almost forgotten in the retelling of the game in the days, months, and years to come. Midway through the third quarter, Alabama mounted a drive that began at its own 12 and moved all the way down to the Auburn 36 before it stalled. Based on his 3-for-3 performance to that point, and with a career-best 57-yard field goal to his name, Tiffin was once again sent onto the field for a field goal try.

The attempt (this is the interesting part) was 52 yards, and Tiffin had the wind behind him. But he didn't have the accuracy, producing his first miss of the game. "I should have made it," Tiffin would say years later. "It was an easy kick, and I had the wind behind me."

After the teams swapped punts, Alabama's Kermit Kendrick intercepted a Washington pass, setting up the Alabama offense with its back against the end zone at the Crimson Tide 4-yard line. One play later, the third period came to an end. What would follow would be a fourth period filled with big plays, drama, and the play now known simply as The Kick, one of the most important and most celebrated plays in Alabama's long football history.

Van Tiffin was only minutes away from hero status.

• • •

Freshman running back Gene Jelks clicked off a 39-yard run on the second play of the final period, moving Alabama from its 10 to its 49 and giving the offense some breathing room. But two plays later in Auburn territory, a Shula pass was intercepted by Kevin Porter in the end zone, giving the ball to the Tigers on their 20.

From there, Jackson and Washington went to work, pushing Auburn down the field. Jackson gained 38 yards rushing and also hauled in a 21-yard pass from Washington. Reaching Alabama's red zone, Auburn faced a fourth-and-goal play at the one-yard line. Everyone in the stadium knew who would be getting the football, and Jackson dove over the top for the remaining yard, the touchdown and Auburn's first lead in the game at 17-16. That's right, Auburn led 17-16, the score of the 1972 Iron Bowl won by the Tigers by that very score—the score that found its way on hundreds of bumper stickers, posters and hand-made signs—in the famous game in which Auburn blocked a pair of Alabama punts and returned both for touchdowns to upset the Crimson Tide. Auburn not only had the lead, but it led by a familiar score, which added to the enjoyment felt by Auburn fans.

The enjoyment and score would be short-lived.

Despite fumbling the ensuing kickoff out of bounds at its 11, Alabama came out with a purpose. Jelks led the way on a first-and-10 play from the 26, darting by and around Auburn defenders for a 74-yard scoring run that ignited the Alabama faithful and returned the lead to the Crimson Tide. But Auburn would deliver a counter punch. Jackson and Company hammered away at the Alabama defense. On a third-and-1 play from the Alabama 23, Jackson caught a pass and picked up 17 yards. A late hit by Kendrick out of bounds gave Auburn some more yards, setting up the Tigers at the Alabama 8. Tommie Agee picked up two yards, then Jackson gained five to the Alabama one-yard line. Instead of going back to Jackson, Reggie Ware got the call, and he scored with just 57 seconds to play. Leading 23-22, Auburn decided to go for the two-point conversion.

"I remember the play Cornelius Bennett made on the two-point conversion," the *Dothan Eagle's* Rogers said. "It was a little flare [pass] to Jackson in the corner of the end zone. I'm standing at about the three-yard line, and they throw the flare and Bennett is coming hard. He takes two steps, already fully committed, and then he realizes where Jackson was going. He broke stride, ran back to Jackson, and just threw his hand up—I don't know that he ever saw the ball—and knocked the ball away."

Auburn had a one-point lead and was about to kick off to Alabama with just 57 seconds to play. Auburn needed only to keep Alabama at bay for 57 more seconds for what would be a third win over Alabama in a four-year span.

As it turned out, it would be 57 seconds too many for the Tigers, though Alabama would need every precious one.

"The similarities to that game and the [1985 season-opening] Georgia game were amazing," Kennedy said. "I had a hunch, just a hunch. I said on the air, 'Don't go anywhere.' Whether that was driven by the fact it would be unbearable to lose that game or if I honestly believed it, I don't know."

• • •

Alabama's final drive—the game's final drive—would feature some fine individual efforts as well as strong teamwork. The Crimson Tide took over possession at its 20 following a touchback on the kickoff and faced the prospect of covering a lot of ground in a short amount of time to score a touchdown or at least get within field goal range. The drive didn't start off impressively. Shula threw an incomplete pass on first down, and on second down, looking for an open receiver but failing to find one, Shula was sacked for an eight-yard loss back to the 12. The Crimson Tide had to use its final time-out, leaving it with just 37 seconds to play, 18 yards from a first down and 88 yards from the end zone.

The Alabama offense wasn't worried. Concerned perhaps, but not yet worried. It had been in this position before. "We knew we could score," offensive lineman Wes Neighbors, now a stockbroker in Huntsville, told the *Huntsville Times* in a 1999 story by John Pruett. "We had already won in the last minute at Georgia, coming from behind. We almost did it against Tennessee. Coming onto the field that last drive, we expected to score, regardless of the time."

On third down, Shula tossed a flare pass to Jelks out of the backfield. He pulled in the pass and managed to get out of bounds to stop the clock, but he exited the field four yards short of a first down, leaving Alabama with a fourth-and-4 situation and 29 seconds to play.

Perkins decided on a bit of razzle-dazzle, considering the situation, not to mention taking a huge chance. It paid off. Shula took the snap from center and pitched out to the right. Wide receiver Al Bell, coming from the left side, took a pitch on a reverse and looked for open field. Shortly after taking the pitch, Bell looked as though he might be in trouble. Auburn's Benji Roland had Bell in his sights in the Alabama backfield, but Shula, who had also reversed his field, waited until the last moment and knocked Roland down with a block that freed Bell, who slipped down the left sideline, picking up 20 yards and the first down before stepping out of bounds to stop the clock. The Legion Field scoreboard showed 21 seconds remaining.

Shula then tried to connect on a pass with Greg Richardson, but the attempt was broken up by the Auburn defense, leaving 15 seconds to play and the Crimson Tide far out of field goal range. Shula dropped back to pass again on second down and he finally found an open man—Richardson—running across the middle of the field.

"They had a three-man rush, and Larry Rose and I were double-teaming their rushers," Neighbors told the *Huntsville Times*. "We looked up and saw Richardson running open over the middle. We were yelling, 'Throw it! Throw it!'"

Shula threw it, dead on target to Richardson, who was being trailed by Auburn defensive back Luvell Bivens. Running hard, Richardson was a long way from being able to get out of bounds, especially once Bivens grabbed him shortly after making the catch. But Richardson managed to stay on his feet, pulling Bivens with him the whole way, until he got himself and the football out of bounds to stop the clock. A mere six seconds remained to play. The Shula-to-Richardson pass had picked up 19 yards to the Auburn 35.

"That's the play that's overlooked," Sylvester Croom, then an Alabama assistant coach, said of Richardson's catch and ability to get out of bounds. "Getting the ball out of bounds, dragging that guy with him, knowing what he had to do and having the strength to get it done. That was a great play. Without that play, it's over."

Sportswriter Ivan Maisel, who now works for ESPN.com, was at the game as a spectator that day. The Richardson pass play stands out in his recollection of the game, too. "Why would you throw over the middle? That play has been lost in the beautification of Van Tiffin, but Richardson made that play," Maisel said. "It was just incredible."

In fact, the drive leading up to Tiffin's game-winning field goal was remarkable on several levels. With one time-out remaining and overcoming a sack deep in its own territory, the odds seemed to be stacked against Alabama. The play-calling was certainly unique, but as was proven, effective.

Consider this: the pass to Jelks was the only catch he made in the game; the reverse to Bell was the only time he carried the ball in the game; and the pass to Richardson was the only catch he made in the game.

Yet the game came down to a player who had made plays earlier in the game, but who also had failed to convert on the same play he was about to attempt again, a 52-yard field goal. The game would be determined by Van Tiffin.

• • •

To be sure, Tiffin isn't the biggest player to ever don an Alabama football uniform. The Red Bay native stood 5-foot-9 and weighed a less-than-imposing 155 pounds. But the little man in the No. 3 jersey wielded a big foot, one that would not miss a single extra-point kick in his college career; one that would produce one of the biggest plays in the Iron Bowl's great history.

He arrived at Alabama as a walk-on, seeking the kicking job along with five others. On his 18th birthday—head coach Ray Perkins didn't realize the significance of the date when he made the call—Tiffin received word he would be the team's starting kicker for the 1983 season. His career didn't start with a bang (he missed his first field goal try, though he made two others in his first game), but his consistency kept him in the starting role.

Tiffin's father had paid attention when it appeared that his son had some talent as a kicker growing up. The elder Tiffin read a *Sports Illustrated* story about Doc Storey, who taught place-kicking in Fort Lauderdale, Fla. At the age of 15, Tiffin went to Fort Lauderdale for spring break, but he went there to work with Storey, not to work on his tan. He returned that summer, and the trips became annual outings for Tiffin. The extra work paid off.

Tiffin always went the extra mile in preparing for a game and season. "I remember seeing him out there in the summer, working all by himself," Croom said of Tiffin. "He had done the work. He had prepared himself for [game-winning] situations, and when they came about, he was ready."

Tiffin was ready on that night, to be sure, though it appeared for a while he wouldn't get a chance to kick a field goal. He watched and waited, and as Croom said, when his time came, Tiffin produced.

"To this day," Tiffin said, "I hate to see a kicker miss a field goal. When you miss a field goal, or you make one, 70,000 or 80,000 people [or more] see you. That's tough. I remember a game when [Auburn kicker Robert] McGinty missed a couple of kicks, and Auburn lost the game. I felt bad for him. . . . Coming into [the '85 game against Auburn], I had had a bad game two games before against LSU. I had missed two field goals in a row . . . and we tied [14-14]. I felt bad about that. But I made a field goal the next week against Southern Miss, and that helped my confidence."

Tiffin now called upon that confidence as he ran out on the Legion Field turf, staring at another 52-yard field goal, this time against the wind. And the odds. Alabama had one chance to win the game, and that chance was riding on the right leg of the kid from Red Bay, a former walk-on who spent every Alabama practice kicking, usually by himself, preparing himself for the moment that was now at hand.

"Auburn scored and took the lead, and normally in a situation like that, you start warming up," Tiffin said. "But on the second play, Mike got sacked, and I thought, *It's going to be a long shot if we get a chance to try a field goal.* But about that time, these two guys who were intoxicated were yelling at me, 'It's going to come down to you!' I thought to myself, *You don't know what you're talking about.* But at that point, I started moving up the sideline so I could see what was happening and be ready in case we got a chance to try [a field goal]."

• • •

Three players would determine the outcome of the game—long-snapper Whitlock, holder Larry Abney, and Tiffin. There was no fanfare, no time-out called to "ice" the kicker. The play would take place as though every player had somewhere else to be. Tiffin ran onto the field, the kicking team set up, Whitlock snapped it to Abney who put the football in place, and Tiffin delivered his kick—"The Kick," as artist Daniel Moore titled it in his painting depicting the play.

Where were you when Tiffin made The Kick? Many remember exactly where they were and what they were feeling.

"Standing on the sidelines, waiting for him to kick it, I knew Van had a great confidence," Croom said. "He never changed his demeanor. He had ice water in his veins."

As Whitlock ran onto the field with the kicking team, he couldn't shake the feeling he had been here before, that the game was taking on the feel and finish he had expected of the Iron Bowl. "You had a feeling it was going to come down to something dramatic," he said. "Are we going to get in range [for a field goal try]? Are we going to do it? Every play was a cheer and a boo.

"When the play happened, I had no idea if we made it or missed it. I had guys on top of me. I didn't know what had happened for a while. It wasn't until the next day that I saw the kick [on a TV replay]."

Abney knew his role in the play was important. He was determined to do his job correctly. "I wasn't scared or anything like that," Abney told the

Huntsville Times. "All I had to do was just put it on the tee. We were still using kicking tees in those days. Heck, people don't remember the holder. The pressure was on Van, not me. Whatever happened, he was the one who was going to be remembered."

That's usually the case, but it seemed people had already forgotten Tiffin kicked a 52-yarder in the 1984 Iron Bowl that had given Alabama a 17-15 win. "But it wasn't a kick in the last seconds, so not too many people remember that," Tiffin said.

They sure remember the kick in the 1985 Iron Bowl.

A few had forgotten Tiffin had missed an earlier try from the same distance earlier in the game.

"Nobody even waited to be told to go in the game," Tiffin said, "and we didn't even look at Coach Perkins [for direction], we just went in, even though we didn't have to rush. I tried to line it up. I'm glad there wasn't a time-out called [to give me time] to think about it. In those days, the snapper dictated when the ball would be snapped. Normally, the holder does that. As soon as Larry put his hand up, [out came] the ball. I was kind of shocked, and I was late leaving [to start the kick]. Kevin Porter rushed the kick, and he jumped offside. I could feel him on my left side, and, if you look at the pictures of that play, he was actually lying on the ground when I kicked it. He actually went past [the kick]. If he had blocked it, it would have been OK because he was offsides and we would have gotten another chance, even closer. But the way it happened, it's almost like it was meant to be.

"I just looked up. It was like an out-of-body experience. I was thrilled that it went through. I was more relieved than anything else. I'm not used to a lot of attention, but I got a lot of attention right then. I'm not a person who likes a lot of attention. I'd rather just be in the background. I kept telling the other guys, 'Don't make such a big fuss over me. Let's just enjoy this.'"

His request was denied. It was the Iron Bowl, and Alabama had overcome a late Auburn score and marched down the field for a 52-yard, game-winning field goal on the game's final play. There was going to be a fuss, a big fuss, and Tiffin would become the focus of the celebration.

In the Alabama radio booth, Kennedy and Doug Layton relayed what was happening on the field to those listening to the game across the state. Here's their call:

Kennedy: *"This would win the game. A 52-yard try. The clock will not start until the ball is snapped. There's the snap, the kick, it's in the air . . . it has the distance. It's good! It's good!"*
Layton: *"It's good!"*
Kennedy: *"It's good!"*
Layton: *"It's good!"*
Kennedy: *"It's good!"*
Layton: *"Van Tiffin has won the ball game."*

"It was great," Tiffin admitted, "the most intense situation I've ever experienced in football. I had never heard a stadium like that before, and it lasted for a long time. That was probably the most electric game of my career. That's always the biggest game of the year. That year we beat Georgia with a late rally at the end, but the game was at Georgia, and we didn't have as many fans there, so the energy wasn't the same."

CHAPTER FOURTEEN
1986 Notre Dame

Alabama 28, Notre Dame 10
October 4, 1986
Legion Field
Birmingham, Alabama

I t wasn't just a sack, wasn't just a win, wasn't just another Saturday afternoon game. It definitely wasn't just another opponent. There was a lot more to it than that. A whole lot more.

When Cornelius Bennett, star linebacker for the 4-0 and No. 1-ranked Alabama Crimson Tide, sacked Notre Dame quarterback Steve Beuerlein on a first-down play in the first quarter of a scoreless game against a 1-2 team, it wasn't just a good play, it was a *defining* play. It was a play that would still be talked about, still celebrated, years later.

It wasn't just a tackle; it was art. Literally. Daniel Moore's painting of *The Sack,* a depiction of Bennett's crunching tackle of Beuerlein, can be found in thousands of homes and offices, not only in the state of Alabama, but across the Southeast and the country. Rumor has it even Beuerlein has a copy of the print. The original oil and acrylic painting on canvas by Moore can also be seen, quite easily, based on its 5-foot-by-7-foot expanse, hanging in the Paul "Bear" Bryant Museum in Tuscaloosa. It's an image visitors can't help but take in given its size and positioning—above the exit of the exhibit hall.

Moore's painting not only captures the motion and result of the play, but its force, too. Bennett's bright, crimson-colored jersey commands the eye of the viewer, as do the subtle streaks of color that illustrate the play's motion. Moore made sure to feature the football out of Beuerlein's grasp, believing as many did that Bennett should also have been credited with causing a fumble and with a fumble recovery.

Fathers viewing the painting, in a style Moore calls photo futurism, can be seen telling their sons the story of The Sack, explaining its impact and importance. Even to those who don't know the story behind the painting, it's just cool to see.

If viewing video of the play without knowledge of the players or teams involved, or the circumstances, one would likely note the athleticism of the linebacker, as well as his speed, quickness, and power. One would certainly deduce that the quarterback found the play to be an unpleasant experience. Otherwise, it was simply a good defensive play. Bennett wasn't blocked as he made his way to the Notre Dame backfield and to Beuerlein, and the play obviously provided quite a momentum boost for the Crimson Tide.

It was more than that. A lot more. To Alabama fans in the stands at Legion Field that day, those who erupted in boisterous cheers and exchanged enthusiastic high-fives and hugs, it represented more than an 8-yard loss. It was a measure of payback, a signal that this would, at last, be Alabama's day, be the fans' day, be the day they had been waiting for since the conclusion of the 1973 Sugar Bowl.

This would be the day Alabama finally beat Notre Dame.

• • •

It wasn't just a sack, it was *The Sack.*

It still is.

To understand why Bennett's play made such an impact, why a victory over a team that would leave Legion Field that day with a 1-3 record would evoke such a response, all that is required is a brief history lesson.

It was Notre Dame. The same Notre Dame that legendary head coach Paul "Bear" Bryant had never beaten. The same Notre Dame that had beaten Alabama the four previous times the teams had played by a combined 13 points, three of the losses coming by a combined winning margin of six points. It was the same Notre Dame that cost Alabama the 1973 Associated Press national championship and a national championship in 1974.

It was the same Notre Dame that played for a tie against Michigan State in 1966 and ended up winning the national championship even though Alabama was unbeaten and untied that year.

That Notre Dame.

That's why The Sack and the win mattered, and mattered deeply.

* 1973 Sugar Bowl; Dec. 31; Notre Dame 24, Alabama 23: The Crimson Tide entered the game at Tulane Stadium ranked No. 1 and looking for another national championship. Bryant had called a trick play—a halfback pass from Mike Stock to quarterback Richard Todd for a 25-yard touchdown play—to give Alabama a 23-21 lead. But Bill Davis missed the extra point kick and Notre Dame produced a field goal with 4:26 left to take a one-point lead. Alabama was driving in the waning moments to get in range to attempt a game-winning field goal. But Todd was intercepted and the Irish held on for the win. To add insult to injury, Notre Dame was selected national champion by the Associated Press. Howard Cosell, who was part of the ABC-TV broadcast team, described the two traditional football powers this way: "Notre Dame, where football is a religion, and Alabama, where football is a way of life."

* 1975 Orange Bowl; Jan. 1; Notre Dame 13, Alabama 11: At the end of the following season, based on the previous bowl game played by the two teams, the Orange Bowl committee looked for a repeat. It got one. In what would be Notre Dame head coach Ara Parseghian's final game with the Irish, Notre Dame denied Alabama the national championship for a second straight year, and the loss to the Irish would, for the second year in a row, be the only blemish on the Crimson Tide's record. The Irish built a 13-0 lead, but Alabama came storming back. The Tide kicked a field goal, then scored a touchdown and a two-point conversion that would open the door for a game-winning field goal attempt. It didn't happen. Southern Cal, which had drummed Notre Dame 55-24 that season, took the national championship Alabama was chasing.

* Nov. 13, 1976; South Bend, Ind.; Notre Dame 21, Alabama 18: Alabama was provided an opportunity to avenge the bowl losses of the previous two seasons, losses that cost it national championships, with a trip to storied Notre Dame Stadium. The Irish proved too much, racking up 484 total yards with a balanced offensive attack (249 yards rushing, 235 yards passing) and a big second quarter in which it scored all its points. A 56-yard touchdown pass started the scoring, the Irish also adding 2-yard and 17-yard scoring runs before the quarter's end. The Irish even overcame four turnovers (two lost fumbles, two interceptions) in keeping the Crimson Tide at bay and picking up a third win over Alabama in three straight seasons.

* Nov. 15, 1980; Birmingham, Ala.; Notre Dame 7, Alabama 0: Again, the second quarter played a key role in the game. It marked the period of the game's only score, Notre Dame producing a 2-yard scoring run that would stand the rest of the way. Alabama's offense and defense was more effective, out-gaining Notre Dame by more than 50 yards, but the offense didn't score and on one series, the defense didn't stop the Irish. That allowed Notre Dame to run its series record against Alabama to 4-0, all of the wins coming in a brief, eight-season period. It only served to add to the frustration (and it wouldn't be incorrect to say irritation) Alabama fans held for Notre Dame. The 0-4 mark, all of the losses to Bryant-coached teams, only served to increase the disdain Alabama fans had for the Fighting Irish.

So when Bennett plowed into Beuerlein in the first period of a scoreless game against a struggling team, it wasn't an 8-yard loss, it was a statement. And that statement, emphasized by Bennett's hit and the crowd's reaction, was this:

Not today.

Not here.

The streak ends now.

• • •

ESPN host and reporter Rece Davis, an Alabama graduate who grew up cheering for the Crimson Tide, remembers what those earlier Notre Dame games meant and the impact they had on fans, including him. "Notre Dame made me cry," Davis said of the 1973 Sugar Bowl when he was just a youngster. "It's the first game I remember that made me cry. I just sat in the bathtub and cried."

These days, Davis said, "as much as I can I try to divorce myself from my passions," but it's not always easy. "I was at the College Football Hall of Fame once and as fate would have it, the Tom Clements' pass [on third down from his end zone for a first down late in the '73 Sugar Bowl that helped seal the victory] came on one of the video screens, and it still bothered me," Davis confessed. "Alabama had never beaten Notre Dame [heading into the 1986 game], and I remember how that felt as a little boy, to lose three games to them by six points."

Everyone associated with Alabama's football team understood the game's meaning. No one on the coaching staff or in uniform, no one in the stands or watching on TV at home or listening to the game on the radio, cared about Notre Dame's record or its coach (Lou Holtz) or its star players such as Tim Brown. Everyone knew what the game represented, and that feeling was evident in the media coverage and the atmosphere around Legion Field.

"We were all aware of the fact Alabama had never beaten Notre Dame," said Jim Fuller, former athletics director at Jacksonville State University who was on Alabama's coaching staff that season and was a former Alabama player himself. "I guess it was as big a game as there could be. All the history that surrounded Notre Dame and their program . . . The reason it was big was because of Coach Bryant and the fact he hadn't beaten them. For our fans, that game was very significant."

For Davis, who now works with Holtz on ESPN's *College GameNight* set during the college football season, reminding Holtz of that day in Birmingham is enjoyable. "To this day, if I bring up that game, he'll begrudgingly admit Alabama was the better team that day," Davis said.

"The Old Gray Lady [Legion Field] was shaking that day," Davis recalled.

The game's first three possessions yielded little offense, and Notre Dame took over for the second time at its own 33-yard line with 7:01 remaining in the first quarter. On the first play of that possession, Beuerlein decided to run a naked bootleg around right end. That's when he was introduced in a most unkind fashion to Bennett. That's when the game, in the view of many who were there, was decided.

"Right flip, go cover two," Joe Kines, Alabama's defensive coordinator that season, said of the defensive call on the play. "It was first down in the middle of the field and they had a little momentum and once they get going and moving they can be tough. They booted [bootleg play] right into [the defensive call]. One of the things I remember from the play is the guard pulling, and Bennett was too quick off the edge and the guard didn't get to him."

Bennett zoomed off the left side of Alabama's line, headed straight for Beuerlein, who on the bootleg turned straight into the oncoming Bennett, who tackled the quarterback under his chin, lifted him off the ground and slammed him to the artificial surface. Hard. As soon as Bennett slammed into him, Beuerlein fumbled the football, which after Bennett had planted him on the ground, rolled directly to Bennett, who recovered it. However, the referees didn't notice the fumble, which is clearly evident in video of the plays from several angles, and Notre Dame maintained possession. But the Irish quarterback was woozy at best, and the Alabama sideline and the thousands of Crimson Tide fans at the game were celebrating.

If the game's momentum prior to that play was in flux, that was no longer the case. The Sack had changed everything.

Kines said he noticed the change right away. "You feel it. You feel the switch," he said. "Everything gets in a faster gear. . . . You'd rather have momentum on your side than anything except the final score. Actually, it was a fumble, and we should have had the ball too, but we definitely had the momentum."

Mike Tankersley, covering the game for the *Montgomery Advertiser*, made note of the momentum swing, too. "I was in the press box and I said, maybe too loudly, that was the play that was going to be the turning point in the game," he said. "After the game, a lot of writers came up to me and said, 'You were right.' I was surprised it became such a big play in Alabama's history, but I guess it goes back to Alabama's psyche because they had never beaten Notre Dame. . . . I just remember it was such a huge hit."

Perhaps no one at Legion Field that day was more excited about The Sack, about Alabama's impending win, than assistant coach Sylvester Croom. He had been on the losing side as an Alabama player in two of Notre Dame's previous wins over the Crimson Tide, and he didn't want his personal string of losses to continue.

"That hit changed everything," Croom, the former head coach at Mississippi State, said. "It took [Notre Dame's] will away. That one play, that one hit, that was the ball game."

As the fans in the stands and his teammates on the sidelines celebrated the now famous hit, Bennett himself was trying to ready himself for the next play and the next opportunity to make a tackle. What others saw as a signal that the game belonged to Alabama, Bennett saw as doing what he was on the field to do: make a play.

"A lot of people made a big deal out of that game," Bennett, one of only two three-time, first-team All-America selections from Alabama (linebacker Woodrow Lowe is the other), said. "I just knew Notre Dame was on the schedule. We were just trying to win one game at a time, but you could sense it was going to be a different game. The media was making a big deal out of the game, and the fans were making a big deal out of it too. When that Saturday came around, if you didn't understand the tradition of Alabama football, you were never going to understand it at all. I never felt like I had to do anything special in that game because it was Notre Dame. I just wanted to play as hard as I could like I did in every game."

Bennett indeed played hard. He had six tackles—four of those being solo stops—The Sack and a pass breakup. But nothing else he would do that afternoon, not the pressure he put on the two Irish quarterbacks, not the other tackles, would have the impact of The Sack.

"It happened just as fast for me as it did for the fans," Bennett said. "It was just reaction. It was almost like [Beuerlein] took the snap, and there I was. It almost happened too fast. In my entire football career I had hit guys with more of a lick than I hit [him], but that was the first time I was worried that I had really hurt someone. He never saw it coming. No one blocked me, and I just went straight at him. He didn't even have a chance to clinch up. You know how you clinch up when you are about to get hit or someone is going to bump into you? Well, he didn't have time to do that because I was on him that fast."

Yet to this day, Bennett—who earned SEC Player of the Year honors that season, won the Lombardi Trophy and was later named to Alabama's Team of the Century, garnering Player of the Decade for the 1980s—insists it was just another play, just another tackle. "I had hit guys harder than that before, and I had made plays that meant more in [a] game before," he said. "But that was a play that got the attention of the fans. My biggest play in the game, I thought, was the fourth down after the sack. If I was going to get an award for making a play in the game or receive a lot of recognition for a play in that game [I thought it would be for] that fourth-down play, not the sack. They punted to us and Greg Richardson returned the punt, and I made a block that cleared him for a touchdown. To this day, that was a much bigger play to me. I still don't understand all the excitement about the sack. I guess if I were a fan I would have reacted like all the fans did. It was a big hit, but I had a lot of big hits in my career. And I'm serious. To me it was just another sack. I hit guys harder than that in practice."

After the game, when asked about Bennett's play, head coach Ray Perkins gushed about his star linebacker. "Cornelius Bennett is at least one of the top five players in America," he said. "If I were still with the [NFL's New York] Giants and wanted to draft a linebacker, I wouldn't look for another one. He's a prototype. And to show you what kind of leader he is, he went about spring training like he was trying to make the team."

• • •

Bennett would have a hard time convincing Beuerlein that he hit other players harder than he did the Irish quarterback on that first-quarter play in 1986. Even though he remained in the game for the remainder of that offensive series, it was clear Beuerlein's senses weren't clear. Jimmy Creed, covering the game for the *Tuscaloosa News* as a correspondent, was assigned to go to the Notre Dame locker room after the game and produce a feature. He chose to interview Beuerlein and get his take on what had happened on the play and what he recalled from the rest of the game.

"I was still bright-eyed and bushy-tailed, just a correspondent for the *Tuscaloosa News*," Creed, who was attending Alabama, said of his assignment as a 19-year-old sportswriter-to-be. "The job got me a pass to the game and I thought that was unbelievable. When I got to their locker room, he had a cut on his chin where Bennett had hit him, and he still had a paper towel or Kleenex or something attached to his chin, trying to stop the bleeding. I couldn't believe he was still bleeding. He told me that after he got hit he was playing on autopilot for a few plays. 'I knew I was in trouble when I could see my teammates' mouths move, but I couldn't understand the words,' he told me. It was amazing how that play really just knocked him silly. Even in the postgame interview, he was still in a daze.

"It was one of those plays, everybody saw it. I remember thinking it was like somebody hit the fast-forward button on the VCR. You couldn't believe Bennett was on him that fast. The impact engulfed the whole stadium. You heard people say 'Ooooohh.' It was like everyone had the breath knocked out of them. . . . I know that's one of those plays, that as many plays as I have seen over the years, it still stands out.

"You knew he was a great player, but that play put a watermark on his career. I can tell you that was Alabama playing Notre Dame and that they played in Birmingham at Legion Field, but I couldn't tell you that Alabama won the game or the score or anything else about the game. That hit, that's what I remember. It was one of those plays that was almost bigger than the game itself. . . . If I had to pick the top five plays in college football history, that would be one of the plays I would pick. Beating Notre Dame for the first time was just icing on the cake."

In his story for the *Tuscaloosa News*, Creed quoted Beuerlein as saying, "It was to the point where I would be trying to figure out where [Bennett] was before the snap, and realize where he was going to be coming from, things you really don't want to be thinking about before the play even gets started." Later in the story, Creed offered this quote from Beuerlein: "I didn't see him, I just felt him hit me and I was on my back. I don't even remember if I had the ball or not. . . . I didn't say anything about it at first, but I probably should have taken myself out. In the second half, I realized I was making some pretty stupid mistakes like going the wrong way on plays and stuff."

It was later learned that Beuerlein, who was quoted in other reports saying, "I have never been hit like that before and hopefully, I'll never be hit like that again," suffered a mild concussion on the play. Notre Dame, on the other hand, would suffer a collapse.

• • •

Three plays after The Sack, Notre Dame punted to Alabama, the Legion Field crowd still abuzz from Bennett's play. Apparently, Greg Richardson was abuzz, too. He fielded the punt at the Alabama 34, made a short, quick move to his right, retreated a bit, and then broke to his left, down the left sideline and away from Notre Dame would-be tacklers. His speed carried him past the Irish as though they were running at half-speed. As he closed in on the end zone, he slipped back to his right and streaked into the middle of the end zone. Just that quickly, almost as quickly as Bennett had reached Beuerlein, Alabama had staked a 7-0 lead on Richardson's 66-yard punt return.

"The punt return was something that we had been working on extremely hard this week," Richardson said after the game. "We had been watching film and we saw that we could get a return on them because they had a lot of big guys that were real slow on their coverage teams. I made the turn and got some key blocks and walked to the end zone. After I broke to the outside and saw Cornelius Bennett stopping the punter, I knew I could go all the way. It's a terrific feeling. It's something I've always wanted to do."

The score stood until the midway mark of the second period when Alabama needed less than two minutes to produce a 64-yard, four-play scoring drive. After three plays that netted 12 yards and a first down, quarterback Mike Shula found Al Bell wide open over the middle for a 52-yard scoring play. Notre Dame tried to counter on its ensuing possession but was halted at the Alabama 29, where a 46-yard field goal attempt by John Carney sailed wide left. But Shula, back to pass three plays later, was hit and fumbled, and the Irish recovered at the Alabama 11. Beuerlein, one play after backup quarterback Terry Andrysiak had thrown an incomplete pass, returned to the field to toss an 8-yard scoring strike to Brown, with 2:59 left in the half.

Alabama fans who, based on past performances against Notre Dame, might have become concerned when the Irish closed the scoring gap, discovered renewed confidence only moments later. Shula directed the Crimson Tide offense on an impressive, two-minute, 80-yard, six-play drive that produced another touchdown. A 14-yard, third-down screen pass to Kerry Goode kept the drive alive early, while a follow-up 18-yard throw to Richardson—with 15 yards tacked on to the end of the play thanks to a personal foul (late hit) penalty against Notre Dame—moved Alabama to the Irish 27. Bell carried for 18 yards on a reverse, then Shula tossed an 11-yard scoring pass to tight end Howard Cross with 59 seconds to play in the half. Alabama held a 21-7 lead and had control of the game and, as Kines suggested was almost as important, the momentum. Momentarily, Alabama lost its grip on the momentum. Andrysiak replaced Beuerlein and directed the Irish on a fast drive from its 25 to Alabama's 4-yard line. With only a few seconds remaining in the half, Carney returned to the field, nailing a 22-yard field goal on the final play of the half, trimming the Alabama lead to 21-10.

If Alabama was concerned by the late score, it didn't show it. The Crimson Tide sealed the game quickly in the second half. Brown, taking the kickoff to start the third period, returned it 19 yards but was stripped of the football by Desmond Holoman who also recovered the loose ball at the Notre Dame

19. Alabama was called for holding on the first play, moving the ball back to the 29. Facing a third-and-13 situation, Shula once again found Bell over the middle for another touchdown. It was now 28-7, and Legion Field was rocking. All that was left was to use up the remaining time.

• • •

To say Alabama fans soaked up every moment of the victory would be as big an understatement as saying simply that Bennett tackled Beuerlein in the first quarter for an 8-yard loss. There was more punch to both truths. Darin Whitlock, who the previous year had snapped the football to Larry Abney who placed it down for Van Tiffin's 52-yard field goal that beat Auburn on the final play of the Iron Bowl, enjoyed the aftermath of this win, too.

"It was really big," he said. "Notre Dame, even though they may not have been in their heyday at that time, was still Notre Dame. We knew Alabama had not beaten Notre Dame and Coach Bryant had not beaten Notre Dame. . . . At the end of the ball game, somebody had a banner that read THIS ONE'S FOR YOU BEAR. For the players, that was pretty emotional. It was the one thing Coach Bryant hadn't accomplished, so it was very rewarding to get that win."

It was especially rewarding for Croom, who could be seen near the end of the game running up and down the Alabama sideline, hugging and congratulating players with great enthusiasm. Kines said it was impossible not to notice what the game, what the win, meant to Croom. "It was Sylvester Croom's game," Kines explained. "I remember the look in Sylvester's eyes and what he was feeling. Back in those days, everybody [including assistant coaches] was responsible for scouting [the opponent] for a few games, helping put the game plan together, and that game was Sylvester's game. I remember how happy, obviously, we all were, but the look on Sylvester's face and in his eyes, that was worth a million dollars."

Certainly, Croom was a happy man, a happy former player, a happy assistant coach, a happy Alabama alumnus. "That was a great feeling, especially for me because I had been waiting since 1973 to beat them," he said. "They had swiped two national championships [from Alabama]. That was a sore spot with me. It still is."

• • •

Alabama won its first seven games of the 1986 season, the Notre Dame win marking its fifth straight victory. A 23-3 loss to Penn State in Tuscaloosa halted the streak and following a win at Mississippi State, the Crimson Tide lost its first game at Legion Field since the Notre Dame win, dropping a 14-10 decision to LSU. It would beat Temple next, but lose a heartbreaker to Auburn in the Iron Bowl before heading to the Sun Bowl where the Tide dropped Washington 28-6 in what would be Perkins's final game as Alabama head coach. The end of Perkins's career with Alabama marked the first post-Bryant coaching stint at the school. Bill Curry would be hired to replace Perkins, and he led the Crimson Tide to South Bend, Ind., for a game against Holtz and Notre Dame in the 10th game of the 1987 season. Notre Dame reverted to its old way, but with emphasis, defeating the Crimson Tide 37-6 in what would be a 7-5 season for Alabama.

CHAPTER FIFTEEN

1992 SEC Championship

Alabama 28, Florida 21
December 5, 1992
Legion Field
Birmingham, Alabama

ormer SEC commissioner Roy Kramer had an idea. He wanted to split the league into two divisions: Eastern Division (Georgia, Florida, Tennessee, Kentucky, Vanderbilt, and new league member South Carolina) and Western Division (Alabama, Auburn, LSU, Mississippi State, Ole Miss, and new league member Arkansas) and have the champion of both divisions play each other at the end of the regular season in the SEC Championship Game.

The idea was financially motivated; the additional revenue such a game would earn would be a great boost to the league and its member schools. It would also add to the conference's substantial national standing as a trend-setting league, especially in football. When the idea was pitched to TV networks, potential sponsors and the SEC's presidents and other athletic administrators, it generally received rave reviews.

SEC football fans, though, would have to be convinced.

It took Alabama and Florida, teams that were at the top of their games at that time, to sell the idea to fans, the media, and other critics. It wasn't as easy a sell as some might have imagined.

In his tenure as SEC commissioner, Kramer led the charge that made the league the most financially stable conference in the country by negotiating better and multiple TV contracts for football and basketball and developing a strong stable of sponsors for the league. He had good vision, some might say 20-20 vision, when it came to recognizing growth potential and ways to assure growth, both in on-the-field competition and revenue production.

He said he always knew a SEC Championship Game would be a winner. "I didn't have any concerns if the championship game would work," Kramer, now retired, said. "I was concerned if fans would like divisional play. That has not proven to be a problem. . . . But at the time, nobody had ever staged a game like that, and no one really knew what to expect."

While there were some grumblings and doubts among SEC fans and some media members who covered the league, nationally the idea was a big hit. "It got such national publicity because it was the first of its kind and everybody was curious about it," Kramer said. "[Then NFL commissioner] Paul Tagliabue asked to come over to see the game. So the game received enormous national media coverage because it hadn't been done before. And because the two teams playing in the game brought a lot of excitement to it too."

There were a few complaints about the site of the game, Birmingham's Legion Field, as well. Technically, because it wasn't a campus site, it was considered a neutral field; that is, until Alabama, which for years had played its most important games on that very field, earned its way into the game. Florida fans complained it was a home game for the Crimson Tide. The site was selected, for the most part, because it was located in the city of the league's office. But after two years in Birmingham—the bitter cold of the first game didn't help Legion Field's cause—the game was moved to the Georgia Dome in Atlanta for the 1994 game, where it has been played every year since that time.

"I always felt like it should be played [in the city] where the league office was," former Alabama head coach Gene Stallings said. "If the league office was in Atlanta, it should be played in Atlanta. The league office is in Birmingham, so I've always thought it should be played there." Stallings and Alabama were 1-1 in SEC Championship Games played in Birmingham. In Atlanta, through the 2012 season, Alabama's record is 3-3 in SEC Championship games.

Interestingly, of those eight Alabama appearances in the SEC Championship Game, Florida was the Eastern Division opponent each time until 2012, when the Crimson Tide played Georgia. The Gators hold a 4-3 edge in those games. Before 2012, Alabama's most recent appearance in the game came in 2009 when the Crimson Tide beat Florida 32-13. That game marked the second consecutive year the country's two top-ranked teams—

No. 1 Florida and No. 2 Alabama—met in the SEC Championship Game. In both cases, the national No. 2-ranked team won the game.

As such, the first matchup in 1992—West champ Alabama against East champ Florida—was a great break for the league in its new venture, especially having the Crimson Tide among the participants with the game being played in Birmingham.

"You knew it was going to be historic," Birmingham sports radio talk show host Ryan Brown said.

If Kramer could have selected the teams to play in that first game, Alabama and Florida are likely the two teams he would have picked that season, especially in the first SEC Championship Game and definitely in that city.

The game, as might have been expected, was a sellout.

But there was still a problem.

The top question mark surrounding the game was the belief by some that the league was taking itself out of the national championship picture by staging a championship game, an extra game that other leagues and teams seeking the national title wouldn't have to play. It was viewed as another possibility of losing a game that would knock a team out of a possible run at the national title. It also set up a scenario where the team with the best overall record and highest national ranking might not win the conference crown.

"When the game was first announced it was a strange thing," Randy Kennedy, then the Alabama beat writer for the *Dothan Eagle* and now managing producer for Sports, Entertainment, and Business for the *Press-Register* in Mobile, said, "It was a very novel idea. But there were a lot of people who thought it was a bad idea. Today, it's as natural a thing as anything in college football. It seems absurd now to think any other way [than having a championship game]. But back then, it was a strange, new thing."

All those factors came into play in the first SEC Championship Game. Alabama entered the game with an unblemished 11-0 overall record, an 8-0 mark in the league and a No. 2 national ranking. Florida, led by Steve Spurrier and his high-powered offense that was starting to reshape the offensive approach of many teams around the league and the country, was 8-3 overall and 6-2 in SEC play. Prior to losing its final regular game of the season to archrival Florida State, the Gators had won seven games in a row.

If the SEC Championship Game didn't exist, Alabama, with its unbeaten record and No. 2 national ranking, would no doubt have already been penciled in as No. 1-ranked Miami's opponent in the Sugar Bowl with the opportunity to play the Hurricanes, the hot team and program nationally at the time, for the national championship.

Now, the possibility existed that the Crimson Tide could lose the SEC title game to the Gators and with such an outcome lose its opportunity to play for the national title. Stallings had faith in his team, but didn't necessarily appreciate having to take the extra risk to achieve the goal that he, his staff, and his players had chased all season.

"We've won 11 games and still won nothing," he said at the time.

Well, the Crimson Tide had the SEC's Western Division title, but in essence, Stallings was correct. That was about to change in a big way, though.

Stallings was philosophical about Alabama's situation. "We were going to have a good year whether we won that game or not," he said. Certainly, that's a true statement, but the season was a whole lot better because Alabama won that game and the one that followed.

Yet some might be surprised at the stance Stallings took concerning the SEC Championship Game that year. "My quote at the time was if it hadn't been for the championship game we might not have gotten the opportunity to play against Miami for the national championship," he said. "Some other team might have leapfrogged us [if Alabama hadn't won the league title game]. That game helped us get that [national championship] shot, in my opinion."

• • •

Alabama's team was preparing to load buses to head for Birmingham and the title game. There was a lot of buzz surrounding the team and what could be in its future. The Florida Gators were headed toward Birmingham too, looking to knock off the previously unbeaten Crimson Tide. If Alabama won the SEC crown, a national title shot would be theirs. The focus, the team's leaders stressed, should be on nothing but football, particularly the game at hand.

Defensive back Willie Gaston supported that line of thinking, but there was another matter he had to deal with first. "Before getting on the bus, I broke up with the girl I had been dating," he said. "Everybody was excited, and I was arguing with her and she slapped me in the middle of all that was going on. I was embarrassed. I just got on the bus. [All-America defensive end] Eric Curry walked up to me after the bus got started and he said, 'I don't care what just happened to you. We've got a football game to play. Everything else is on the backburner. You got me?' I told him, 'Yes, I got you. I'm ready.'"

When the team arrived in Birmingham, after dinner the secondary spent a little extra time going over game films with defensive coordinator Bill Oliver. He was concerned about the Gators' offensive abilities, especially its quick-strike capabilities through their passing game, directed by Spurrier.

"The Alabama defense had played really well all year, but this was when everybody [in the league] was scared to death of Spurrier and that offense," sportswriter Ivan Maisel of ESPN.com said. "There was a rational fear among Alabama fans and SEC people in general about Spurrier and Florida and that offense. People were asking, 'How can they do this? How did they score 21 points against that [Alabama] defense [in the SEC Championship Game]?' Spurrier was proving that kind of football could work. If you think about it, Antonio Langham's [game-winning] play was the last gasp for Alabama against Florida. They didn't win again for a while."

Although it would lose the first SEC title game to the Crimson Tide, the Gators and Spurrier certainly made their mark in the title games to follow. Florida would win the next four SEC Championship Game crowns, beating Alabama in three of the games and Arkansas in the other. And except for a 24-23 decision over the Crimson Tide in the 1994 game, the Gators won easily, outscoring its opponents by a combined 61 points. Florida would play in five more league title games, winning three of them (2000, 2006, 2008) but losing convincingly to Alabama (34-7) in the 1999 game and in the 2009 game.

• • •

This wasn't just any matchup. It was *the* matchup in terms of the SEC and making the title game idea work. Alabama, in Stallings's third season as head coach, was unbeaten and aiming for a shot at the national title. Florida, led by Spurrier, had all the bells and whistles and athletes a college team could want, especially on offense. With Oliver leading the Alabama defense, the Crimson Tide had a counterpunch to the Gators' offensive abilities.

"Florida probably had as good a personnel as anybody we lined up against that year, and we lined up against some pretty good teams," Oliver said. "They just had so much talent. I think we were fortunate to win that ball game. . . . If we had gone into overtime I'm not sure we would have won the ball game.

The respect and admiration is mutual between the two coaches. In fact, Spurrier tried to hire Oliver as his defensive coordinator as many as four times, Oliver said. Each time, though there was interest from Oliver, he didn't feel the situation was right. Either he stayed in the state of Alabama because of retirement considerations or other factors. The last offer came in 2006, when Oliver was asked to join Spurrier's South Carolina staff. "I would have loved to have coached with him," Oliver said.

• • •

As became common for Spurrier-coached Florida teams, the Gators didn't like to waste time; they tried to score on the very first play. That was the case against Alabama in the SEC title game. Alabama won the coin toss and deferred its decision to the second half, leaving the Gators to start the game on offense, which they enjoyed.

Starting the game's opening possession at its own 23, Florida moved quickly down the field. Quarterback Shane Matthews tossed a third-down pass to Errict Rhett for 13 yards and a first down at the 43. Not only would Rhett be the Gators' leading rusher in the game—in fact, the only ball-carrier with positive yards, with 59 yards and a touchdown—but he would also be the Gators' leading pass-catcher in the game, with 10 catches for 82 yards and another touchdown. Willie Jackson would catch nine passes for 100 yards and a touchdown.

Later, another third-down play gave the Gators another first down at the Alabama 45. From there, Matthews threw strikes of 13 yards to Terry Dean, 17 yards to Jackson and another 13-yarder to Dean that moved Florida to the Alabama 2. After Rhett lost five yards on a pitchout, he gained it all back and added a touchdown on the next play when Matthews tossed him a shuffle pass for five yards and the score. Less than five minutes into the action, and in front of what Florida fans felt was a "road game" crowd, the Gators were on top 7-0.

The Crimson Tide responded right away, as if saying to Florida, "We know you can score; we can too."

Starting its first offensive drive at its own 28, Derrick Lassic was given the football on the first three plays, gaining 7, 8 and 3 yards to the Tide's 46. Martin Houston was given the ball on the next two plays, picking up nine total yards and leaving Alabama with a third-and-1 situation at the Florida 45. From there, quarterback Jay Barker connected with David Palmer on a 17-yard pass play that gave the Tide a first down at the Gators' 28.

Lassic took over from there. He took four consecutive pitchouts, as Alabama set to establish its running game as a counter to Florida's passing attack and made each one count. He picked up eight yards each on the first two carries, then seven to the Florida 5. From there, he covered the remaining distance and scooted into the end zone for a touchdown, tying the game at 7-7.

With that kind of opening to the first SEC title game, the more than 83,000 in attendance, despite the chilly weather and 10-15-miles-per-hour winds, settled in for what would prove to be a terrific game.

After five consecutive combined punts, Alabama took possession at the Gators' 42, thanks to a 20-yard punt return by Palmer and another 15 yards tacked on to the end of the run for a facemask penalty against Florida. Barker threw a nine-yard pass to Palmer on first down, but Lassic and Houston both failed to gain on the next two plays, leaving Alabama facing a fourth-and-1 play at the Gators' 33. Chris Anderson tried to slip around right end, and he was stopped for no gain, but Florida was hit with an illegal substitution penalty that gave Alabama five yards and a first down and kept the drive alive.

Lassic was stopped for a two-yard loss back at the Florida 30 on the next play, but Barker, going to the air for only the fourth time in the game, found Curtis Brown for 30 yards and a touchdown, capping a 5-play, 42-yard drive with 4:49 left in the first half.

Neither team would score again in the second period, though Alabama, as if telling the Gators' defense to expect anything, produced a 30-yard pass play between Barker and Palmer again on the final play of the half. It started at the Crimson Tide 36 and ended at the Florida 34 and was more flash than substance, but it was no doubt a strong way to end the first half, Alabama holding the lead and showing the Gators it could produce quick-strike tactics too.

While the score showed Alabama in front, the halftime stats pointed to a closely played game. Both teams had nine first downs, four penalties, no fumbles or interceptions, and Florida had punted just once more than Alabama. While taking different routes to collect yards, Alabama had just 26 more total yards than the Gators. There was still a lot to be proven, and there was 30 minutes of play left in which to do so.

The third quarter started slowly, both defenses stepping up their play, forcing the opponent to punt the ball away. On its second possession of the half, Rhett and Jackson combined for 29 yards—10 on a run by Rhett, 19 on a reception by Jackson—that helped move the Gators to the Alabama 27. After a pair of incomplete passes from there, Matthews was sacked by George Teague for a loss of seven yards back to the 34. From there, Judd Davis attempted a 51-yard field goal, but the try fell short of the mark.

Barker and Palmer, the duo that ended the first half with a sign of things to come, demonstrated what could be gained. On the first play of its ensuing possession from its 34, the duo hooked up for a 39-yard pass play that featured Palmer's speed. Suddenly, Alabama was knocking on the door again at the Florida 27.

After Lassic picked up nine yards, Houston added a 3-yard run for a first down at the Gators' 15. That's where Lassic took yet another pitchout around right end, scoring a touchdown. Kicking the extra point was harder than scoring the touchdown. After nailing two kicks, only to be disallowed because of Alabama penalties, Michael Proctor finally picked up the one point by kicking the ball through the uprights (barely) from the 28, a 45-yard extra point try. The Crimson Tide led 21-7 with 5:14 left in the third quarter.

It was time for Florida to re-introduce Alabama and the fans to its quick-strike offense. The Gators needed less than four minutes to cover 68 yards and score its second touchdown. Harrison Houston returned the kickoff 19 yards to the Gators' 32 to start things off. Matthews hit Greg Keller with a 19-yard pass, and Rhett ran for 12, pushing Florida to the Crimson Tide 37. Three more plays netted just nine yards, leaving the Gators with a fourth-and-1 decision. Matthews tossed a short, 3-yard pass to Jackson for the first down, keeping the drive alive at the Alabama 25.

A shuffle pass to Rhett gained 14 to the Alabama 11, so the Gators tried it again and picked up seven more to the Alabama 4. That's when Matthews turned back to Jackson, hitting him with a 4-yard scoring strike and trimming the Crimson Tide's lead to 21-14 with just 16 minutes and 21 seconds left in the game.

An Alabama mistake would give Florida good field position midway through the final period. Bryne Diehl's 19-yard punt set up the Gators at their own 49. Florida put together a methodical drive, Matthews completing passes for 9, 6 and 4 yards, the last of the trio of passes another shuffle pass, before trying a flea-flicker play to Rhett for 5 yards to the Alabama 27. Rhett then took a pitchout for four yards, an Alabama offsides penalty moved the ball five yards closer to the end zone, and Matthews threw to Jackson in the end zone, but the pass was incomplete. The duo tried once again, this time collecting 16 yards and a first down at the Alabama 2. After Rhett gained a yard on a pitchout, he gained the remaining yard on another toss sweep for the touchdown and a tie game.

• • •

A combined three more punts, two by Alabama, gave Florida the football late in the game at its own 21. It was there that the game took a dramatic turn. Florida, looking to make a late charge and win the game, was introduced to Antonio Langham and a defense that had decided that enough is enough.

With the Gators looking to pick up the win, Langham and Alabama would pick off the victory.

Matthews, who to this point in the game had completed 29-of-45 passes for 270 yards, two touchdowns and no interceptions, would discover that sometimes a good game ends before the allotted time has expired. He was looking to continue the strong second half he had produced, looking to get the ball to Monty Duncan, looking to put the Gators in front so they could take home the very first SEC Championship Game trophy.

Yet Langham had other plans. The Crimson Tide defensive back read the play, saw where Matthews intended to throw, stepped in front of the pass, picked it off and high-stepped himself into the end zone to complete the 27-yard interception return for a touchdown.

It was the Gators' first-down play, the first and last play of that drive.

"In the fourth quarter, we couldn't figure out how to stop them," Langham recalled. "No matter what we tried, we couldn't stop them. We weren't used to that. We had had teams have a little success against us, but not like this. They were running the same routes all game long—high-low routes. I told George [Teague] to set his man up, to get them to make a mistake. I'd been giving them some ground too, but not letting them get something over my head.

"I told [defensive end] John Copeland and the others up front to put some pressure on [Matthews]. . . . I figured if they could get some pressure on him, he would throw too quick and somebody—not necessarily me, but somebody—could take advantage. And that's what happened."

Gaston said there was a lot of talk in Alabama's defensive huddle before the interception. "Everybody is looking at each other, and Eric said, 'Somebody needs to make a play.'" Gaston recalled, "Teague said the same thing. When we broke the huddle, just before the play, I said to myself, *Lord, somebody needs to make a play, but don't let them throw the ball over here.* It had to be one of the happiest moments of my life when they threw the ball to Antonio's side and he picked off the pass and took off. Being a sophomore and winning a championship like that, it was special. So when Langham intercepted that pass and scored, we just went crazy.

"It was nothing new; we had been winning games all year, even close games, but that one sure felt good."

Melick said the Langham interception return for a touchdown is another example of how Oliver, with his game plans, forced teams to be on the lookout for anything and everything, even at times when nothing had changed.

"The play was one of those deals late in a game where Langham had been playing off the receivers a little, setting them up late in the game. You have to give Oliver credit for that. Spurrier had great respect for Oliver—he tried to hire him as his defensive coordinator a couple of times—and always called him for advice. Spurrier was just gashing Alabama with a little play, and had made a play on Sam Shade's side of the field. Spurrier got confused and thought Oliver had made an adjustment, so they quit going to that play, which had been working the entire first half."

The Alabama defense took advantage of the mistake. "It was a great defensive team, and you just knew that's how they were going to win the game, with a defensive play, if they won it at all," Melick said of Alabama. "A great defensive team versus a great offensive mind; it was the perfect matchup. Alabama executed that play perfectly. They forced Matthews into a bad throw, and Langham was there to pick it off."

Langham doesn't take sole credit for the game-winning play. He said it was a team effort that started with the defensive line. "Matthews was pressured, and he just let the ball go," he said. "When I saw it, I knew I could get to it. I had a perfect shot at the ball, and I kept telling myself, *Whatever you do, don't drop the football. And when you pick it off, you've got to take it to the house.*

"As I ran to the end zone, out of the corner of my eye I saw John Copeland wipe somebody out. To this day, I still don't know who he blocked, but it was the best block I've ever seen in my life. When I was in the end zone, one of my teammates kept yelling, 'Lift up your jersey! Lift up your jersey! You've got an *S* on your chest!' He was talking about me being Superman. He said I had three big games in a row—versus Mississippi State, Auburn, and Florida— and that I was a superhero.

Certainly it was the defining and deciding play of the game. It was the kind of play Stallings said is made in almost every football game played, regardless of the opponents or the circumstances. "You play 50 or 60 plays for the privilege of making two or three," he said.

• • •

Florida still had a little time to try and get back in the game. The Gators were reeling from Langham's play and the buzz of the pro-Alabama crowd in its ears, but they had overcome such situations before. This, however, would not be one of those times. Matthews hit Jackson for a 17-yard gain and then tossed an incomplete pass to Keller. His next try would all but seal the Gators' fate, making a throw that was batted around and ended up in the hands of Alabama's Michael Rogers.

The Crimson Tide tried to run out the remaining time and keep the ball away from the Gators, but it wasn't successful in that effort. Diehl came on and, from the Florida 41, dropped a 32-yard punt at the Gators' 9 that would require nothing short of a miracle for Florida to produce a game-tying touchdown. An Alabama penalty and four straight incomplete passes gave the ball back to Alabama. Barker took the game's last snap, dropped to one knee and Alabama had the first SEC Championship Game crown.

"The locker room was chaotic," Gaston said of Alabama's celebration of the victory. "Everybody was hugging each other and giving each other high-fives. We knew somebody was going to make a play, it was just a matter of who. It was like, we did it. We're going to the Sugar Bowl and play for the national championship.

"For most of us, that's why we went to Alabama, to play for a national championship. So to have it come true, to have that chance, was a dream come true."

• • •

Alabama received an invitation to play in the Sugar Bowl against unbeaten and No. 1-ranked Miami. The winner would claim the national championship. Despite what some believed, that adding a conference championship game might knock a SEC team out of contention for the national championship, Alabama would get that chance.

"If you look at [the league's] history over the years, that hasn't been the case," Kramer said in reference to the can't-win-the-national-title talk surrounding the SEC Championship Game at the time. "I think it gave Alabama the spark it needed to win the national championship.

"We didn't have the best of weather [for the game], but the game itself took care of that problem. . . . [The SEC Championship Game] has taken on a life of its own now, with people attending no matter what teams are playing. But that first game was very important. We had a great game in the first year and because that first game was so exciting—I think it is one of the best championship games we've ever had —it developed into an important game. If that first game had been a blowout, we probably would have had a lot of criticism."

This would have been especially true if Alabama had lost and the league's only team with a chance to play for the national championship had lost that opportunity.

And as for the concerns that first year as to whether the SEC would be handcuffed in trying to win the national championship with the extra game, the concerns have proven to be unfounded. Alabama won the national title that first year in 1992 by whipping Miami in the Sugar Bowl. In 1996, Florida won the national crown, with Tennessee claiming the national title in 1998. LSU won national titles in 2003 (with current Alabama head coach Nick Saban leading the Tigers) and 2007, with Florida winning the national championship in 2006 in a situation where winning the SEC Championship Game probably created the opportunity for the Gators to play for the No. 1

national ranking. The same was true in 2007 for LSU, which parlayed its SEC Championship Game win into an opportunity of earning a spot in the BCS national championship game, where it, like Florida had done the previous year, defeated Ohio State for the crown.

At this writing (spring of 2013), SEC teams have won seven consecutive national championships, including Alabama in 2009, 2011, and 2012. In fact, the BCS national title game following the 2011 season was an all-SEC affair featuring a rematch of Alabama against LSU in the Mercedes-Benz Superdome in New Orleans.

And somewhere, Roy Kramer is still smiling.

CHAPTER SIXTEEN

1993 Sugar Bowl

Alabama 34, Miami 13
January 1, 1993
Louisiana Superdome
New Orleans, Louisiana

Go ahead, pick a sports matchup, any matchup, and the pairing of Alabama vs. Miami in the 1993 Sugar Bowl was on equal standing in terms of interest and intensity.

On paper.

Ali vs. Frazier. Borg vs. McEnroe or Connors. Nicklaus vs. Palmer. Red Sox vs. Yankees. Celtics vs. Lakers. Giants vs. Eagles.

There were a couple of other comparisons that, in the days leading up to the teams playing for the 1992 season's national championship in the Superdome in New Orleans, were inescapable; comparisons that labeled the matchup and heightened the interest in the game.

The first was attitude; Miami had it, displayed it and in fact wore it as a badge of honor; Alabama had it, but kept it under wraps, choosing to remain silent until kickoff. The second was a comparison as obvious as the domed stadium's presence in the old-world city and it became the theme that fans and media, and even the players and coaches in some respects, attached to the game:

Good vs. Evil.

"It's hard to think about that game as David vs. Goliath," Randy Kennedy, then the *Dothan Eagle*'s Alabama beat writer and now managing producer for Sports, Entertainment, and Business of the *Press-Register* in Mobile, said.

"Miami had all the swagger, the long winning streak and everything was going well. They were at the height of their badness."

The Hurricanes, national champions the previous season and winners of 29 straight games, were heavy favorites to win the game. In the previous 11 seasons, Miami had won four national championships (1983, '87, '89, '91) and was looking to claim its fifth. The Hurricanes' program was considered the program of the '80s and had a jump on extending that dominance into the '90s.

Alabama, which had begun the 1990 season with three losses, had hit its stride under third-year head coach Gene Stallings and on the strength of a defense that refused opponents any breathing room. Alabama, with a long and rich football history, was seeking its first national championship since 1979.

Throughout the days leading up to the game, both teams played their projected roles to perfection; the Canes strolled around New Orleans and the French Quarter, telling anyone who would listen (and some who tried not to) how easily they would beat Alabama. The Crimson Tide players took on an almost "ah-shucks" attitude, speaking of Miami's team in respectful terms and saying they looked forward to the challenge that was ahead. The respective approaches only fed the Good vs. Evil tag the game was receiving.

Although they remained quiet, that didn't mean the Alabama players were in awe of their opponent. Nor did they lack self-assurance.

"The confidence was there," All-America defensive end Eric Curry said of Alabama's demeanor that week. "We just went about our work at practice and went about our business. We had our own attitude, and we kept it to ourselves. Miami was talking all week long about what they were going to do to us, and we just kept on working and stayed away from that sort of thing. But we were never afraid of those guys or intimidated by them at all, not at all. . . . Everything was building up for us. We were ready to play right then [days before kickoff]. We didn't care if we were on the field or not, we were ready to play."

In the French Quarter one night a few days before the game, members of the Miami team and members of the Alabama team met near Bourbon Street, and a ministandoff of sorts ensued. Challenges were made, verbal jousts were exchanged, and tempers rose, but in the end, nothing happened.

"Miami tried to bait the Alabama players," Ray Melick, former sports columnist for the *Birmingham News* who at that time was the Alabama beat writer for the *Birmingham Post-Herald*, said. "The Alabama players said, 'We don't play the game in the Quarter, we'll play it in the Superdome.'"

Willie Gaston recalled the showdown. "I remember [Miami's] Rohan Marley saying to us, 'You guys decided to show up, huh?' But E. C. [Curry] just looked at them and shook his head and said, 'We'll see you on the field.'"

Miami wide receiver Lamar Thomas was perhaps the most vocal of the Hurricane players, making boasts throughout the week. "He kept showing his national championship ring and talked about getting another one, and of Miami becoming a dynasty," Melick said.

George Teague would find a way to silence Thomas's boastfulness on New Year's night.

• • •

David Crane, then a student assistant working in Alabama's media relations office, had managed to get four tickets for the game through a good friend in the Alabama athletic department. That meant he, his brother and sister, and one of his sister's friends would be in the Superdome for the game. The good friend in the athletic department had even been able to secure rooms at the team hotel. The morning of the game, Crane and his brother Mac played tennis. When they had finished playing a friend approached them with some interesting information.

"I don't know if it's confidence or stupidity, but I just talked to one of the defensive assistants and he told me if we didn't win by three touchdowns he'd be surprised," the friend told the Crane brothers. Then the friend added, "I think he's crazy."

Turns out, the defensive assistant knew what he was talking about, of course, probably after watching defensive coordinator Bill "Brother" Oliver run the Crimson Tide defense through the game plan he had devised for the offensively talented Hurricanes.

As it turned out, it was confidence, not stupidity.

If Alabama, which had just won the first SEC Championship Game over a talented Florida team, was going to have a chance against Miami, that chance would be granted by its tenacious defense. The number of outstanding players on the defensive side of the football was high, beginning with the bookend All-America defensive ends Curry and John Copeland. Teague, Antonio Langham, and Sam Shade led the secondary. There were others too, the entire unit developing a national reputation based on the group's stinginess in allowing points and yardage.

No one recognized the talent of Alabama's defensive roster more than Oliver, and he was going to fortify that talent by producing a defensive game plan that would keep Miami guessing, as well as consistently favor Alabama's defensive personnel.

Oliver's defensive plan would become the blueprint for Alabama's success against the No. 1-ranked and previously unbeaten Hurricanes. He spent a lot of time developing the plan of attack, which would give the impression that Alabama had all 11 defensive players up near the line of scrimmage, but in reality, provided several options for the Crimson Tide in terms of coverage. Out of the alignment, Alabama could blitz, drop its linebackers, drop the safeties, employ the use of six or seven defensive backs, or spread the defenders out vertically or horizontally.

The plan, which was different than anything Alabama had employed all season, was devised to create confusion for the Miami offense as well as address the Canes' obvious offensive talents. In order to install the new plan, Melick said, Oliver not only would put the defense through basic practice sessions during the day, but would also institute more intricate and detailed preparations at night by way of walk-through sessions in ballrooms, watching films on Miami, and by simply talking his players through their responsibilities.

At 5:15 AM on Christmas morning, the day players and coaches were to leave for New Orleans, Oliver was in his office, still looking for ways to better explain his plan to the players, trying to make it easier to understand. It must have worked. "We didn't have a bad practice after that," he said.

What made the "11-man look" work, Oliver said, was the 11 players charged with carrying out the plan. "The biggest thing was how smart our guys were," he said, "how calm and collected they were and how well they played out of it. They did a great job of executing what we had taught, of understanding how the technique worked and how we were going to attack them, how we would come at them from inside and outside." It began with "walk-and-talk" sessions in which Oliver described what he wanted each player to do, based on a specific defensive call, and so they walked through the respective positions and the players' respective responsibilities, over and over and over again.

"The thing I think of when I think of that game is Bill Oliver," Kennedy said. "He is one of the greatest defensive coordinators there has ever been in the game, and I don't think that's overstating it. He had a great, quiet confidence. And this is not a plan he stole, this was his plan."

The most valuable sessions were the ones that took place at night, sessions away from the possibility of those who might relay such information to those for whom it was not intended. "It was almost like the [implementation of] the wishbone [offense by head coach Paul 'Bear' Bryant] in 1971," Melick said. "It was a complete secret. No one knew it was coming. They worked on it in ballrooms throughout the week, away from the field."

As the game drew closer, and his observance of practices and the ballroom walk-throughs led him to believe the plan was going to be successful, Oliver opened up a bit to those who regularly covered the team. Yet he did so only with the assurance the information was for background information only and would not be reported before the game.

"He was holding court one day at a practice in one of the end zones [in the Superdome]," Phillip Tutor, the editorial page editor at the *Anniston Star* who then was the newspaper's Alabama beat writer, said. "He was telling us about the goal-line stand against Penn State [in the 1979 Sugar Bowl], and he gets out on the field and starts showing us [the alignment Alabama would use against Miami]. He had such a great game plan for [Miami], using that great defensive line. It was unorthodox and it looked crazy, but it was really neat watching that game and thinking back to a couple of days before and what he said, because it was happening just like he said it would. It was going to take a superhuman effort to win against that defense and that plan."

Miami had no such effort in it, or if it did, the plan stripped that effort and the Hurricanes' will from them.

Oliver was quoted as saying he wished Bryant was still alive so he could have seen that defense play. "I really do," he emphasized a few years later. "He loved great defense and he would have cherished getting to see those guys play, how hard they played. He really would have."

It was apparent from the start that Miami was confused as to how to attack Alabama's defense or if they had a plan to stage such an attack. Torretta was especially flustered, trying to read the defense and get the Miami offense in a position to make some yards and score some points against it. While the Canes had a moment or two of success, the game and the night belonged to the Alabama defense and Oliver's plan.

A few years later, at a pro-am golf event prior to a PGA Champions Tour tournament at The Moors in Milton, Fla., just outside Pensacola, Torretta and Oliver met again. Torretta didn't recognize Oliver until one of the tournament officials asked the former quarterback if he recognized the man across the table from him. Torretta said no, he didn't know him, and was then told he was the man responsible for making his life miserable in New Orleans on a certain New Year's night. After dinner, Torretta introduced himself to Oliver, and the men shook hands and chatted for a few moments.

"He put his arm around my shoulder and he said, 'I get out there and look at that defense and I don't know what to think,'" Oliver recalled Torretta saying. "'We go three-and-out and I get on the phone [up to the coaches in the press box] and ask them what was happening, and they told me to just keep playing and they'd get back to me.' Torretta said one time he called [to the coaches] and no one answered the phone."

Oliver said that when watching game films on Miami, they would give teams a lot of different looks, but all those looks were run out of the same basic formations with the same personnel. And while it appeared at times that Alabama's defense was just winging it, that it was taking chances that happened to pay off, Oliver said that was far from the truth.

"It wasn't gambling," he said. "That plan was as sound as a silver dollar. The biggest thing was how they approached it, but we felt like we could put them in some difficult and different situations and it would create problems for them. But that plan was sound, very sound."

And effective.

• • •

Despite the quiet confidence of the Alabama players, everyone else seemed to believe that the Miami players, though the message was delivered in a brusque manner, were probably right: the Canes would likely win the game going away.

"I remember being in New Orleans and there was no buzz about Alabama having any chance to win," Gregg Dewalt, sports editor of the *Florence Times Daily*, said. "I don't even think a lot of Alabama fans thought they had a big chance to win the game. I don't think we realized how strong Alabama's defense was at that time, but now when you look back on it, that was one of the great defenses ever."

Dewalt isn't alone in his assessment. "I was as brainwashed about Miami as the rest of the national media," sportswriter Ivan Maisel of ESPN.com said. "Alabama's offense was OK, but Miami was the defending national champion and had won 29 games in a row. Gino Torretta had won the Heisman Trophy, and that was a legendary team."

Despite the Canes' role as the heavy favorite in the No. 1 vs. No. 2 game of undefeated teams, Alabama fans, as is usually the case, traveled by the carloads to New Orleans. By contrast, there were only a few Miami fans who had made their way to Louisiana.

"It felt like an Alabama home game," Birmingham sports radio talk show host Ryan Brown said. "Inside, there were thousands of Alabama fans, and outside, there were hundreds more, all dressed in red, holding fingers up in the air for how many tickets they needed. Nobody was selling tickets. You couldn't find any."

Alabama graduate Jimmy Creed, a former sports editor for the *Anniston Star* who at the time was working in New Orleans covering the NFL's Saints, said he wasn't surprised. "I think it was one of those games where [Alabama fans] just packed up and went to New Orleans without tickets, hoping to find them when they got there or just wanting to be in the same place where the game was being played."

Working for Host Communications at the time, Mark Meadows, now executive director of the BBVA Compass Bowl in Birmingham and a former manager for the Alabama football team, was one of the lucky ones to secure tickets. In fact, he and his wife had their choice of seats—in one of the luxury boxes or in the regular seats. "I've never been to a louder place in my life," he recalled. "We started out in the [luxury] box, but only stayed there a few minutes. It didn't feel right. So we moved to the other seats and we couldn't hear each other speak. It was great. I was hoarse for two days after that game."

• • •

Miami's Torretta was not prepared for what he would see as the game began. As the Heisman Trophy winner broke huddle and headed to the line of scrimmage for the game's first play following Alabama's kickoff at the Hurricanes' 18-yard line, he saw red. A lot of red. And all of it really close. This was something he had never seen before outside of a goal-line defense; Alabama was putting all 11 of its defenders up near the line of scrimmage. What the heck was going on?

It must have seemed as though Alabama hadn't watched a single game film of the Hurricanes' offense. Didn't the Crimson Tide coaches know Miami had one of the best passing games in the country? Was Alabama *daring* Miami to pass? Torretta decided to oblige. His first pass was good for just three yards as Sam Shade made a quick stop.

The next two plays, both passes, wouldn't fare any better. Lining up in the shotgun on second down, Torretta was sacked by cornerback Tommy Johnson. On third down, Torretta's pass fell incomplete. Miami's first offensive series resulted in zero yards. It would be a sign of things to come. Alabama fans, enjoying the defensive stand, revved up its noise level a bit as the defense left the field. The noise, which grew louder as the game progressed, was just getting unwrapped.

"A Miami writer was sitting next to me during the game and when he saw Alabama's defense line up, he said, 'What the hell are they doing? They'll never get away with that,'" Melick recalled. "But they did."

Moments later, another noise level was reached when David Palmer took in a Miami punt at the Alabama 38 and returned it 38 yards to the Miami 24. The offense would take over from there.

"When Palmer broke that punt, there was a tremendous roar that broke out," Brown said. "It was incredibly loud."

Derrick Lassic made the first of his 28 carries of the day on the Crimson Tide's first play from scrimmage, gaining four of his 143 total yards for the game. He then bounced off the right side of the line for 14 yards on second down to the Miami 6. The Hurricanes called time-out to try and readjust. Jay Barker threw an incomplete pass, Lassic picked up three more yards and Barker then scrambled for a yard, leaving Alabama with a fourth down-and-goal at the 2. Stallings decided to go with the safe choice, and Michael Procter was called on to kick a 19-yard field goal.

Miami's offense returned to the field, starting at its 21, and enjoyed some success. After a 1-yard gain on a run, Torretta completed passes for five and 34 yards from the shotgun formation. After an incomplete throw, he completed another pass for 10 to the Alabama 29. A draw play lost three yards, and Torretta's next two passes fell incomplete. Miami settled for a 49-yard Dane Prewitt field goal, tying the game.

Turnovers would rule the next three possessions. Barker had a pass intercepted on Alabama's follow-up possession, but two plays into Miami's ensuing series Torretta passed to Lamar Thomas, who was hit by Johnson, the loose ball recovered by Willie Gaston at the Alabama 23. But Alabama gave the ball back to the Canes when Barker was intercepted again with 1:53 left in the first period.

Miami could get nothing on its final series of the quarter, Torretta sandwiching two incomplete passes around an 8-yard loss on a reverse, and punted to Alabama. The Crimson Tide drove from its 48 to the Miami 1 but was hit with a costly unsportsmanlike conduct penalty, moving it back to the Miami 16. It could gain no offensive steam after the penalty and settled for another Proctor field goal, this one for 23 yards.

Some fans took exception to the penalties being called against Alabama. David Crane remembers a fan nearby becoming especially upset over a series of calls against the Crimson Tide, and the fan let the officials—and everyone else around him—know exactly how he felt. After a play in which Alabama had picked up a first down on a long third-down play, the man directed a statement to the officials, who probably could hear him over all the noise being generated in the dome. "Deny that, [expletive]!" the man yelled, adding a multisyllable curse word onto the exclamation. Several in the area, including Crane and his group, cast a glance at the man that suggested the third word of his rant was not only unnecessary but inappropriate.

A few moments later, when an exciting play took place on the field, a youngster around the age of five, according to Crane, who was seated near the ranting fan, stood up and shouted, "Deny that!" providing the same, multisyllable expletive he had heard just moments before. The father of the boy immediately turned to the fan, who had just heard how his own words sounded when yelled by a youngster, stared hard at him, and said, "Thank you," with as much sarcasm as could be mustered.

The game continued with Alabama delivering a bit of "Deny that!" play at the Hurricanes' expense.

Shade came through again when the defense returned to the field, picking off a Torretta pass and returning it 33 yards to the Miami 31. Lassic put the Alabama offense in gear, gaining three, 25 and two yards to the Miami 1 before losing a yard on a second-and-goal play. Giving Lassic a rest, Alabama gave the football to Sherman Williams on the next play. He covered the remaining two yards off the left side for the touchdown and a 13-3 Crimson Tide lead.

After the teams swapped punts, Miami put together another drive. Starting at its own 16, Torretta moved the Canes all the way to the Alabama 28 with one second to play and set up for a field goal try. Alabama called two time-outs in an effort to "freeze" the Miami kicker. It didn't work as Prewitt, a high school teammate of Barker, booted a 42-yarder on the final play of the half.

Alabama had a 10-point lead, but it had something more, too: momentum. The Alabama defense had held Miami's vaunted offense to just two first downs in the first period and only six yards rushing in the half. The Alabama offense, though it let a couple of scoring opportunities slip away, was doing its part.

The third quarter would define the game—on Torretta's first two passes, Miami's first two offensive plays of the second half.

Alabama received the kickoff to open the second half but did little with its first opportunity, punting to the Canes, who did nothing with its first possession, thanks to another key play by Alabama's Johnson. Torretta passed on first down and Johnson picked off the throw, returning it 23 yards to the Miami 20, and Lassic picked up seven yards on a second-down reverse.

Barker scrambled for nine yards and picked up some extra yardage when Miami was penalized for grabbing his facemask, setting up the Tide at the Canes' 2. Lassic gained nothing on a run and Barker picked up a yard a play later before Lassic got the final yard and the touchdown.

Obviously feeling the pressure to make something happen quickly to get back in the game, Torretta looked to pass again on the Canes' first play of the ensuing possession, and he was intercepted again, with a twist. Defensive back George Teague stepped in front of a pass intended for Jonathan Harris at the Miami 31, slipped down the sideline, and raced into the end zone for another Alabama touchdown, high-stepping the final yards.

Just more than five minutes into the third quarter, Alabama held a 27-6 lead and the Superdome, now as much a noise factory as a multipurpose dome, was owned by Alabama's fans, who now knew the team, led by its stellar defensive unit, was going to win a national championship.

• • •

Teague wasn't finished. In what was perhaps the greatest college football play that didn't count, Teague would make a play that produced the loudest cheers on a night of pretty loud cheering.

The Canes' possession started with a run up the middle for no gain, which led to Torretta turning to the pass again. He found Thomas, one of the most vocal Miami players in the days leading up to the game, open on the left sideline with a pass. It appeared Thomas was headed for what might have been an 89-yard scoring play if not for Teague. It probably would have led to another quick Alabama touchdown if not for an offsides penalty against the Crimson Tide. As it turned out, the play didn't count, at least not officially. Unofficially, it was perhaps the biggest play of the game.

Thomas pulled the pass in and was sprinting down the left sideline, using the speed for which he was so noted. He didn't see that Teague, before this play considered one of the slower members of the Alabama secondary, chasing after him. And not just chasing, but catching Thomas. And not just catching Thomas, but stripping him of the football around the five-yard line and heading back the other way.

Here was Thomas, who talked of how easy it was going to be for the Canes to win their second straight title against Alabama, being caught from behind and, just as important in the eyes of the Alabama team and its fans, being embarrassed on a play that had been his bread and butter—getting behind a defender and scoring.

"He made the catch in my area. The way I saw it, if he scored, it was going to be my fault," Teague said in Ray Melick's 1993 book *Roll Tide Roll: Alabama's National Championship Season*. "I just thought about [stripping away the ball] and did it. And the ball came right back in my belly."

Thomas had at least a six-yard head start on Teague when he caught the pass and was in full stride down the sidelines. The difference was covered pretty quickly and the result put the final stamp on a game that, for all intents and purposes, had been decided when Teague intercepted the pass and returned it for a touchdown a couple of plays prior to the Thomas pass.

"That was the greatest non-play I've ever seen," Maisel said. "The individual effort, refusing to give up on the play, I think it spoke volumes of who Miami was and who Alabama was. . . ."

Brown, sitting in the stands, said fans didn't react to Teague's play right away, but certainly did when a replay was shown on the video screens in the dome. "I think that play was the game in a nutshell," he said. "Alabama just wanted it more."

Instead of producing a touchdown that might have given Miami some life, might have generated some momentum, Teague's play was the final uppercut that knocked out the Hurricanes. What little hope was left in them had been chased down and taken away.

• • •

After Alabama's offsides penalty, Miami received the ball back, but two lackluster plays later the Canes punted again. Later in the third quarter, Miami reached the Alabama 11, but on a fourth-and-2 play Torretta's pass was off the mark, giving the ball back to Alabama. On the final play of the third period, Alabama punted back to Miami. The Crimson Tide was just 15 minutes of playing time away from claiming the national championship.

The Miami offense, once again, could generate nothing, punting to Alabama, and the Crimson Tide returned the favor. That's when the Canes finally produced a big play. Kevin Williams fielded the Alabama punt at the 22, made a few moves and was on his way to a 78-yard punt return for a touchdown. The Canes had trimmed Alabama's lead to 14 points with 12:08 to play. Could Miami mount a late push and get back in the game?

In a word, no. Alabama's offense responded to the Canes' score by producing a matching touchdown of its own. Miami's ensuing kickoff was fielded by Palmer at the Alabama 5, and he produced some moves and speed of his own, returning the kick 36 yards to the Alabama 41. He lost four yards on a reverse on the first play of the drive, but Lassic picked up 13 on the next play and, after Barker failed to get the first down on a quarterback sneak, Houston completed fourth-and-1 play to set up the first down.

A pass interference penalty against Miami on a third-down throw gave Alabama a first down, and three running plays produced yet another first down, placing Alabama at the Miami 20. Running back Tarrant Lynch, who had just five carries in the game, slipped off the right side of the line for 16 yards to the Miami 4. Two plays later, Lassic was back at it, covering the final four yards for the Alabama touchdown. It was 34-13, and Alabama fans already had the celebration party in full swing.

More than six minutes remained to be played, but they were a mere formality. Miami's intensity had been taken away—stripped away, to be sure—and Alabama's defense had produced one of the most dominating performances in recent history. The Canes would get two more offensive possessions, one ending at its own 45 on an incomplete pass on a fourth-and-12 play, the last on a third-and-goal play from the Alabama 4 when yet another Torretta pass fell incomplete as the final seconds dwindled down.

How dominating was the Alabama defensive performance? Dominating enough to support an offense that received 135 rushing yards and two touchdowns from Lassic, but no other Alabama rusher had more than 39 yards. Dominating to support an offense whose quarterback was a mere 4-of-13 passing for 18 yards and two interceptions, an offense that produced a total of just 285 yards.

• • •

With the game well in hand, Alabama Assistant Coach Jim Fuller, located in the coaches' box in the press box, informed Assistant Coach Danny Pearman he was headed down to the field. "'I'm coming down,' I said, and he said, 'No, you're not.' He was superstitious," Fuller recalled. "I said, 'The hell with you, this thing is over. It's been over for a while. I'm coming down because I want to be on the field with the players and celebrate their winning the national championship.'"

As a player at Alabama, Fuller had been a part of two national championship teams and a third team, the 1966 team, that went through the season unbeaten and untied but without a national crown. "I should have played on three [national championship teams]," he said. Fuller didn't believe the feeling of winning a national championship could ever be topped. "They kept telling me all week, 'Relax, we're going to win,'" Fuller said. "I guess I should have seen the signs. . . . Being on the field with them, that was a totally different feeling, just watching those kids react to winning. I wanted to share that moment with them. I had a great feeling of joy for them."

In all of Miami's previous games that year, Torretta had been intercepted only seven times. Against Alabama on New Year's night, he was picked off three times, one of those returned for a touchdown, against a team that often put all 11 players up near the line of scrimmage and challenged Miami to do what many believed it did better than most teams in the country: throw the football.

The Canes not only lost the game and their No. 1 ranking, but some mystique as well. The fast-talking, high-stepping, extremely confident Hurricanes had allowed Alabama, a team Miami players had boasted earlier in the week on the streets of the French Quarter and all around New Orleans couldn't stay on the field with them, to gain 67 more rushing yards than any team had totaled against them all season.

"I said all along we had the best football team, just no one would listen to me," Stallings said. "Miami had a great team, and they could throw the football. But we led the nation in three or four defensive categories. . . . I don't think football games are won with schemes; football games are won with football players making plays, and we made more plays."

Stallings's place in Alabama's football history was secured with the victory and national title. He said he was proud to be a part of that team, a part of what was accomplished. "I know this, the people of the state of Alabama loved Coach [Paul] Bryant, they just tolerated the rest of us," he said. "To be a small part of that tradition is special. I loved every day that I was coaching. I loved getting a team ready to play and working with the coaching staff. If you can't enjoy yourself in that environment, there's something wrong with you."

"I cried," Willie Gaston said of his reaction to being part of a national championship team. "So many things happened that year, and for us to win that game, it was special. I had fulfilled a dream I'd had all my life. It's a dream a lot of people never achieve. I felt so many things.

"I had leg cramps late in the game, and one of the coaches told the trainers, 'Go ahead and take Willie to the locker room.' I said, 'Y'all ain't taking me no place. I'm staying to watch the clock run down. I'm not going anywhere.' We had worked too hard for me to go to the locker room and wait around. I wanted to be out there, celebrating with everybody else. To do something everyone said you couldn't do, that's an unbelievable feeling."

Whether it was No. 1 vs. No. 2, Brash vs. Reserved, Defense vs. Offense or Good vs. Evil; however one viewed the 1993 Sugar Bowl matchup of Alabama vs. Miami going into the game, there was only one way to look at it after the fact:

Alabama, led by its stellar defense and a little bit of moxie of its own, was the best college football team in the country.

CHAPTER SEVENTEEN

1998 LSU

Alabama 22, LSU 16
November 7, 1998
Tiger Stadium
Baton Rouge, Louisiana

Tiger Stadium—known lovingly as "Death Valley" to LSU fans, and certainly by opposing teams, too—is considered one of the toughest places in college football for an opposing team to win. The LSU faithful turn out loud and strong in support of their Tigers.

And Tiger Stadium at night is an even louder, more intimidating place for opposing teams to play.

In October of 2007, then-ESPN.com writer Bruce Feldman produced a list of the "Top Ten Scariest Places to Play" in regard to stadiums where opposing teams find it tough to win. LSU's Tiger Stadium was No. 1 on his list. LSU's home record from 2000-07 was 49-7, and the home field advantage helped pave the way for national championships in 2003 and 2007, although the Tigers lost one home game both of those seasons.

Perhaps one of the most famous Tiger Stadium games took place in 1988, when LSU scored a touchdown on a Tommy Hodson-to-Eddie Fuller pass with 1:48 left in the game that gave the Tigers a 7-6 victory over Auburn. The crowd noise from the stadium following Fuller's touchdown catch was so loud it registered on the seismograph in LSU's Howe-Russell Geoscience Complex. As such, the victory, still celebrated and talked about today, has become known as the "Earthquake Game."

Still, with all the advantages Tiger Stadium mustered for the LSU football team and for its fans, for all the times opponents have entered Death Valley only to leave beaten and disappointed, Alabama was unaffected for a 15-game run in Baton Rouge. After a 20-15 LSU victory over the Crimson Tide at Tiger Stadium in 1969, Alabama did not lose again in Death Valley until a 30-28 defeat in 2000.

Not only did Alabama post a 14-0-1 record at Tiger Stadium from 1971 through 1998, but it usually won those games in a convincing manner. The average score for those games was 23-10 [actually 9.8], and in two of those Alabama wins LSU's offense failed to register a point.

So when the teams were scheduled to meet again in 1998 at Tiger Stadium at night, even with LSU at 4-4 overall and 2-4 in SEC games, there was still a sense among Tiger fans that this would be the year Alabama's string of victories on LSU's home field would finally come to an end. Alabama was 5-3 overall and 2-3 in SEC games heading to Baton Rouge, the Crimson Tide having already lost to Arkansas (42-6), Florida (16-10) and Tennessee (35-16).

As the teams began the fourth quarter of play in 1998, it appeared those who felt the streak would come to an end were not correct. Instead, the charm or strength or jinx Alabama possessed when it played in Tiger Stadium during that period would remain intact.

It didn't hurt that Alabama had Shaun Alexander on its side.

• • •

Alabama's broadcast team for the pay-per-view and tape-delayed broadcast of the game didn't have a place to work in the Tiger Stadium press box, which was undergoing some construction. A small area was made available for the crew, but it didn't provide enough room for monitors and equipment, much less people, including play-by-play announcer David Crane and color commentator Chris Stewart. Instead, the group went to Plan B, which placed them outside the stadium, positioned next to the company's production trucks, watching the game that was going on inside the stadium via TV monitors.

OK, so Plan B wasn't ideal. But as it turned out, it would be quite a vantage point later in the evening.

"The game wasn't being televised by the [Southeastern] conference, so we were doing it on pay-per-view," Wright Waters, then general manager of Crimson Tide Sports Marketing, and now executive director of the Football

Bowl Association, said. "I'm pretty sure we can get it for pay-per-view and I'm using a favor with [then LSU athletics director] Joe Dean. He said there was a little construction going on in the press box but that he would find a place for us. . . . There's no room in the press box, so Chris and David decide they will broadcast off TV, like the old days of radio when the announcer would fake the sound of a bat hitting a baseball and tell the listeners it was a base hit."

Stewart remembers showing up at Tiger Stadium on the Friday before game day and how he and Crane were greeted. "We had been told all season that the LSU game in Baton Rouge might be challenging because there was no auxiliary broadcast space available at Tiger Stadium," he said. "We even joked that we might have to broadcast the game from outside the stadium. As it turned out, the joke was on us."

It would be, Stewart said, "the greatest game I never saw."

Waters had other problems, too. He was also in charge of getting Alabama's radio team of Eli Gold and Ken "Snake" Stabler taken care of in the press box so they could do their show. The group produced its usual pregame show from a location outside the stadium, soaking up some atmosphere and fan reaction and comments, then headed up to the press box where they would provide the play-by-play and commentary on the game. The press box reserved for the radio team wasn't as tight-quartered as what had been set aside for the TV crew, but it was close.

Waters, who had spent the first half with the TV crew, decided to head up to the press box for a few minutes in the third period to check on his radio crew. When he looked in the broadcast room, he was surprised. "Eli tried to stand up—they both went to stand up and give each other a high-five after a big play—and there was no room," Waters said. "I'm looking at Snake, who ought to be in the [Pro Football] Hall of Fame, one of the greatest quarterbacks of all time, and I've got him in a cramped press box."

Despite the restrictions, both crews pressed on with their work, and both had quite a game to relay back to their respective viewers and listeners.

• • •

LSU received the opening kickoff and appeared ready to make an immediate statement. Quarterback Herb Tyler and running back Kevin Faulk hurried out of the gate, Tyler throwing for five yards on the game's first play, and Faulk following with runs of three and four yards respectively.

After an incomplete pass, Faulk ran for seven yards, then Tyler hit Faulk for a two-yard pass play before Faulk gained a yard on a third down-and-1 play for a first down. The Tigers had moved from their 26 to their 48. They would get as far as the Alabama 45 when the drive stalled and an 11-yard punt gave the Crimson Tide good field position at its 34. The Tide was unable to take advantage of the field position, going three-and-out on its first possession and punting back to the Tigers.

LSU tried again, but ended up attempting a 40-yard field goal that missed its mark.

Alabama's offense would fare a little better the next time, but the result was the same—a punt to LSU. The Tigers returned the favor after a three-and-out performance, and on the final play of the first quarter, Daniel Pope boomed a 56-yard punt that was returned 11 yards by Faulk, with an additional five yards because of an inadvertent facemask penalty against Alabama, putting the Tigers at their 33 to start the second quarter.

The drive would look similar to the first two LSU drives and come up with the same result—no points, after attempting another field goal, which was off the mark.

LSU's offense had been productive in terms of yards, but had failed to garner any points. Alabama's offense had yet to get going, and its next drive would not change that trend, the Tide getting 16 yards from Alexander on five carries but having the drive falter, bringing Pope back on the field for another punt, this one a 44-yarder.

With 8:44 to play in the half, LSU's offense began the game's first scoring drive. Starting at its 14, Tyler tossed a pass to Kyle Kipps for 18 yards on the first play, then hit Booty with a 10-yarder, followed by a Faulk run for 13. Tyler, feeling confident, tossed to Booty again, this time for 14 yards. In four plays, the Tigers had earned four consecutive first downs and moved the football 55 yards to the Alabama 31.

Tiger Stadium was rockin' now. Tyler hit Kipps for nine yards before Faulk lost two on a run but gained three on the next carry. Facing third-and-3, Faulk picked up three for the first down at the 21. The rest of the drive belonged to Faulk. He gained five to the 16, then 15 to the 1, getting the last yard on a follow-up carry that gave the Tigers a touchdown. But the kicking game, which would play such an important role in the game, failed LSU again with a failed Danny Boyd extra-point attempt.

Alabama's offense produced another three-and-out series and Pope punt. The teams would swap punts again and LSU, getting the ball back with five seconds to play in the half, had Tyler take the snap and take a knee, sending LSU to its locker room with a 6-0 halftime advantage.

There were other advantages, too. LSU recorded 15 first downs to Alabama's three, 254 total yards to just 78 for the Crimson Tide, and the time of possession advantage was almost 19 minutes to 11. LSU was disappointed it hadn't scored more points—two missed field goals and a missed extra point represented seven points that could have been collected. Tyler was 15-of-23 passing for 141 yards and no interceptions at the half.

Alabama head coach Mike DuBose was not at all pleased. "I have to explain it this way: when we arrived at the stadium our fans had already accepted the challenge," he said. "They deserve our best, and we didn't give it to them in the first half."

But there was at least one person who saw something he liked, saw the possibility of an Alabama victory. Waters, during his visit to Alabama's cramped radio booth, spoke briefly with Stabler. "We're down at halftime, and people were talking about the streak coming to an end," Waters said. "This isn't good. I was in school [at Alabama] when the streak began. And Snake says, 'We're going to win.' He just said, 'We're going to win.' He called it at the half, and it turned out he was right and it happened pretty much like he said it would, with a big fourth quarter."

The Crimson Tide immediately stepped up its offensive production in the second half. Taking the kickoff to start the third period, Alabama began at its 18 with Alexander gaining three yards on a run before quarterback Andrew Zow completed a pass to Freddie Milons for 22 yards. Alexander then gained four more yards on a run in front of a 53-yard Zow-to-Quincy Jackson touchdown pass that, with Ryan Pflugner's extra-point, put Alabama in the lead 7-6. The drive required less than two minutes to complete and almost ended badly. LSU cornerback Robert Davis, who would experience this feeling again later in the game, tipped the pass, but Jackson still managed to pull it in and parlay it into a score.

LSU responded. Starting at its 28, Tyler threw a 32-yard pass to Larry Foster that moved the Tigers from their 28 to the Alabama 40. Faulk had a 14-yard run, followed by a five-yarder and a 15-yarder that ended up getting three more yards for the Tigers when Alabama was called for a personal foul penalty. The Tigers now had a first-and-goal situation at the Alabama 3. But the Tide defense stiffened. Faulk got a yard, then nothing on a second-down run. On third and goal he lost a yard, putting the Tigers back at the 3. LSU opted for the field goal, kicking a 20-yarder for a 9-7 lead.

Leaning on Alexander, Alabama's next series moved from its 20 to the LSU 48, but there Zow was sacked on third down, losing eight yards, forcing another Pope punt. LSU took over at its 11, where it would start another scoring drive and get the LSU faithful thinking about the end of the streak.

Tyler found Foster on a seven-yard pass to start things off, and Faulk made a big run, gaining 34 and putting the Tigers at the Alabama 48. Faulk then picked up nine more in front on a three-yard Mealey run. That's when Tyler handed the ball to Faulk again, the small but flashy and speedy back picking up 29 yards to the Alabama 7. On the following play, Tyler let his arm do the rest, hitting Kipps with a seven-yard scoring strike that lifted LSU to a 16-7 lead with 2:37 left in the third quarter.

It would mark LSU's final points in the game.

Alabama's follow-up possession that moved the game into the fourth period produced little, and Pope was called on to help out the defense again, which he did by backing up the Tigers to their 22 with a 50-yard punt that was returned eight yards by Faulk. A few small gains to start the LSU drive led to a Tyler-to-Foster pass for 11 yards to the LSU 44, where a Tyler-to-Booty pass was good for 12 yards. Faulk had three straight runs for a total of 25 yards to the Alabama 19, and Tyler tacked on a 16-yard run of his own to the Alabama 3.

Faulk picked up two yards to the Alabama 1 on the next play, but lost a yard back to the 2 to set up a third-and-goal situation. The Tigers called time-out to set up their next play, which would be a Tyler pass, but instead of picking up a touchdown, huge momentum, and a bigger lead, Alabama's Marcus Spencer intercepted the throw and returned it out of the end zone to the Alabama 26.

"We had watched them on film and we had taken a time-out to talk about the type of defense we were going to run," Spencer told the *Mobile Press-Register*. "The ball just hit [Booty], and I think he had it for a second, but then I grabbed it and ran as far as I could." Spencer had also made the tackle on the two running plays prior to the pass and interception.

That was the play that would trigger the game's turnaround. Instead of taking control of the game, LSU had missed yet another scoring opportunity. The interception, with 9:28 to play, would be yet another disappointment to be relived later by LSU fans.

Looking to use the bit of momentum it had just seized—or rather, intercepted—Alabama's offense attempted to get things going again. A trio of pass plays between other, smaller plays aided that goal. Zow threw to Michael Vaughn for eight yards and then later hit him again for 15. After the 15-yarder, Zow threw to Alexander for 29, putting the Crimson Tide at the LSU 11. A one-yard Alexander run was followed by an incomplete pass and a Zow run for no gain, leaving a fourth-and-9 situation. The Crimson Tide chose to kick a field goal, but Arnold Miller blocked Pflugner's 27-yard try.

David Crane's brother Mac, who was inside Tiger Stadium watching the game, believed that play had ended Alabama's hopes of winning the game and the streak was coming to an end. From his seat outside the stadium, Crane saw a few Alabama fans and LSU fans start to exit the stadium. The Alabama fans were leaving so they didn't have to absorb the LSU celebration; LSU fans were making their exit for only one reason: to avoid getting stuck in the postgame traffic jam.

"My brother was one of the ones to leave early," Crane said. "He left after the blocked field goal. He tried to pass it off the next day on the first tee with his buddies, saying he had stayed, but my mom had already told them he left early and they rode him about it all day. He regrets leaving early that night to this day."

The blocked kick brought the LSU crowd back into the game in a big way, and a victory celebration was under way. Less than five minutes remained to be played, and LSU had the football at its 19. Faulk ran on three straight plays, gaining a total of six yards, and Alabama called a timeout to stop the clock with 3:25 to go. Corey Gibbs delivered a 41-yard punt that was returned four yards, and Alabama had the ball at its 38 with 3:16 left.

Striking immediately, Zow and Jackson hooked up on a 30-yard pass on the first play of the drive, which ended in a 21-yard touchdown pass to Alexander. Pflugner's extra-point kick was good, and the score was 16-14 in LSU's favor with 2:24 remaining to be played.

"At one point, I was really down, but Coach [Charlie] Stubbs [offensive coordinator] got on the headphones and told me to keep my head up," Zow said. "He said we were going to win the game. . . ."

Alabama had just one choice: an onside kick. Everyone in Tiger Stadium knew it was coming, and LSU lined up in preparation for just such a play. But Alabama's fate and Pope's perfect onside kick would win out. Pope topped the kick that bounced a couple of times low to the ground before bouncing high right after the required 10-yard distance to make it eligible for recovery by the

Crimson Tide. Receiver Jason McAddley slipped behind the pile of players awaiting the ball's descent and recovered it for Alabama at the LSU 40. There was 2:17 left to play.

"Daniel Pope absolutely nailed the kick," DuBose said. "He could kick it 100 times and not make it as good."

Pope liked the view he had. "I kicked it, I looked up and it went pretty high," he told the *Press-Register*. "Their guy touched it, and all I saw were red jerseys going towards the end zone." The perfectly placed onside kick was just one of Pope's contributions in the game. He also averaged 46.9 yards per punt and kept LSU backed up much of the game.

Alexander made a quick punch at LSU's hopes, picking up 14 yards on first down to the LSU 26. He then rushed for another yard and was held for no gain, putting Alabama's offense up against a third-and-9 situation from the 25. That's where Zow looked to Jackson again and where he would deliver again, hauling in another tipped pass for a 25-yard touchdown play.

The play was called sprint rub, with Zow rolling right and hoping to locate an open receiver coming across the middle of the field. "Charlie [Stubbs] said, 'This is there, it's open,'" DuBose said after the game. Stubbs said he told DuBose that LSU was in man-to-man coverage and stacking the line of scrimmage and that it was a safe play. The play call surprised Zow, who thought the team was just trying to get in position to try a field goal. "I looked at Quincy, and he had his guy halfway beat," Zow said. "I just threw it and let one of our playmakers make a play."

Tiger Stadium, so rowdy and loud and electric a few minutes earlier, was now almost silent with the exception of the Alabama contingent that was celebrating its team's 15 points—Zow hit Vaughn on a two-point conversion pass play following the TD throw to Jackson—in a span of less than two minutes.

"I think you make your own luck, and that's what I did," Jackson told the *Press-Register* after the game. "The ball got tipped. I just kept my eyes on it, and it hit me right in the middle of my [jersey number] seven. Hey, the Tide don't lose in Baton Rouge."

LSU cornerback Davis, who was also defending Jackson on his previous touchdown catch, couldn't believe it had happened to him again, especially at that point in the game, in that situation. "I thought I had it," Davis said, "but it fell into his hands. We played great football if you take away the two tipped balls. Both of them I should have had."

That's not how Jackson saw it. "We work tip drills, tip drills, tip drills," he said. "We got ourselves in a bowl with this win. . . . We wanted to make it back to a bowl and this was the first step. Hey, 1969 baby!"

Alabama began celebrating its 15th straight visit to Tiger Stadium without a defeat.

Only 35 seconds remained. LSU fumbled the kickoff, though it recovered the loose football at the Alabama 49. On the first play, Tyler looked for some more magic from his throwing arm but found only heartbreak when Spencer again intercepted him, this time at the Alabama 16. That allowed the Crimson Tide offense, with Zow taking the snap and dropping to one knee, to simply run off the 27 seconds left in the game for the victory.

Spencer credited good timing for being able to come up with the two key fourth-period interceptions. That, and some incentive. "We didn't want to be the first team to lose here in 29 years," he said. "We were down 16-9 in a hostile place and we still won, and it's a great feeling."

Alexander said other forces might have been involved. "I think God's just with us when we come down here to play," he said.

Since the 1998 game, LSU has managed to reverse the trend, The Tigers have beaten Alabama in Baton Rouge in 2000, '04, '06 and '10—four times in a six-game span.

• • •

Back at the card tables-turned broadcast desk outside Tiger Stadium, the Crimson Tide Sports Marketing TV crew was seeing a great deal from their unusual location, and learning a lot too. "The stadium went from being so loud, which was basically all but the last four or five minutes, to quiet," Stewart said. "It was amazing to hear and to see. You could see the looks on the faces of the people who were leaving the stadium, and it was an incredible show. You saw the LSU fans who had this I-can't-believe-it-happened-again look, to the Alabama fans who were just ecstatic."

Crane said he enjoyed the view and perspective as well, though it isn't something he would like to take on permanently. "I know a lot of people really loved that broadcast and they enjoyed watching it again on our re-broadcast," he said. "LSU fans were certain that was going to be the year the streak ended. And then to lose the game the way they did, you could feel for them."

After the game, the crew had to start the long drive back to Tuscaloosa. Waters treated the crew to a steak dinner at the first place they found that was open and could handle the number of people they needed to feed. It's fair to say the restaurant did not have a five-star rating.

"We stopped to eat dinner, and it may have been the single-worst dinner I've ever had," Crane said. "But even with that, it was a great day and we had so much fun at dinner."

No matter where one sat at that game, the view was the same—another Alabama win in Tiger Stadium.

CHAPTER EIGHTEEN
1999 Florida

Alabama 40, Florida 39 (OT)
October 2, 1999
Ben Hill Griffin Stadium
Gainesville, Florida

The odds were in Florida's favor. Stats, streaks, success, home field. Everything it seemed.

When Alabama traveled to Gainesville to face the Gators in 1999, Steve Spurrier had Florida football on a very fast track. Taking over as the head coach, Spurrier had led the Gators to a 93-18 record from 1990 through the 1998 season. In that time, the Gators had become known for their productive and quick-strike offenses and for winning titles. Florida had won five SEC championships and the 1996 national championship under Spurrier's direction.

The Gators were especially dangerous at home. So when Alabama traveled to Gainesville to play the Gators at Florida Field at Ben Hill Griffin Stadium, known as The Swamp, in 1999, the Crimson Tide faced a lot of obstacles.

Alabama would overcome them all.

Florida entered the game having won 30 consecutive games at The Swamp; this time, Alabama would be the victor.

In the previous 77 games when the Gators gained more rushing yards than its opponent, Florida won all but one of those contests. Florida would collect more rushing yards than the Crimson Tide; yet Alabama won the game.

Two weeks before the teams met at The Swamp, Florida defeated defending national champ and SEC Eastern Division rival Tennessee, while on the same day the Crimson Tide allowed Louisiana Tech to complete a Hail Mary pass for a one-point victory at Bryant-Denny Stadium; but Alabama would make the big plays late to beat the Gators two weeks later.

With possession of the football the Gators' high-flying offense would have 1:25 left to play in a tie game, more than enough time for the quick-strike Gators to get on the scoreboard, especially when cheered on by a boisterous and encouraging crowd of more than 85,000 fans. The Gators didn't score; Alabama would win the game in overtime, and in a quickness usually displayed by the Gators' offense.

There was more. The previous season the Gators posted a 10-2 record and, late in the season, garnered national attention while Alabama struggled to a 7-5 finish. Fan support and enthusiasm was high at Florida, as the Gator Nation held high expectations for the season that could be in 1999; in Tuscaloosa and across the state, the Bama Nation was whispering and wondering aloud as to the program's future, and that of head coach Mike DuBose. The usual enthusiasm that surrounded the team and the program was at low tide.

On paper, everything pointed to another Florida win, another Florida celebration, the continuation of the Gators' win streak at The Swamp, and its chase of another SEC crown.

So what was Alabama defensive lineman Kenny Smith thinking on Tuesday afternoon the week of the game, when he guaranteed a Crimson Tide victory over the Gators? Yes, he *guaranteed* Alabama would win.

Apparently, at least for Smith, coming to such a conclusion was elementary.

"I knew Florida wasn't a much better team than we are," Smith told reporters after the game. "But they put on their clothes just like we do."

Smith's guarantee was golden, though not easily secured. When the game that required an overtime period had ended, when all the paper with the lists of stats, intangibles, and reasons Florida would win the game had been pushed aside in favor of the playing of the game, there was one, undeniable aspect of that matchup that weighed in Alabama's favor, the one thing that could not be rejected, the point that trumped every other reason and stat, the one fact that literally was written in lights on the Florida Field scoreboard: Alabama 40, Florida 39.

• • •

It wasn't as though Alabama arrived in Gainesville ill-equipped. The Crimson Tide had future NFL Most Valuable Player Shaun Alexander in its backfield, available for powerful runs and just-as-effective pass catches. It had perhaps the country's best offensive lineman in Chris Samuels, Alexander's favorite lead blocker. It had quarterback Andrew Zow, a Florida native who wanted nothing more than to beat the Gators and earn bragging rights for a year, a player who was coming into his own as a talent and as a leader. Alabama also had Chris Kemp, another Florida native, who would miss an extra-point kick but make good on a second chance only moments after his high school teammate had failed. It had Antonio "A. C." Carter, who would make a big touchdown catch. It had Marcus Spencer, who made five tackles and returned a fumble recovery 13 yards, leading to a field goal.

And Alabama had a huge intangible in its corner: it had heart.

According to former *Birmingham News* sports columnist Ray Melick, who was the Alabama beat writer for the former *Birmingham Post-Herald* at the time, Alabama also had two players who as much as anyone refused to allow their team to do any less than its best—Samuels and Cornelius Griffin.

"Those guys were the real leaders of that team. Samuels and Griffin made up their minds [Alabama] was going to win that season, despite everything else, and they pushed the other players on that team. And the players responded. . . ." Melick said.

Assistant coach Neil Callaway, a former Alabama player who would later be head coach at UAB, said the leadership actually appeared the week before when a 35-28 win over Arkansas "really flipped the season."

"The win over Florida kept things going," he said. "I really think the Arkansas win gave us confidence. To beat Arkansas after a terrible loss to Louisiana Tech was big. Then to beat Florida in Gainesville, I think, solidified that we were going to have a good year."

• • •

Both teams had talent. Considering the players concerned—Alabama's Alexander, Zow, Samuels, Griffin, Carter and Freddie Milons; Florida had Doug Johnson, Bo Carroll, Robert Gillespie, Darrell Jackson, Reche Caldwell and Alex Willis—it was no surprise the teams combined for 79 points and 997 total yards.

Those in attendance didn't have to wait long before the scoring began, though the start of the scoring wasn't by the team that most of those fans would have preferred.

After swapping punts to open the game, Florida took possession for the second time at its 34-yard line. On the first play, Johnson tossed a pass to Gillespie for 11 yards before being hit and fumbling. Alabama's Spencer picked up the loose football and returned it 13 yards to the Florida 38.

In four plays, Alabama advanced 16 yards to the 22, but that's where the advancement ended. A pair of incomplete passes left the Crimson Tide with a fourth-and-4 situation. Chris Kemp was called on to attempt a 47-yard field goal, which he made. Midway through the first period, Alabama had taken a 3-0 lead.

As was the trademark of Florida teams under Spurrier, master of the big-play offense, the Gators came right back. And very quickly. After a 16-yard Carroll kickoff return to the 27, Johnson tossed a postpattern pass to Jackson for 73 yards and a touchdown. Alabama's lead had lasted for a kickoff and one play.

The Crimson Tide offense wasn't successful in its next turn and the team in turn punted to the Gators. Johnson threw an incomplete pass to Jackson on a fade route, but Alabama was penalized for holding, moving the ball 11 yards to the Gators' 25. Later, an 18-yard Gillespie run gave Florida a first down at the Alabama 40, but on the next play Johnson fumbled and Alabama recovered.

Taking a page from the Florida playbook, Alabama struck quickly. Zow tossed a pass to Alexander that collected 39 yards to the Gators' 20. Alexander picked up a yard on a carry, with Zow hitting Jason McAddley for four yards on second down that ended the first period. Zow followed with a 14-yard pass to Milons to the Gators' 1. Alexander tried to reach the end zone but failed, and then Dustin McClintock was given a chance but was stopped too. Alexander got a second try and he accomplished the task, going off left tackle behind Samuels for the touchdown to give Alabama a 10-7 lead.

Florida embarked on a follow-up drive that almost provided points. Starting at their 20, the Gators picked up four first downs in five plays and quickly found themselves at the Alabama 22. The biggest of the first five plays was a 38-yard run by Carroll. But the drive screeched to a halt as quickly as it began when a Johnson pass missed its mark and, after a follow-up six-yard pass play, Johnson was penalized for intentional grounding, resulting in a loss of nine yards and the down. That forced a 42-yard field goal attempt by Jeff Chandler from the Alabama 25 that sailed wide right.

Taking over at the Florida 25, the Crimson Tide put together a time-consuming and point-producing drive that would use up all but 17 seconds of the remaining time in the half. It ended in Kemp's 22-yard field goal to put the Crimson Tide in front 13-7 with 17 seconds left in the half. The 18-play scoring drive used up 8:58 of the second quarter, not only producing three points but keeping the ball out of the hands of the Gators' offense.

Florida's Carroll returned the kickoff 34 yards out of the end zone, and a Gillespie draw play picked up 19 yards before Santonio Beard tackled him and the half ended at the Alabama 47.

The staggering differences between the teams during the first half were time of possession and the number of offensive plays run. Alabama had the ball for more than 21 minutes of the first half, leaving the Gators' offense less than nine minutes of possession. As the time difference would suggest, Alabama ran 41 offensive plays to just 18 for Florida, but the Gators had 215 total yards, with Alabama gaining just 176. Yet Alabama had the six-point lead, and it would receive the kickoff to open the second half.

The Crimson Tide didn't take advantage of the possession, advancing the ball only 15 yards before punting to the Gators. Florida's offense struggled, too, getting nothing going and punted back to Alabama. But the Gators' defense would soon lend its help. After Alexander picked up five yards on a run, Zow dropped back to pass but the throw was intercepted by Bennie Alexander, who would return it 42 yards for a touchdown. Just that quickly, the Gators were in front 14-13.

Alabama had an answer. Starting at its 30-yard line after a 21-yard kickoff return by Beard, Alexander picked up 11 yards and then made a 1-yard run. After Zow was sacked for a 10-yard loss to the Alabama 32, Zow found Carter once again on a crossing pattern for 21 yards and a first down to the Florida 47. Zow went back to the air, throwing a deep pass to Alexander who hauled it in and completed a 47-yard touchdown play. Alabama attempted a two-point conversion, but the pass was incomplete, leaving Alabama in front 19-14 with 6:07 remaining in the third quarter.

Three minutes later, Florida would be in front again. When Johnson found Jackson open on a slant pattern for the touchdown. Alabama's score had been matched again, and the Gators were back in front 22-19 after a successful Johnson-to-Kirk Wells two-point conversion pass.

The teams weren't close to being finished. Six more combined scores awaited, as well as some important extra-point kicks, before the game would be decided. An extra period would be needed as well, as regulation ended with the teams tied at 33.

Alabama won the coin toss prior to the overtime period and, as is usually the case, elected to play defense to start the overtime. Starting at the 25, Florida picked up a yard from Gillespie on a first-down run, followed by four yards on a Johnson-to-Caldwell pass. On third-and-5, Johnson threw to Jackson for eight yards and a first down at the 12. Gillespie picked up seven on a run and then one yard on second down. On another third-down play, Johnson completed a pass to Caldwell in the end zone for a touchdown.

That's when things became interesting. Chandler lined up for the extra-point kick and missed it to the right. Florida fans were stunned into silence as the group of Alabama fans cheered. On the Crimson Tide's first play of the overtime, Alexander was handed the ball. He crashed off left tackle behind a block by Samuels and stormed into the end zone on a 25-yard scoring run.

With the game tied, all Alabama had to do was kick the extra point, and the Tide would win the game.

So here was Kemp, attempting a routine—at least that's always the way it is usually viewed by fans—extra-point kick that would give Alabama a nothing-close-to-routine victory over Florida in The Swamp.

Talk about a set up. Ryan Pflugner was Alabama's starting kicker at the beginning of the season, but Kemp had taken over when Pflugner pulled a muscle while warming up for the Louisiana Tech game. Suddenly, he was the Crimson Tide's No. 1 guy. "Five minutes before kickoff [for the Louisiana Tech game] they told me I'm kicking," Kemp told the *Huntsville Times'* Gene Duffey.

Three games later, Pflugner was still recovering and Kemp was the starter. Against Florida. In The Swamp. What a turnaround, and what a storyline. Kemp's father had graduated from Florida, and Kemp himself was born in Shands Hospital on the Florida campus. The family had later moved to Jacksonville, where Kemp was the kicker for Mandarin High School, which happened to be the same high school where Florida's kicker, Chandler, had played, actually following Kemp as the team's starting kicker.

So after Chandler had missed his extra-point kick in overtime—"He's a good friend," Kemp told Mark McCarter of the *Huntsville Times.* "It's unfortunate for him"—here was Kemp with a chance to win the game for Alabama by making an extra point kick in overtime. He missed it too. His excuse for the miss: he was "too relaxed," adding, "I wasn't feeling anything; I couldn't hear a thing or feel a thing."

His demeanor changed pretty quickly. No longer relaxed, Kemp started to trot over to the Alabama sideline, keeping his head down and trying to avoid eye contact. It would be best just to find a spot to try and blend into the scenery and others wearing Alabama's colors. But Kemp heard a voice calling to him. It was DuBose, telling him to turn around and head back to the field. The officials had dropped a penalty flag; Florida's Alexander, who had returned an interception for a touchdown earlier in the game, was offsides. Kemp was going to get a second chance.

"I got back out there and just took a deep breath and looked at the goal post," Kemp told McCarter. "I looked down and hit it." In fact, he kept his gaze down so long he was the only person in the stadium who didn't see the end result, but he knew it was good. "I listen to the crowd. They tell me if it's good or not," he said.

As the game ended with Alabama in front, one of the Alabama fans joined the celebration with the Alabama band.

The celebration would continue in Tuscaloosa. When the team's plane landed late that night, hundreds of fans were on hand to welcome the Crimson Tide home. The team loaded on buses for the drive to campus, and along the way, lining University Boulevard, were hundreds more fans, there to cheer on the team.

"The crowd at the airport was unbelievable," DuBose said. "What it meant to the players and staff can't be put into words. The people on the street when the buses went down University was an unbelievable feeling. I heard several of the young guys saying, 'I love this; I never expected this.'"

Many of those fans hadn't expected, in their heart of hearts, Alabama to stop Florida in the Swamp, either.

"I kept saying, 'Please let something good happen, because we deserve it,'" Finus Gaston, senior associate athletics director for the university, said as he watched the end of the game. As for the team's arrival back in Tuscaloosa, he gave his support. "It was a mob scene at the airport," he said. "I remember how glad I felt for Mike [DuBose]."

When it was all said and done, Alabama's offense had controlled the football for more than 41 minutes, leaving Florida just 18 minutes of offensive possession. "Alabama was well-prepared, especially on offense," McCarter said. "[Offensive coordinator] Charlie Stubbs controlled the ball for 41:22. That shows you how dangerous Florida's offense was. It only had the ball for 18 minutes, but it still put up [39] points. . . . The Florida defense was on the field so long, they had to be leg-weary, especially in the overtime."

Zow had turned in a stellar performance, completing 28-of-40 passes for 336 yards and two touchdowns with just one interception and one sack. "I never got down," he said after the game. "I know if there's time on the clock, I think we can win." DuBose praised Zow's play. "I thought Andrew Zow played his best game since he became a starter here at Alabama," he said. "He showed tremendous poise and tremendous leadership in a very loud, very hostile environment."

The win probably meant more to Zow than any of the other Alabama players, with the possible exception of Kemp. The previous season, he was the quarterback when Alabama lost to the Gators 16-10 in Tuscaloosa. It was a tough loss to handle. "My wife and I were walking in the mall [in Gainesville] before [the 1999 season], and some of the people who recognized me came up and gave me a hard time," Zow said. "That was a little tough."

He would get the last laugh in 1999. Twice. But the win in Gainesville was probably the sweetest, even though the second win, in the SEC Championship Game, gave Alabama the league crown. "I think it is a game that ranks right up there with the Auburn game [of 2001, won by Alabama]," he said, adding its importance was based on the fact that it was played near his hometown of Lake Butler and gave him the opportunity to play against Florida, one of the teams that had recruited him but backed away.

Alabama football radio play-by-play announcer Eli Gold, who has also written two books on Alabama football, said the 1999 Florida game "is still to this day one of the most special games I've ever had the privilege of calling."

• • •

The victory kept Alabama's record unblemished in SEC play at 3-0 and gave the Crimson Tide a 4-1 record overall. The loss, which ended the Gators' 30-game home win streak, the longest in the nation at that time, was Florida's first of the season and left it at 4-1 overall and 2-1 in league play. It was the first time Alabama had won in The Swamp since 1979, when the stadium wasn't known by the endearing nickname.

The Alabama win also added to the interesting history between the two schools. In 1921, Florida beat Alabama 9-2 in Tuscaloosa to snap the Crimson Tide's 31-game home win streak, the second-longest in the nation at that time and the second-longest in the school's history. In 1963, Florida beat Alabama 10-6. Following that loss, Alabama won a then-NCAA record 57 straight home games that ended with a 1982 loss to Southern Miss and Brett Favre, in head coach Paul "Bear" Bryant's final season.

The win over the No. 3-ranked Gators was Alabama's first win over a Top 5 team since the Tide slapped Miami in the 1993 New Year's Day Sugar Bowl to claim the 1992 national championship. It marked the first win over a Top 10 opponent in the regular season since a 1991 win over No. 8 Tennessee at Legion Field. The previous Top 5 road win had come in 1990 in Knoxville against Tennessee in a 9-6 victory in which kicking provided all the offense— three Philip Doyle field goals, the third coming on the game's final play. Another interesting note: Alabama's 13-7 halftime lead marked the first time Alabama had scored against the Gators in Gainesville in the first half since 1979.

But most important was what the win meant emotionally for Alabama. The win over Florida was a significant confidence-booster. For starters, it raised the Crimson Tide's national attention, jumping from No. 21 in the Associated Press poll to the No. 11 spot after the win. As the season progressed, Alabama would move to No. 10, up and down a couple of times and eventually finish the year No. 8 after losing to Michigan 35-34 in the Orange Bowl.

The win in Gainesville would play a significant role when the teams met again in the SEC Championship Game. Armed with the knowledge it could match the Gators' offense and with the increased confidence the Tide defensive unit had gained, Alabama claimed a 34-7 victory.

Zow wasn't called upon to throw as much in the title game, but remained on target against the Gators' defense, completing 10-of-17 tries for a touchdown and 134 yards. Alexander had 30 carries for 116 yards and a touchdown, while Milons, on six carries, accounted for 116 yards and a score, earning Most Valuable Player honors. He played three positions in the game: quarterback, wide receiver and kick returner. The Alabama defense allowed the Gators, who held a 7-0 lead early, but didn't score again, to their lowest output in total offense (114 yards), passing yards, pass completions and first downs since Spurrier's arrival as head coach. The defense also accounted for four interceptions.

"To go on and play them in the championship game, I thought it would be hard to beat them two times in one year. But the guys had great confidence and really, really played well," Callaway said.

Once again, as it would most of that season, Alabama had defied the odds.

CHAPTER NINETEEN
2005 Florida

Alabama 31, Florida 3
October 1, 2005
Bryant-Denny Stadium
Tuscaloosa, Alabama

Jason Kirksey had a feeling there was going to be something special about this game. Of course, to be fair, he usually felt that way when it came to Alabama football. He had been a season ticket holder for a couple of seasons, and although he didn't attend Alabama, he has been a lifelong fan of the Crimson Tide, especially its football team. While most games on campus produce anticipation and excitement, Kirksey noted a little something extra, a different buzz, about the 2005 Florida game.

He wasn't alone.

"I always took off work on Friday [before an Alabama home football game], and I couldn't find a hotel room. None were available anywhere," Kirksey said. "We were only going to be sleeping for a few hours anyway, so we decided to take a tent and camp out in the quad. Me and my friends—Jimmy Alford, Rebekah and Matt Blocker and their [then] four-year-old son Peyton—all camped out there in a tent they brought. We usually took the tent to keep food and beverages in the shade for tailgating, but this time we had to use it. The funniest part of the whole thing was, right behind the quad, there are emergency washers, in case someone gets chemicals on them. We used those as a shower the next day.

"We got there about 1 o'clock Friday afternoon, and the quad was already half-full. By six o'clock, it was completely slammed. We barely found a place to set up. People came in all night, putting their stuff out for the next day, getting ready, cheering. We woke up at about six the next morning because it was so noisy you couldn't sleep. People were waking up and getting ready. It was an incredible atmosphere. People were psyched. But an hour and half before the game, the quad was almost empty because everyone had already walked over to the stadium for the game. . . . There was definitely a different atmosphere to that day."

"The campus was absolutely crazy," Quarterback Brody Croyle said in describing the buzz that seemed to engulf the school in the days leading up to the game. "People would come to [the closed] practices and hang on the fences and cheer, even if they couldn't see anything. They'd cheer if they saw a football in the air."

John Croyle, former standout defensive end for the Crimson Tide and Brodie's father, had left his seat to get a soft drink before kickoff. When he was returning to his seat, there was a fly-over of military jets that streaked across the sky as low as the pilots dared fly. "The roar after that was the loudest I had ever heard," the elder Croyle said. "You could sense something special was going to happen and everyone was ready. Brodie told me later that DeMeco said to [Florida quarterback] Chris Leak [at coin toss shortly after the fly-over], 'You're going to lose today.'"

Birmingham radio show host Ryan Brown, on the sidelines for the start of the game, said it was obvious the Gators didn't expect the kind of reaction that was being generated around the stadium. "You could tell, Florida was just stunned by it," Brown said.

ESPN.com's Ivan Maisel had selected the game as an indoctrination for his then-13-year-old daughter Sarah to "real" college football. Maisel had grown up in Alabama and attended Stanford. As a sportswriter for the *Dallas Morning News* and *Sports Illustrated* and now ESPN.com, he had attended his share of big college football games. Living in Connecticut, Sarah hadn't been exposed to big-time, Southern college football.

"That game will always have a special place in my heart because I took Sarah with me to the game," said Maisel, whose brother Elliot is a season ticket holder who has been attending Alabama games since his youth and as such could provide a ticket and adult supervision for Sarah while her father covered the game. "I wanted her to see what I do and why I enjoy doing what I do.

"We went to Dreamland [famous Tuscaloosa barbecue joint] Friday afternoon, and Florida fans started talking with me about the game. Sarah asked me, 'Who are those people? And how do they know you?' We walked across campus that night and went to the stadium early the next day. . . . To see a home stadium erupt the way it did that day, I think she understood what I had been telling her."

Sarah would learn a lot more, too, like how to sing "Rammer Jammer," what song the Alabama band plays when the Crimson Tide scores, and how loud a big-time college football stadium can get when everything falls into place. She also learned that her uncle still has a bit of little boy in him.

"A kid like Sarah, she knows me as Uncle Elliot, and there's a certain line of decorum at home," Elliot Maisel said. "She lives in Connecticut, so we don't see each other that often during the year except for holidays and other family events. There's a certain line of demarcation. Well, that line of demarcation ends for football games. Everybody's a kid."

And the kids were about to take over Tuscaloosa.

• • •

Kirksey, who would later work in Alabama's media relations department and currently works for Atlanta's Georgia Dome, took his seat in Section K, row 56, on the press box side to the left of the 50-yard line when facing the field. He didn't use the seat much that day. He and everyone around him would stand for the majority of the game, sitting only at halftime to rest for the second half. Kirksey took a photo of the stadium and the crowd from his vantage point at that seat that day, a photo that later served as the screensaver on his computer. "The place was nuts," he said.

Florida would learn right away what the day would be like. Mark Anderson sacked Leak on the game's first play for a loss of four yards after the Gators had been penalized 10 yards to their own 10 on the kickoff return for holding. Leak fumbled on the sack, but Florida maintained possession. A run up the middle provided no gain, and a third-down pass fell incomplete. The Bryant-Denny Stadium crowd exploded.

The excitement would soon dissipate, at least momentarily. Florida punted to wide receiver-kick return specialist Tyrone Prothro, who fumbled. Florida recovered the miscue and took over at Alabama's 43-yard line.

"That first series set the tone," Joe Kines, then Alabama's defensive coordinator, said. "It just fell into place. The game plan from the first play just gelled. It was just like we expected it to be, just like we planned it. If it had been a five-and-out, six-and-out first series, it might have been different. But we had held them three-and-out. When Tyrone fumbled, they wanted to be back out there. They were just glad to get back out again so quick and play again.

"They went out there excited about playing. They weren't mad at Tyrone or anything. I saw it in them, the way they went out there. I said to myself, 'This is the way it's going to be.' And they stopped them again."

Ryans was one of the defensive players looking forward to getting back on the field, looking forward to showing Florida what was in store for the rest of the day. "They were close, but we had our swagger that day," Ryans said. "They weren't going to get in the end zone. We were playing at a different level than they were. . . ."

Believing it had been given a second chance, Florida discovered it would instead get more of the same. The Gators began with a false start penalty, moving them back to the Alabama 48, then gained just a yard on a first-down run. A four-yard run was followed by an incomplete pass and another punt, this one a 31-yarder that was downed on Alabama's 13.

"That's when I knew it was over," Ryans said of the game. "It was over right there. They weren't going to be able to do anything against us."

The Crimson Tide fans expressed their appreciation to the defense once again, and they were a play away from offering kudos to the offense, too.

Head coach Mike Shula decided to use the momentum the defense had created by trying to generate a big play on offense. On first down, he borrowed an approach made famous by former Florida head coach Steve Spurrier: go for it. Now. Alabama broke the huddle and, with his back to the end zone, Croyle delivered a strike. With speedster Prothro on the left side, Croyle took the snap and saw that Prothro had zoomed by the Florida coverage. Using his potent arm, Croyle laid the pass out to Prothro, who pulled it into his chest and raced into the end zone.

Now, Bryant-Denny Stadium was *really* going crazy, no matter one's vantage point of the play.

In the CBS-TV booth where Verne Lundquist, who said later that Bryant-Denny Stadium "exploded in ways I had never heard before," was offering the play-by-play coverage of the game. As Prothro hauled in the pass, the veteran announcer called out, "He's down there. He's got it and he . . . is . . . gone!"

Backup quarterback John Parker Wilson was pretty excited, too. "I had been to plenty of Alabama games there, but it had never been like that [in the stadium]. . . . On that play, the safety bit on the dig underneath, and Tyrone was open up top. Brodie just laid it in there."

In the radio booth, Crimson Tide play-by-play announcer Eli Gold could barely hear himself talk. "My ears are still ringing," he said two seasons later. "There was just the volcano of sound that engulfed everything. . . . The crowd had started yelling a half-hour before the game started and they never stopped."

Kirksey didn't get to hear Gold's call of the play, even though he had his radio, complete with headphones, with him. "As soon as the ball was out of Brodie's hand, you just saw it. You knew what was going to happen," he said. "Everybody was screaming. I was yelling as loud as I could. Jimmy was next to me, and he couldn't hear me yelling because of the noise. . . . I had the sound maxed out on the radio and my headphones on, and I still couldn't hear a word. As soon as Prothro scored, you realized the defense had had two three-and-outs and the offense had run one play and scored a touchdown. We knew it was going to be our day. . . . Even the people around us who [usually] never stood up, they were standing up and they stood up the whole first half. Nobody used the bleachers that day. Nobody."

Ken Stabler had a wide grin on his face. "That game is the game I use to measure noise by now," Stabler, the former Alabama All-America quarterback who then served as color commentator for Alabama broadcasts, said. "It was the loudest I've ever heard it there. The Arkansas game [in 2007] came real close, but that Florida game is the measuring stick. The crowd noise and the passion and the fans, that's the way it ought to be."

Sitting in the stands along with several other prep recruits was offensive lineman Andre Smith, the state's most sought-after recruit that year. Still weighing the decision of where he wanted to play college football, the crowd and the game he would witness certainly didn't hurt Alabama's chances of signing him to a scholarship offer. "Everybody was into that game," Smith, who did sign with Alabama, earning a starting nod in his first game with the Crimson Tide and later gaining All-SEC honors, said. "It was so loud after that first touchdown I couldn't talk to my mom, and she was sitting next to me. I had never been in a place that loud."

The 87-yard Croyle-to-Prothro touchdown pass gave Alabama a 7-0 lead and much more than that. The team that had entered the game with more confidence than its fans realized had now kicked that confidence up a notch or two. As he watched Prothro catch his pass, Croyle didn't wait to see his receiver find the end zone. He knew the end result. So he turned to face the Alabama student section behind him and raised his arms in triumph.

"I got carried away," he said. "I really didn't know what to do. . . . I just got caught up in the moment. I had never done anything like that before. I knew Florida wasn't going to catch Tyrone. Standing on the field, it felt like the earth was shaking because of the noise and everybody jumping up and down.

"After that, we just wanted the ball. That's what we kept telling the defense—get us the ball, we're going to score. It was one of those games when everything went right, when we did everything we wanted to do. That game showed what we could do."

Florida was only just learning what Alabama—offensively and defensively—was capable of doing. It would be a daylong lesson. On the second down of Florida's ensuing possession, Chris Harris intercepted a Leak pass and returned it to the Gators' 2-yard line. Three plays later, Tim Castille scored from a yard out. Another three-and-out possession for the Gators led to yet another punt—and yet another Alabama score. With 5:52 left in the first period, Jamie Christensen kicked a 22-yard field goal for a 17-0 Alabama lead after a third-and-goal pass from the 3 fell incomplete. On the final play of the quarter, Florida, finally mounting some offense, gained three yards on a third-and-goal play from the 4. On the first play of the second period, the Gators went for the touchdown. They failed when Mark Anderson and Freddie Roach stuffed the play for no gain.

A 37-yard field goal midway through the quarter finally produced some points for the Gators, but Alabama countered with yet another touchdown. Another one-play, big-play, scoring drive. Positioned at its own 35 when Florida's kickoff went out of bounds, Croyle tossed a simple over-the-middle pass to Keith Brown, who had slipped away from a defender, then turned on his speed up the middle of the field, outrunning the Florida defense for 65 yards and a touchdown.

As Brown headed for the end zone, Croyle had another move for the crowd. The quarterback then held both his arms outstretched at his sides, did a little spin move, and then faced the Alabama sideline as he started to sprint to the other end of the field to greet Brown. As he started to run, his eyes met those of Shula. Croyle pointed at his coach, and the coach returned the salute with a two-handed point and perhaps the biggest smile of his coaching career in Tuscaloosa.

"When Brodie was little and he would be excited, he would do a little spin," John Croyle said. "I remember seeing him throw the ball to Keith, and Coach Shula pointing at him with both hands and him dropping his shoulders and doing that little spin. That was a little boy playing a game. It was priceless. People say things are priceless and it's overused, but that was priceless. It really was. For me, that was the best game I ever saw my son play. It was just a joy to see that."

For all intents and purposes, the game was over. There was still 7:22 left to play in the second quarter, but the game had been decided. Gold said his radio partner "Snake" Stabler made an interesting observation about the Gators. "Snake said [Florida head coach Urban] Meyer had brought the West Coast offense to Gainesville, but he had also brought along a West Coast defense," Gold recalled.

• • •

In a word, the Alabama defense was awesome. Ryans was a buzzsaw at linebacker, chasing down running backs and swarming Leak as he tried to pass. Defensive back Harper also had a big day, as did Anderson and Roach and others on that side of the football.

Kines watched how his defense made play after play, and its consistency amazed even him. The defense had allowed only a field goal in the first half, and that was all it would allow. Whatever the Crimson Tide unit decided to do, it worked. The frustration level that Leak and the Florida offense felt was obvious.

"From the opening kickoff to the final whistle, I've never been in a game where more things went right for you," Kines said. "I've never been in a game when guys were so ready to play. Freddie Roach wore [Leak] out. That was probably Freddie's best game at Alabama. All those guys played great. For those 60 minutes, we probably had more things go right than in any other game. There were only three or four plays, maybe, that you would change on the defensive side of the ball.

"At halftime, I kept saying, 'We get the ball first [to open the second half], and if we score, it's over,'" Croyle recalled. If he was looking for an amen of sorts, he got it. "DeMeco came up to me and said, 'If you score [on the first possession], it's over. They're not going to score.'"

Croyle and the offense achieved that goal. Prothro returned the kickoff 16 yards to the Alabama 20. A Croyle run for two yards was followed by a nine-yard pickup by Ken Darby and a first down. Croyle threw a short pass in the flats to Le'Ron McClain that went for 20 yards, and Darby got loose off left tackle for 33 yards, and just like that, Alabama was at the Florida 16. After an incomplete pass and a Castille carry for a yard, Alabama faced third-and-9 at the Gators' 15.

It was time for Croyle and Prothro to hook up again. "I remember Pro was jammed, and it took him off his route," Croyle recalled. "But I watched him. That's what happens when you play three years together— you know what the other guy is thinking and what he's going to do. He broke free, and I got him the ball and we scored again. There's a picture of me and Pro jumping way up and celebrating. I was way up there. It was over."

Indeed it was.

Alabama wouldn't score again, but neither would Florida. The Gators got close once, but the defense held. Leak would throw another interception, this time at the hands of Ramzee Robinson, on Florida's first possession of the fourth quarter. The pass pickoff signaled the end of any fight that might have been left in the Gators.

Throughout the game, No. 35 (Ryans) seemed to be everywhere, seemed to be in on every tackle or big play. Kines, who displayed a photograph of Ryans tackling Leak from that game in his office at the school before leaving for Texas A&M to become the Aggies' defensive coordinator, just smiled when asked about Ryans, who would be named the NFL's Defensive Rookie of the Year in 2006.

"Cornelius Bennett, DeMeco Ryans, Wilbur Marshall, those are players who have something extra in them, something you can't teach, a sixth sense," Kines said. "I'd like to say I taught DeMeco Ryans how to play, but my goal every day was not to mess him up. He is the hardest worker I have ever coached.

"That game—for DeMeco and the whole defense—it was one of those games you'll remember until your last day. Everything just clicked."

• • •

Alabama, set up at the Florida 43, wanted to cash in with another score. The attempt would prove more costly than could have been imagined. On a fourth-and-5 play from the 27, Croyle dropped back to pass deep, looking for Prothro. He found the diminutive receiver in the end zone, Prothro having to leap high to try and make the catch. The pass fell incomplete in what would be the final play of Prothro's Alabama career. When he landed in the end zone, he suffered a fracture in both major bones, the tibia and fibula. The crowd that had been so energized, so involved, so loud throughout the day, suddenly fell eerily silent.

Lundquist knew right away the injury was serious. "It was one of those things that when it happened, you knew right away something was really wrong," he said. "It reminded me of the infamous night on *Monday Night Football* when Joe Theismann's leg was broken. . . . We showed a replay of it, and I silenced my mic and called back to the producer and said, 'Let's not show that again.' It was awful to watch.

"You think about the explosiveness he had in that game, the impact, and to see that happened. It was the alpha and omega of that afternoon. Until that moment, the afternoon was a great success for Alabama. As well as Alabama played that day, I can't quite get away from [seeing] Prothro laying on the ground near the end of the game."

Gold recalls looking at Lundquist through the glass that separated the CBS announcing booth next door from the one used by the Alabama radio broadcast team. "Looking at Verne, our eyes locked and we both had that look on our faces, of knowing what we had just seen and making the comparison. We were both thinking the same thing, I believe, that we had just seen a Joe Theismann-like play. And of all the things that happened that day, that's the play that stands out to me more than any of the others. That's the one that always comes to mind."

Players, coaches, and medical personnel rushed to the end zone to check on Prothro. For several minutes, everyone's attention was directed to that one spot, the place where Prothro lay in the end zone. Soon, medical personnel rolled a stretcher out on the field, and Prothro was gently placed on top and taken off the field. As he left, the silence was broken and the crowd presented Prothro a standing ovation as he was taken from the field.

"It broke my heart," Croyle said. "Keith [Brown] and I were the first ones to get to him. To see his leg that way, it just put a bad feeling in your heart."

It was easy to spot the emotion—this emotion was obviously much different than what had been expressed throughout the day—being felt by the fans in Bryant-Denny Stadium. "Even after Tyrone broke his leg, the way they cheered for him, giving him a standing ovation even though it was obvious what the outcome of that was going to be, was amazing," Crane said.

On the stretcher, the crowd cheering, many chanting his name, Prothro delivered a salute of his own: he held an arm upward, the index finger indicating his team was No. 1. The crowd cheered even louder.

Prothro, who had won a national contest for the Game-Changing Play of the Year the previous season for his spectacular touchdown catch against Southern Miss in which he caught the ball behind the helmet of defensive back Jasper Faulk and held on as the two tumbled into the end zone, had made quite a mark before the injury. For the day, he had five catches for 134 yards and two touchdowns, carried the ball once for six yards and returned a kick 16 yards. It seemed every time he placed his hands on the football, something big happened.

"It leaves you with an empty feeling to see the nature of the injury," Shula said after the game. "My heart goes out to him. He's been a big impact in every game [that season], even if he doesn't touch the ball. It was good to see him have a great game, but sad to see the injury."

A pass interference penalty was called against Florida on the play, and Alabama was given a first down and another chance to score. The Crimson Tide got as close as the Florida four-yard line, but on a fourth-and-2 play Jimmy Johns gained just a yard, turning the ball over to the Gators on downs. The rest of the game was merely an exercise in running out the remaining time.

• • •

Up in Elliot Maisel's suite, Sarah Maisel was well into her lessons of the day, and the big moment, joining in the singing of "Rammer Jammer" at the end of the game, was close at hand. "I had arranged for the cheerleaders and Big Al [Alabama's mascot] to come by before the game so Sarah could meet them," Maisel said. "We were beating the stew out of them, and every time we scored I have this ugly facemask that I put on, so we had that on a lot. Sarah was having a great time. I told her I had to teach her to sing 'Rammer Jammer.' She said, 'What's that?' I said, 'You people in Connecticut don't "Rammer Jammer"? So we practiced during the game and toward the end of the game, when the band played it, that was a big deal for Sarah.

"I thought she was going to fall out of the box. She had a shaker in each hand and she was really into it. She was singing as loud as she could. She had been hanging out the box the entire game, and she was really into it at that point."

The crowd, like Sarah, had returned to the celebratory aspect of the day, having now been removed from Prothro's injury by several minutes. If Florida's team thought the first part of the day was loud, they were learning it wouldn't compare to those final seconds of the game and the jubilation that would be displayed. They were just getting started.

Shula was given a Gatorade dousing by his players. Defensive lineman Wallace Gilberry grabbed a flag sporting the team logo and made a couple of laps around the field, waving it as high as he could reach. After the players and coaches had soaked in the moment (as well as the crowd noise) for all it was worth, they all made their way to the team locker room.

In the stands, fans weren't leaving. It was the biggest win the program had enjoyed in a long time, and they were not going to let go of the moment either. It was a win that overshadowed the many difficulties the members of the team had faced, including NCAA sanctions and several coaching changes. It was time to celebrate.

"I've never been in a locker room like that before," Croyle said. "I've never seen one like that on TV or seen one in-person like that. It took about 20 minutes before Coach Shula could say anything. It was crazy."

At the family's tailgate set-up near Tutwiller Hall, Ivan Maisel, having finished his work from the game for ESPN.com probably three hours after the final whistle had blown, left the press box to join the rest of his family. As he neared where the others were gathered, Sarah spotted her father walking toward them. "Sarah sprinted up to me and said, 'Dad, dad, I want to go to a *big* school,'" Ivan Maisel remembers. "And I thought to myself, mission accomplished." Sarah Maisel enrolled at Stanford, her father's alma mater, in the fall of 2010.

Croyle broke the school record for career touchdown passes in the game, setting the new mark with his second TD throw to Prothro. He was 14-of-17 on the day for 283 yards and three touchdowns, including a 10-of-12 showing for 235 yards and two touchdowns in the first half alone. Just as important, he helped Alabama to its first-ever win in Bryant-Denny Stadium over a Top-5-ranked team.

He had help. Aside from Prothro's contributions, Darby rushed for 101 yards on 15 carries, a tally that moved him, at the time, to No. 16 all-time in career rushing yards (1,760). Florida, which was averaging 34.5 points a game heading into the meeting with Alabama, was hounded by Ryans and company all day. Ryans had nine tackles, a sack-and-a-half, and a quarterback pressure, with Roman Harper producing eight tackles. Juwan Simpson had seven stops and a sack, and Roach and Robinson had six tackles each, with Robinson adding an interception and Roach a pass breakup.

"I thought Florida would win the game," Brown admitted. "I thought they were the better team all-around, and I thought Florida would expose Alabama. But as it turned out, Alabama exposed Florida. The exact opposite was true."

• • •

Jason Kirksey and his friends were right in the middle of the celebration. There was nowhere else they wanted to be than in the epicenter of it all. "What was incredible was as soon as the clock hit one minute to play, the band cranked up and everyone started singing 'Rammer Jammer,'" he said. "It had to be the loudest it has ever been sung before. I remember thinking, *Did we really just beat Florida 31-3?* And when *Sports Illustrated* put 'Bama's Back' on the cover the next week, it put everything we were feeling on a national level.

"As you were sitting there and watching the game, you realized the fans really had an impact on that game. The players celebrated with us, and that was their way of saying thank you to the fans. Everybody played a part. For me, it was the first really big game I'd ever been at, the first big game where I could say, 'I was there.' I was there for Prothro's catch the year before, but that was Southern Miss and it wasn't a big, big win like the Florida game was. It wasn't a win that, 20 or 30 years from now, I can say, 'I was there,' and it would mean something. But I know years from now, that's what I'll be telling people when they talk about the Florida game. I'll be able to tell them, 'I was there.'"

CHAPTER TWENTY
2008 Georgia

Alabama 41, Georgia 30
September 27, 2008
Sanford Stadium
Athens, Georgia

Following Alabama football isn't a weekend hobby for Ray and Kathy Walker. It's an every-day passion that intensifies on football weekends. The Walkers married in 1968, and Ray took Kathy to her first Alabama football game in 1969. It wasn't just any football game. He escorted his young bride to the Alabama-Ole Miss game, the first college football game to be televised in prime time and a game that featured quarterbacks Scott Hunter for Alabama and Archie Manning for Ole Miss in one of the darndest, back-and-forth games that has ever been played between the two schools. Fans for both teams still talk about that game to this day, won by Alabama 33-32 at Birmingham's Legion Field.

As it turned out, it was an evening that potentially could have had a great impact on the Walker marriage.

"At that point," Ray recalled, referring to a moment in the game when the Rebels had taken the lead, "it was pretty exciting, and I was misbehaving pretty badly and ripped up my program and broke my glasses and cussed everybody out around me. Kathy just patted me on the shoulder and said, 'Honey, it's just a game.' Well, I explained to her in very graphic language that it was not just a game and so she had to make a decision then whether she was going to remain married to me or whether she was going to go on down the road."

Kathy Walker decided to stand by her man and stand behind the Crimson Tide. "Now, she's as big a fan as I am," Ray proudly boasts.

So it has been for the Walkers, who lived in Birmingham when they were first married and now live in Macon, Ga. From that famous Alabama-Ole Miss game to today's schedules, regardless of the opponent, the Walkers cheer for their beloved Alabama football team. Together, they have formed a tailgating partnership that is equal parts social activity and football fandom, as well as equal parts tradition, responsibility and, they are quick to add, just plain fun.

Their support for the team has taken them to every game Alabama has played some seasons, just home games during other years. It has taken them to Memphis for the Liberty Bowl against Colorado, to Pasadena, Calif., for a game against UCLA, and to Tiger Stadium in Baton Rouge for games against LSU. There are scrapbooks filled with photographs that chronicle their travels and the people they have met along the way. And there are stories. Lots and lots of stories.

Most of the stories come from the couple's tailgating experiences, which began small and have grown over the years, moving from various spots on campus to their current location in the alley behind Trinity United Methodist Church and sometimes feature as many as 20-25 people. Included in the group are family members, acquaintances, and friends.

"We generally go over to the Quad," Ray said. "We have different friends that have different tailgates. A lot of others go to the Walk of Champions and watch the team arrive and listen to the band play. Just all the things that usually happen on a typical game day."

• • •

Alabama's fifth game of the 2008 season against Georgia at Sanford Stadium in Athens matched an up-and-coming Alabama team that started the year ranked No. 24 and had subsequently moved up to the No. 8 spot, against Georgia, a team of deep talent that was picked by at least one preseason magazine to win the national title that season. The Bulldogs, who had defeated Alabama 26-23 in overtime in Tuscaloosa the previous season and had won the previous three games against the Crimson Tide (2002, '03, '07), were ranked No. 3 and appeared to be a team that indeed could make a run at the national championship.

Added to the evening was the announced plan of a "blackout" game for the Dawgs; fans were encouraged to wear black to the game, and the Bulldogs would wear black jerseys. Georgia fans participated overwhelmingly, making the stadium a sea of black except for the small patches where Alabama fans were seated, most donning white and crimson attire. It was expected to be a too-close-to-call game matching two of the SEC's top teams. What it became wasn't a blackout as much as it was a knockout. Alabama, in a 31-point first half, dominated what had been a dominating Georgia team. It silenced the crowd quickly and for long periods of time as it turned what was expected to be a showdown into a beat down.

The Walkers were there to see it all. They rode to the game with long-time Macon friends Jimmy and Maebelle Joyner. The Joyners, staunch Georgia fans, had been the Walkers' neighbors for 11 years, but although they no longer live in the same neighborhood they have remained good friends. The Joyners asked the Walkers to ride to the game with them and to take part in their tailgate, and the Walkers agreed. Ray found tickets to the game for himself and Kathy, and the Joyners had their tickets. It provided an opportunity for the friends to spend some time together doing something they all enjoyed— watching college football. At this particular game, the Walkers would have a bit more fun than the Joyners.

They're decked out in their black, and we're in our Alabama stuff," ray said of the Joyners. "We go to the tailgate, and all the Georgia fans are anticipating a victory. All I'm doing mostly is keeping my mouth shut. … The atmosphere was good, and the people were yelling and screaming."

Strength and conditioning coach Scott Cochran, during an Alabama practice the week of the game, mentioned the "blackout" plan, telling Crimson Tide players the only reason the Bulldogs would be wearing black for the game was because they were going to a funeral. The remarks were captured on video and broadcast in both states, stirring the pot between the two fan bases even more leading up to the game.

As it turned out, Cochran was right. Everyone could see that, even those whose seats weren't ideal.

"When we get to the stadium we go to the gate to get to our seats, and we take an escalator up three levels," Ray Walker said. "Then we walk up three more levels. We're at the 600 level, and when we get there our seats are two rows from the top, so we walk to the top. People don't believe this, but I'm telling you it's true: from our seats looking northeast you could see the lights at the Clemson stadium. That's how high we were. You look down on the field, and it's almost like ants were playing." Ever the optimist, Kathy added, "But my goodness, we were in the middle of the field. We don't ever get to sit there."

The view would be just fine for the Walkers and all Alabama football fans.

• • •

Once the game began, the dominant colors were crimson and white. Dressed in its road white uniforms with crimson numbers, helmets and trim,

Alabama would be a blur of motion and activity. Its offense, which scored on its first five possessions, would be an almost blinding white as it moved up and down the field with precision and effectiveness. The defense, failing to allow the Bulldogs any momentum and any reason for optimism at the start of the game, was a vision of strength and aggressiveness.

For the first 30 minutes of the game, of which Alabama had possession for 21:05, the Crimson Tide had a stranglehold on the momentum, the scoreboard, and certainly the atmosphere. The home field advantage was non-existent, the team in charge was clear. Crystal clear.

Alabama's scoring drive started simply enough at its own 20-yard line, with Glen Coffee producing a two-yard run. It was followed by a seven-yard pass from John Parker Wilson to B. J. Scott and a pair of three-yard runs by Coffee to the Alabama 35. Doubling its pleasure again, Alabama completed a pair of 13-yard passes from Wilson to Julio Jones, putting the Tide at the Georgia 39. Another three-yard run by Coffee preceded an incomplete pass to Marquis Maze that turned into a 15-yard gain for Alabama via a pass interference penalty against the Dawgs, moving Alabama to the Georgia 21.

Mark Ingram gained a yard on a run and then lost three on a second-down carry, moving the Tide back to the Georgia 23. Wilson completed a 16-yard pass to Coffee, who fumbled the football. It was recovered by Georgia's C. J. Byrd at the six-yard line, but the Dawgs' celebration was short-lived; a roughing the passer penalty against Akeem Dent erased the play, giving the ball back to Alabama at the Georgia 11. Instead of stopping Alabama's drive and gaining possession of the football, Georgia now had its back against the end zone.

That's right where Ingram wanted the Dawgs, as he gained four yards and then covered the remaining seven yards into the end zone for the score. The touchdown and Leigh Tiffin's extra-point kick capped an 11-play, 80-yard drive and put Alabama in front 7-0 with 8:32 left in the first quarter. The Crimson Tide, the black-attired Georgia fans would soon learn, was just getting started.

Armed with an offense that featured quarterback Matt Stafford and receiver A. J. Green, both of whom would have good games, the Bulldogs looked to match Alabama's score right away. That wouldn't be the case. Instead, after a 13-yard pass on the first play from scrimmage, Georgia was limited to a seven-yard Knowshon Moreno run, a four-yard loss by Moreno, and an incomplete pass.

Alabama's offense was back in business, and business, certainly in the first half, was good. Coffee started the drive with another three-yard run, and Wilson picked up seven more on the next play for a first down. Georgia was called for holding, moving the Tide 10 more yards, and Coffee rushed for four yards to the Georgia 41. Wilson tossed a pass to Nikita Stover for 14 yards to the Georgia 27, and a roughing the passer penalty against Georgia's Jarius Wright moved Alabama to the 13. Ingram rushed for eight yards but lost a yard on his next two carries. That brought Tiffin into the game to attempt a 23-yard field goal, which he made.

Remarcus Brown returned the ensuing kickoff 25 yards to the Georgia 28, when Moreno gained a yard and Stafford threw an incomplete pass to close out the first period. Another incomplete pass led to another Georgia punt that was downed at the Dawgs' 48.

It wouldn't take Alabama long to finish off its drive from that distance. Coffee rushed for nine yards, then three. He fumbled on the second carry when he was hit by Rennie Curran, but recovered his own fumble at the Georgia 36. Wilson tossed a 31-yard pass to Jones that moved the Tide to the Dawgs' five-yard line, where Coffee ran for two yards, then the remaining three for the touchdown. Alabama held a 17-0 lead that was going to increase before halftime.

Starting at its 22, Georgia received a three-yard run by Moreno and a five-yard pickup by Stafford. On third down-and-2, Stafford completed a pass to Green, but the ball was jarred loose on a hit by Justin Woodall and was recovered by Dont'a Hightower, who returned it eight yards to the Dawgs' 33.

Wilson completed a 12-yard pass to Mike McCoy. Roy Upchurch added runs of three and one that preceded another Wilson-to-McCoy pass play, this one for 10 yards to the Georgia 7. After an incomplete pass to Jones, Upchurch managed runs of three and four, the latter good for the Crimson Tide's third touchdown.

The pressure was on the Georgia offense to make something happen in a hurry. It would not be able to answer that call, at least for the remainder of the first half. Instead, the Dawgs used a handful of plays to move only 10 yards.

Arenas returned the ensuing punt 10 yards to the Alabama 37, where the Crimson Tide would put together another scoring drive. Wilson connected with Coffee for a 6-yard pass, and then Coffee added runs of 15 and five yards to the Georgia 37. Wilson went back to the pass, hitting Nick Walker on an 11-yard strike before Coffee chipped in a four-yard run. The drive was complete when Wilson, 3-for-3 passing in the series for 39 of the 63 yards, found Jones on a 22-yard scoring strike, the freshman receiver making an over-the-shoulder catch. It was the kind of play expected by the highly touted and recruited receiver from Foley, Ala. Tiffin's kick made it 31-0.

"He's good. He's really good," Wilson said of Jones after the game. "He gets open and he puts pressure on the defense. They were playing him one-on-one with no safety over the top [on the touchdown], so we were going to take it." Saban described Jones's performance as a "breakout game."

To say the crowd had been taken out of the game would be a gross understatement, and the Bulldogs' final drive of the half would end with an interception.

The Crimson Tide rolled up 231 total yards and 31 points, while Georgia was limited to 86 yards and no points. What's more, the Dawgs had just four first downs, while Alabama had produced 17.

Bulldog fans didn't get the "blackout" they had expected and for which they had planned. They received only a black eye.

"One of the biggest problems," freelance journalist Ray Glier, author of *How the SEC Became Goliath: The Making of Southeastern Conference Football,*' recalled, "was Alabama had too much muscle up the middle for Georgia. Back in 2008, that's when Georgia was losing its size on defense. They were going with smaller defensive guys and fast guys that didn't weigh 200 pounds. And that's been one of Georgia's issues [during the following three seasons]."

Saban would later describe the first two quarters of play by saying, "We probably played the best half of football we've played all season. It couldn't have come at a better time."

Georgia's Mark Richt, who was 3-0 against Alabama heading into the game, said of the first half afterward, "It was such a big hole. We weren't getting out of it."

• • •

There would be some redemption, even some thoughts of a huge comeback, for Georgia fans in the third period. After watching Alabama have its way with their Dawgs in the first two quarters, the third period would be owned by Georgia. Opening the second half at its 27, Moreno gained four yards, which were wiped out by a five-yard false start penalty on the next play. Stafford connected with Kris Durham for a pair of 22-yard pass plays, moving the Dawgs to the Alabama 30, and Moreno gained six before an ineligible player downfield penalty cost the Dawgs five yards. A three-yard Stafford run and incomplete pass led to a Blair Walsh field goal of 43 yards that finally put Georgia in the scoring column.

Alabama's P. J. Fitzgerald was called on for his first punt of the game on Alabama's first possession of the second half, concluding a three-and-out series. But Georgia returned the favor with a three-and-out series and punt of its own. Alabama repeated the three-and-out offensive effort, punting back to the Dawgs who took over at their 42.

Stafford went to work, tossing a seven-yarder to Green and, following a no-gain run by Moreno, completed passes of seven to Massaquoi and one to Moore before an incomplete throw. Stafford picked up the pace again, completing passes of five to Massaquoi, 10 to Moore and 26 to Green that moved Georgia to the Alabama 2. After an incomplete pass, Moreno scored from two yards out and the Dawgs, with Walsh's extra-point kick, had trimmed Alabama's lead to 31-10.

One more three-and-out series for Alabama led to another Fitzgerald punt on the first play of the fourth quarter. Prince Miller fielded the kick at the Georgia 8 and returned it 92 yards for a touchdown. Just like that, Georgia had cut the Crimson Tide's lead to 31-17, it had brought the crowd back into the game, and the momentum shifted to the home team.

Arenas gave the Alabama fans something to cheer about, when the drive ended on Tiffin's 32-yard field goal, which he made.

"At some point in that game I screwed up a kickoff," Tiffin said. "If I'm being completely honest, I probably went out there thinking, *I better knock this down or somebody's going to want to kill me.*"

The pressure of playing at Sanford Stadium in front of a loud, enthusiastic crowd—at least at the start of the game—was something Tiffin said he learned to enjoy. "I always really enjoyed road games," he said. "Once I finally hit a certain point in my career—it was the Auburn game of my sophomore year—I finally realized the mental approach you have to take into a road game. I realized, 'Wait a second here, this is actually a source of energy here for me, the fact these people are wanting me to miss, the fact that there's a lot of energy here.'"

Back stormed Georgia. The big play came on fourth-and-18 from the Alabama 43, when Georgia decided to go for the first down. It appeared it had picked up the first down when Stafford connected with Green on a 19-yard play to the Alabama 24, but a holding penalty overturned the play. Now facing a fourth-and-28 situation at its 47, Georgia, with time running out, decided to try again. Stafford's pass fell incomplete, and Alabama took over possession on downs.

Coffee had a four-yard run, followed by a one-yard run before Wilson and Upchurch connected on a 29-yard pass play that moved the Tide to the Dawgs' 13. Coffee rushed for a yard before breaking free on the next play for 12 yards and a touchdown that, with 4:13 to play, sealed the game for the Crimson Tide, even though Georgia would not go down without a few more swings.

A 41-yard kickoff return by Georgia's Richard Samuel put the Dawgs at the Alabama 40. After an incomplete pass, Caleb King ran for five yards.

Another incomplete pass set up a fourth-and-5 play for the Dawgs, who got that and more on an 11-yard Stafford-to-Kenneth Harris pass play. That was followed by a 24-yard touchdown throw from Stafford to Moore that ended the five-play, 68-second drive. Georgia had trimmed Alabama's lead to 41-23, but only three minutes remained to be played.

There was still hope for the Georgia team and its fans. Georgia successfully recovered an onside kick at its own 42. Stafford ran for 10, and then 11 yards before completing a four-yard pass to King. An incomplete pass and false start penalty slowed the Dawgs' momentum, but Stafford threw to Harris for 17 yards and then connected with Green on a 21-yard scoring throw with 1:35 to go, 41-30.

Still, the 11-point Alabama lead with just 95 seconds to play spelled defeat for Georgia, which had managed a solid second half of play. The Bulldogs kicked off, and the ball went out of bounds at the 29. Three plays later, each one a snap of the football followed by Wilson dropping to one knee, closed out the game and the victory.

The stats would even out at the end, just as the score seemed to indicate a much closer game. But the game was neither even nor close. Against a higher-ranked, fan-fueled opponent on its home field, Alabama had proven its worth. It not only quieted a crowd ready to explode, but it completely silenced that crowd in the first half. When Georgia mounted a comeback of sorts in the second half, Alabama maintained its poise and scored enough to keep the game out of reach of the Bulldogs. The win would move Alabama from No. 8 in the country to No. 2 in the next Associated Press Top 25 poll.

It wasn't, as Georgia fans had envisioned, a blackout at all. It was instead an awakening for Alabama. For a program that had produced disappointing finishes the previous two years, it would be the game that signaled an impending return to prominence.

"Without question, I think that's where the tide turned for us," Tiffin said four years later. "That game sticks out in my mind so vividly."

The Crimson Tide would jump to the No. 2 national ranking after the win, and after a ninth consecutive victory to start the season, it took over as the No. 1-ranked team in the country. National title hopes was not a subject in which Saban wished to engage after the game. "I'm not interested," Saban told *New York Times* reporter Ray Glier when the reporter asked him about Alabama entering the national title chase discussion. "These are not the kind of things we're worried about right now."

Wilson was 13-of-16 passing for 205 yards, one touchdown and no interceptions. "He just abused Georgia and they never saw him coming,"

Glier said of Wilson. "Georgia was saying, 'We're going to make you beat us,' and damn if he didn't."

Coffee rushed for 86 yards and a pair of scores against a defense that had been allowing opponents just 45 rushing yards a game. Jones caught five passes for 94 yards and a touchdown, and Wilson threw to seven different receivers. The Alabama defense, led by Woodall and Rolando McClain with five tackles each, allowed Moreno just 34 yards on nine carries, sacked Stafford twice and picked off one of his 42 throws. It was a blackout to be sure, but not the one that had been planned.

"At the time, people forgot how good that Georgia team was supposed to be. They had so much NFL talent, first-round NFL talent," said Gentry Estes, former Alabama beat writer for the *Press-Register* in Mobile who now covers Georgia sports for 24/7 Sports.

"There were some signs [that Alabama was improving], but it was still a surprise to me. The whole thing was crazy with the blackout thing Georgia was doing; they had done it once before against Auburn, so it was a big deal. Everybody wore black to the stadium, and the team came out in the [black] jerseys. It was a pretty electric atmosphere. . . . I remember that season I only missed one game in my [Alabama] predictions, and that was the only game I missed all year."

• • •

The Walkers were thoroughly enjoying themselves from their seats high above the action. They watched Georgia fans start to leave the stadium at halftime, the number of black-attired fans taking their leave growing in the third period. Their friends the Joyners were included in that number.

"We were just saying, 'Let us score.' Then it was, 'Let us score one more time.' And it just continued and continued," Ray said of the start of the game.

Though the Joyners went back to their car during the third quarter, the Walkers remained in rapidly emptying Sanford Stadium until the end of the game, then stayed a little longer to celebrate the victory with the other Alabama fans, who had also elected to stay and soak up the moment. "Georgia people were leaving in droves," Ray said. "I mean, no laughing, no nothing, just gone. We celebrated for 15 or 30 minutes in the stadium and we celebrated all the way back to the tailgate.

"So we get in the car and it's a pretty quiet ride back until they finally loosened up about halfway back. They weren't mad at us, Jimmy was just mad at the way his team had played. I would have been too. I don't lose good."

CHAPTER TWENTY-ONE
2009 Tennessee

Alabama 12, Tennessee 10
October 24, 2009
Bryant-Denny Stadium
Tuscaloosa, Alabama

In a way, they could be considered a kind of before and after team, though it would be unclear exactly who should represent "before" and who the "after." In many ways, they couldn't be any more different. But when Alabama faced longtime rival Tennessee in the Crimson Tide's eighth game of the 2009 season, nose tackle Terrence Cody and place-kicker Leigh Tiffin stood together in aiding their team's cause, both saving the day in their own way.

Alabama's offense failed to generate a touchdown, calling on Tiffin's kicking talents for all of its points. Defensively, Cody was there to block, quite literally, a couple of Tennessee scoring opportunities, including the last play of the game, a play that if successful would have given the Volunteers the victory.

So there they were, the 6-foot-5, space-eating, running back-crunching; field goal-blocking; 350-plus-pound Cody, a Florida native who transferred to Alabama after two seasons at Mississippi Gulf Coast Community College; and Tiffin, son of a former record-setting; big-win clinching place-kicker for the Crimson Tide in the mid-1980s, joining forces not only to lead Alabama to a win, but keep it on an undefeated path to the national championship.

• • •

Terrence Cody was a mystery to many. He was wearing size 10 shoes when he was just eight years old, and when he reached high school in Fort

Meyers, Fla., he played varsity football only two seasons—as a freshman and a senior. Recruiters would marvel at the size of the young defensive lineman, who weighed well more than 350 pounds, but they were more impressed with the athleticism he displayed despite his size. He was a terror on the defensive front, manhandling opposing blockers and simply filling up any bit of running room up the middle. Cody had offers from Division I schools, but he did not qualify academically and was signed by Mississippi Gulf Coast Community College.

As a junior college player he earned All-America honors for his play, which continued to improve. He helped lead MGCCC to an undefeated season in 2007, when he made 48 tackles and had 2.5 sacks. His sophomore season, Cody added another 31 tackles and 3.5 sacks. Alabama expressed an interest in him, and Cody was interested in the Crimson Tide.

He made a name for himself right away, making four tackles, including one for a loss, in Alabama's season-opening win against Clemson in 2008 in Atlanta's Georgia Dome. Soon, he was being referred to by Alabama fans as "Mount Cody."

"You talk to other coaches after you play them," Alabama defensive coordinator Kirby Smart told Chris Dufresne of the *Los Angeles Times* prior to the 2010 BCS national championship game against Texas at the Rose Bowl. "Talk to other SEC teams. They just couldn't get movement. If you can move people you can create space. And there is no space created when Cody is in there."

At MGCCC, Cody weighed more than 400 pounds. At Alabama he tipped the scales at 354 the first day of fall practice in 2008. Head coach Nick Saban told him if he wanted to be an every down player he would have to get down to 345. He made it to 349. Cody would earn All-America honors both years at Alabama, but did so more for his presence, his athleticism and his ability to take on two and sometimes three blockers and still plug up any running room along the line of scrimmage. His statistics were not staggering: in 2009 he was 11th on Alabama's team in total tackles, with 28 in 14 games. He had no sacks and just 12 solo tackles. He did have six tackles for a loss, three quarterback hurries, a pass deflection and a pass breakup. And he had two blocks. Two monumental blocks.

"I think Terrence deserves a lot of credit," Tiffin said. "He was a really good player and he did a lot of special things. And he was part of a special team."

• • •

Tiffin knew all about Alabama's tradition, its national championships, and its pressures. He grew up with that knowledge, as the son of Van Tiffin, whose 52-yard field goal on the final play of the 1985 Iron Bowl had led to the defeat of archrival Auburn and ensured Tiffin's place in Alabama lore forever.

"I can't recall a time not knowing that he played football at the University of Alabama," Tiffin said of his father. "I think that's a by-product of being a huge part of the culture here and everyone, no matter where I lived or where I was, recognizing him. . . . In that respect, it was almost a given for me that he played football. But honestly, I didn't think it was that special at the time because it was kind of normal."

When colleges recruited Tiffin, Alabama among them, his signing to play for the Crimson Tide seemed a natural choice. Yet it was also somewhat of a risk. There was the pressure of following a legend who also happened to be your father. "I'd like to be able to say, 'No, of course not,' but the fact of the matter is, when I look at it in retrospect, if you're human you realize you're part of a legacy and it's a very, very awesome tradition at the university," Tiffin said. "Just the football program in general, it's a great program, great tradition, great pride there and a family member of yours was a forerunner of yours who was part of that. I do think whether you acknowledge it or not, on some level, even subconsciously, there is some pressure there. I tried not to let it affect me as an individual or player, and I think the longer I was there the better I got at that. But I have to admit that early in my career that was certainly a factor.

"I think I handled it as well as I could have at that point in my life. With the maturity that an 18-year-old male has in that situation, I think I did the best that I could do. That being said, I don't know that it ever affected my performance on the field because frankly, when you go out there in that environment and under those circumstances with that much on the line, you're not worried about what happened 20 years ago. You're worried about what's happening today. So I can honestly say I never took the field and prepared to execute a kick and thought to myself, *Oh wow, my dad played football here.* That was the last thing on my mind. I was thinking, *holy crap, I've got to make this [kick], and that was pretty intense.*"

For his part, Van Tiffin maintained a hands-off approach when it came to his son's play, and that worked perfectly, Leigh Tiffin said, noting that his father had never pushed him to play football, never encouraged him to be a kicker, and didn't try to persuade him to go to Alabama. A bond developed between father and son during Leigh's time at Alabama, he said, noting that together that bond and his father's support gave him great strength.

"Whether you admit it or not, everyone wants their dad's approval," he said. "I think that was a big part of what drove me to really excel and what really pushed me to be the best that I could be in that particular endeavor. I would be remiss if I didn't acknowledge that. But I think we certainly bonded and we could relate on a level that we couldn't have before. He was an absolute, 110 percent, unequivocal asset during my time there.

"I suffered a tremendous setback early in my career there, and I think I would have probably been in the trash heap of kickers who have kicked a couple of games at the University of Alabama had I not had someone I could rely on and who had been there. In that regard, he was an invaluable asset to my career. I owe him a lot of gratitude for his unconditional acceptance."

• • •

The Legacy and The Mountain would have their day together.

Tennessee was a team that created uneasiness for opposing teams. That was true as Alabama prepared to play the Vols in the annual Third Saturday in October meeting, even if this one happened to be played on the fourth Saturday of the month. The Vols were coming off a 45-19 demolition of Georgia in Knoxville. They had beat Western Kentucky and Ohio University easily enough, and had sufficiently scared Florida in Gainesville, losing 23-13 in a game that was closer than the score indicated, and 26-22 to Auburn at the Vols' Neyland Stadium.

Saban said he felt his team looked sluggish in practice all week heading into the Tennessee game, and with the Vols gaining some momentum with the Georgia win, they were a dangerous team, even on the Crimson Tide's home field. Lane Kiffin was a brash coach in his first—and what would be his only—year at Tennessee after a successful stint as an assistant coach at USC and a not-so-successful turn as head coach of the NFL's Oakland Raiders. But he was getting more out of his team, a team that had finished 5-7 the previous year, than most had anticipated.

After the Alabama game, the Vols finished the year by winning four of their final five regular season games, including a win over South Carolina the following week, and earned a spot in the Chick-fil-A Bowl against Virginia Tech.

On this particular Saturday, Alabama held the No. 1 ranking in the Associated Press Top 25 poll. The Vols were unranked, but still dangerous, dangerous enough to almost pull off an upset win, an upset bid that was blocked by Alabama. Twice.

• • •

The teams started slowly. Alabama took the opening possession, ran three plays for five yards and punted to the Vols. Tennessee didn't fare much better in its initial offensive effort, moving from its own 46-yard line to the Alabama 39 where, facing a fourth down-and-14 situation, it chose to punt. But Chad Cunningham's punt traveled just 19 yards, with Javier Arenas calling for a fair catch at the Alabama 20.

An incomplete pass on first down preceded a Mark Ingram run of two yards and a 10-yard pickup by Greg McElroy on the next play. A screen pass to Julio Jones was good for 14 yards, and on a third-and-10 play after two plays without a gain, McElroy threw a sideline pass to Jones for 12 more, moving the Crimson Tide to the Vols' 42. Trent Richardson picked up three yards on a first-down run, and McElroy threw a two-yard pass to Richardson on second down, but a follow-up incomplete pass left Alabama with a fourth-and-5 situation at the Vols' 37. Saban and his staff decided to go for the first down, but a McElroy-to-Roy Upchurch pass gained only two yards, giving the ball back to the Vols.

Tennessee picked up 26 yards on the first play when Jonathan Crompton connected with running back Montario Hardesty, pushing the Vols all the way to the Alabama 35. A false start penalty moved the Vols back five yards and a Hardesty run picked up two yards before Mark Barron intercepted a Crompton pass at the 19 and returned it 11 yards to the 30.

This time, Alabama's offense would put points on the scoreboard, on the game's first field goal attempt by Tiffin. He booted the 38-yarder true, and the Crimson Tide held a 3-0 lead with just 1:22 left to play in the first quarter. It would be the first of eight field goal attempts on the day, four by each team.

A 28-yard kickoff return by the Vols put them at their 31 to start the ensuing possession. After a one-yard run by Bryce Brown, Hardesty caught a slant pass from Crompton for 27 yards. A seven-yard run by Brown on the final play of the first period placed the Vols at the Alabama 34. From there, the Vols received a five-yard run by Brown, who lost one yard on the next play. Hardesty added a three-yard run to make it third-and-8, when Crompton tossed a 19-yard strike to Denarius Moore on a crossing pattern for another first down at the Alabama 8.

The Crimson Tide defense stiffened. David Oku gained two yards, but two follow-up passes by Crompton fell incomplete. On fourth-and-goal from the 6, Kiffin sent Lincoln out for his first field goal try of the game, which he made from 24 yards out, tying the game 3-3. It would be Lincoln's only successful field goal of the game.

Terry Grant put Alabama in great field position with a 30-yard kickoff return to the Alabama 45. On the first play from scrimmage, McElroy returned to his favorite target, Julio Jones, who would catch seven passes for

54 yards against the Vols. The pass was good for 12 yards. Richardson rushed for four yards, McElroy threw a sideline pass to Michael Williams for four more yards, and Richardson added a five-yard run for a first down at the Vols' 30. But Richardson failed to gain on a first-down run, a McElroy pass fell incomplete and a third-down pass to Jones lost three yards, moving the Tide back to the 33 facing fourth-and-13. That sent Tiffin onto the field for a 50-yard field goal try, which he made to put Alabama back in front with 7:54 to play in the first half.

"I was in a state of flow that day," Tiffin said more than two years later. "It was not a state that was normal for me. I didn't experience that regularly. I had a lot of good games where I was not in a flow state. I don't think you have to be in a zone to play well, but that day I particularly remember being in that zone. I was in that zone maybe three or four times in my whole career on a game day. And that day—that whole season for me was a good season.

"That day I just didn't even want to know [the distances of the kicks] or care. I don't even think I knew how far those kicks were when I was doing them. It was just one of those days when you're just there, you just are. I just remember going out and being relaxed and not thinking a thing and just hitting them."

The Vols' offense followed with a three-and-out series, with Alabama taking possession at its 32 after a 34-yard punt by Cunningham. McElroy hit Dial for a short four-yard gain, and Ingram followed with four straight runs, gaining a combined 20 yards to the Tennessee 44. McElroy threw a five-yard pass to Darius Hanks, and Ingram gained four on a run. A third-and-1 pass from McElroy to Baron Huber picked up four yards and another first down. McElroy then hooked up with Marquis Maze for 19 yards to the Tennessee 12. Ingram got Alabama to the 4 on an eight-yard run, but two consecutive pass attempts fell incomplete. On fourth-and-2 from the 4, Tiffin got the call again. And again, he was successful, this one from 22 yards out with 1:11 left in the half.

The Vols made a strong effort to score before the end of the half, but Lincoln's 47-yard field goal attempt fell short, leaving Alabama with a 9-3 lead heading into halftime.

Neither offense had established itself, and neither had managed to grab the momentum. The Crimson Tide offense had control of the football for more than 18 minutes in the first half but managed just three field goals and a six-point halftime lead. The game was far from being decided.

• • •

The second half started much the same as the first, with both offenses producing three-and-out series with the first possession. The Vols generated

13 plays on their second drive of the half, but it was good for only 30 yards and ate up almost eight minutes of playing time. Getting as far as the Alabama 32, a sack of Crompton by Arenas pushed the Vols back to the 42, followed by a delay of game penalty to the 47 and a loss of three yards on a pass play back to the 50. At that spot, Tennessee faced a fourth-and-30 outlook and of course elected to punt. Once again, Alabama's offense generated little, and after three plays it punted the ball back to the Vols.

Starting at its own 21, the Vols put their running game into play, and on fourth-and-18, Lincoln got the call to attempt a 43-yard field goal.

Enter Terrence Cody.

Alabama called for its "max block'" defense, which calls for a big push up front and on the corners, all 11 players aiming to block the kick. Cody did his job and made the play. The big man pushed through the line of scrimmage, broke free and extended his left arm. Lincoln's kick was low and Cody's arm high, a bad combination for the Vols. Cody slapped the kick away a split-second after Lincoln made contact. After knocking down the kick, Cody kept running, raising his left hand, his index finger pointing skyward.

The ball bounced around the 35, where Tennessee's Bram Cannon picked it up, but he lost two yards trying to advance the ball, stopped by an Arenas tackle, and Alabama took over at its 37. Cody's play had re-energized the Alabama faithful, and Bryant-Denny Stadium was jumping. The Alabama offense used that energy. Ingram produced a three-yard run in front of a 10-yard McElroy-to-Smelley pass. McElroy then rushed for 12 yards to the Tennessee 38, where Richardson lost two yards on a carry. A pair of four-yard passes, one to Hanks, the other to Upchurch, left the Tide at the Tennessee 32 facing fourth-and-4. That meant just one thing: it was Tiffin Time. Again. The steady kicker proved up to the task, booting a 49-yard field goal that gave Alabama a 12-3 lead with 6:31 left in the game.

When Alabama's defense held the Vols to three plays and six yards on Tennessee's next offensive series, it appeared the Crimson Tide had claimed the game's momentum and would have the opportunity to run out the clock for the victory. That wouldn't be the case. Instead, something that hadn't happened before took place—Ingram fumbled for the first time in his college career. After 322 touches as a college player, Ingram had the ball jarred loose by All-America defensive back Eric Berry, who also recovered the loose ball for the Vols at the Alabama 43.

"Probably the worst feeling I've ever had," Ingram would say later of the fumble. "Ever."

Crompton was sacked on the first play, losing seven yards, but he tossed a screen pass to Hardesty for a gain of 16 on the next play. Brown rushed for two yards to get a first down, and Crompton tossed an eight-yard pass to Moore. Brown rushed for eight yards, then lost two, and the Vols called time-out with 1:46 to play. After the time-out, Crompton threw a seven-yard strike to Stocker before finding Jones on a crossing route for 11 yards and the game's only touchdown. Lincoln added the extra point, and the Vols trailed by two points, 12-10, with 1:19 left to play.

Tennessee completed an onside kick, with Denarius Moore recovering the ball for the Vols on their 41-yard line. An incomplete pass was countered by a 14-yard strike from Crompton to Jones on second down. The Vols were now at Alabama's 44. A false start penalty pushed them back to the 50, where an incomplete pass was followed by a 23-yard, well-thrown strike by Crompton to tight end Stocker to the 27. Hardesty lost a yard on a run, and Crompton spiked the ball to stop the clock with four seconds to play.

Tennessee had a chance to win the game. That opportunity was being handed over to Lincoln, who faced a 44-yard field goal.

Alabama, after a time-out to allow Lincoln to consider the moment just a little longer, placed its hopes on its "max block" defense. And Terrence Cody.

Cody would win the battle and the game. Lincoln's kick again started low, and it never had the opportunity to get better. Cody pushed the Tennessee blocker in front of him out of the way and stuck up his left arm again, swatting away the kick like a pesky fly. Caught up in the moment, Cody immediately yanked off his helmet, his long hair flying, put both of his hands in the air and just ran, some of his teammates draped around him in celebration.

The stadium exploded, and no one was ready to leave. They stayed, chanting Cody's name, singing and enjoying a victory that kept their team unbeaten. They celebrated Mount Cody. He joined in.

Surrounded by reporters after the game, Cody said of the second block, "After I blocked that thing I knew I was a big hero," he said.

As he described it after the game, Cody said he didn't even have to leap to make the play. "I didn't really get off the ground. I just reached up and stuck my arm up. That's when I got it."

That's when the Alabama fans, so nervous and quiet just moments before, exploded in cheers. "I looked up and everybody was still in their seats," Cody said. " . . . The fans were going crazy."

• • •

While Alabama celebrated, Tennessee's players quietly made their way back to the visitor's locker room. The Vols had fought all day, put themselves in good position to win the game, only to have that opportunity slapped away on the game's final play. Lincoln felt the sting perhaps a bit deeper than most.

Tiffin said he could relate to what Lincoln must have been feeling.

"I could totally empathize with the guy. Heck, I could sympathize. I've been there, and it's not a lot of fun. So in that respect, I totally felt for the guy. But in another respect, I was totally removed from it. I tried to train myself mentally to never judge my performance relative to anyone's but my own. It was bad for him, but it was good for our team. That's how I looked at it."

Tiffin was good for his team, too. During the 2009 season, his senior year, he would score a team-high 132 points, making 30-of-35 field goal attempts and 42-of-46 point-after kicks. He and his father Van are mentioned often in Alabama's record book. Leigh's 132 points in a season is second all-time in school history, and his 385 career points is first all-time. He made 136 career extra-point kicks, also the best in school history; Van is No. 2 with 135 in 135 attempts. The 30 field goals in 2009 is a school record, and his 25 in 2007 ranks second. Leigh Tiffin also holds the school mark for most field goals in a career; Van is fourth. Dad has the school's longest field goal made at 57 yards, while the son ranks third at 54.

"I think it's very cool, not that I do that," Leigh Tiffin said when asked his thoughts on sharing space in Alabama's record book pages with his dad. "To realize that we both had significant accomplishments during our time there, that's important, that's special and that's unique.

"But more than anything, I think it's a testament to his character and to my character. I don't think that position is a position that is necessarily born of an innate talent. I think the only talent—and I can only speak for myself, but I think my father would tend to agree—the only talent the two of us possessed was this ability to execute consistently and drive, drive, drive; just gut it out when the other guy says, 'You know what, I've had enough of this.'

"I think it's more a testament to our ability to persevere and to always be the same guy and bring it every day. I really think that's the only thing I did that was special there."

• • •

Some might argue that point; most would certainly agree that, above all else, the performances by Tiffin and Cody against Tennessee that season were special. Very special. Most would agree that when the opportunity to make a play was presented to them, both players delivered, more than once. Most would agree that they provided the focal point and the key plays that enabled Alabama to continue on its journey toward an unbeaten season and a national championship.

Cody, the mountain of a defensive player who rejected a pair of Daniel Lincoln field goal tries, was right; on that day and still today, he attained "big hero" status with Alabama fans everywhere. Tiffin, a model of consistency that season, was right too—he was in a flow at a time his team needed him to be in that zone.

Together, they added another chapter to the Alabama-Tennessee rivalry and added to their own legacies in the process. They were part of a special time and a special moment.

"To me, that's really what that game and that season was about," Tiffin said. "It wasn't about me. It was about being a part of a special team. At the end of the day, the one thing I probably appreciate the most about that game is the one day my teammates needed me, I came through. To me, that's the most special part of the whole deal."

CHAPTER TWENTY-TWO

2009 SEC Championship

Alabama 32, Florida 13
December 5, 2009
Georgia Dome
Atlanta, Georgia

Nothing had changed in a year except the rankings. And the motivation. That's how revenge—payback if one wishes to be more politically correct, though both are exactly the same—works.

The 2008 season had found Alabama push its way through the regular season with an unbeaten record. It arrived at the SEC championship game in Atlanta's Georgia Dome ranked No. 1 in the country, facing a once-beaten and No. 2-ranked Florida team. A win over the Gators would mean a spot in the BCS national championship game, a return to glory for the program. It appeared that would be the outcome, at least until the fourth quarter arrived. It was in the final period that Florida took over and in so doing, won the SEC crown, earned a spot in the BCS title game, and came away with the national championship. Alabama lost to Utah in the Sugar Bowl after the loss to Florida and the next day began its quest for a return to the SEC championship game in 2009, where everyone associated with the team hoped to once again get a chance to play the Gators.

Both wishes were granted. Alabama once again made its way through the regular season without a loss, as did Florida. This time, Alabama would be the team holding the No. 2 ranking in the country; Florida was ranked

No. 1. It was billed not only as a battle for the SEC title, but in effect, a national championship game semifinal. The winner would head to the BCS title game with a chance of providing the SEC with a fourth consecutive national championship. Florida won the crown in 2006, and LSU was the 2007 winner.

The incentive for Alabama, other than moving on to play for the national championship, was revenge. Payback, if you will. The Crimson was happy to be playing for the SEC crown, but it was *really* pleased it would play against Florida, a team it had kept an eye on throughout the season; a team it had wanted to play again since the 2008 SEC title game. There was something to prove, as much to itself as to anyone else, and the only way to make such a point, the only way to prove itself, was against the Gators. It was perfect, the way Alabama players viewed it, that Florida was the top-ranked team in the country. That made the matchup all the stronger, all the better.

Alabama had the Gators right where they wanted them. They had the opportunity, they had the game they had waited a year to play.

"I think everyone realized what was on the table and what we had an opportunity to do, and everybody applied themselves like that," quarterback Greg McElroy said. "Everybody worked at it. Everybody watched extra film. Everybody did whatever was necessary in order for us to be successful."

• • •

It would be a huge game for McElroy, a defining game in his first year as a starter at Alabama. He had waited patiently for his turn and had grown in the role throughout the season and through some close and tough games. It started with a win over Virginia Tech in Atlanta, followed by easy wins against Florida International and North Texas. SEC wins over Arkansas, Kentucky, Ole Miss and South Carolina followed. The Tide slipped past Tennessee, thanks to Leigh Tiffin's field goal kicking and Terrence Cody's two blocked field goals, the second of those coming on the game's final play. A close win over LSU was next, followed by wins over Mississippi State and Tennessee-Chattanooga before a last-minute rally was required to beat archrival Auburn on the road.

Alabama's confidence grew with each win, McElroy's confidence expanding as well. When he prepared for the SEC title game, he was as sure in his role, as confident in his play, as he had been all season. And he was ready. It was his time, and he didn't want the opportunity to end in disappointment.

The red-haired Texas native, who said he chose Alabama because of "the conservative nature of the school, the tradition and pageantry, everything that football meant to the state," couldn't wait to get the game under way, though it was his patience that placed him in that spot at that particular time.

"Anything worth doing is worth waiting for," he explained, adding that he understood the situation in terms of quarterback play at Alabama when he accepted a scholarship to join the Crimson Tide program. "You just have to make the best of what you're given, and every opportunity I've been given I've been able to make the best of, both in high school and at Alabama. I knew I would make the most of my opportunity once I got my chance. Patiently waiting never really bothered me because I understood there were other things, that I could grow as a person and as a player in the time I spend as a backup."

The lessons were valuable. McElroy said he was nervous but excited in his first start, which just happened to be nationally televised and against a Virginia Tech team that some believed would beat the Crimson Tide. He admits to starting a bit shaky but finishing strong. He also understood he wasn't just filling a starting spot on the offensive roster, but more importantly he was stepping into a prominent position—the starting quarterback at Alabama, a role that has been filled in the past by players such as Gilmer, Namath, Stabler, Todd, Lewis, Shula and Croyle. "I was ready," he said. "Playing high school football in the state of Texas prepared me to handle the nerves. . . ."

The story McElroy was writing during the 2009 season was special. He was blessed with a one-two punch at running back in Mark Ingram, who would win the Heisman Trophy that season, and Trent Richardson, who would be a Heisman candidate in 2011. He also had an offensive line that, like himself, was gaining confidence and experience as the season progressed. He had a good group of receivers, too. But he was charged with making it all work, using all those parts to produce an effective, efficient offensive attack. He had to be a leader as well as a performer. Each game, each victory, helped in his development; some games helped more than others.

On the game against LSU, McElroy said: "That was one of those times when we didn't play our best game at all, but we made the plays necessary to be successful and it was another game that we felt strongly about the way it finished out."

Of the matchup against Auburn, McElroy recalled: "You can't really understand it and appreciate [the rivalry] until you actually start the game. The heckling that the fans give you at Jordan-Hare Stadium and just the way that whole rivalry is, just totally magnified in the fact [it was played on] the Friday after Thanksgiving, that it's the only game on TV.

"Really, we stepped into the huddle, we completed a couple of passes, ran the ball a couple of times and really just got right where we wanted to be. We wanted to move it the length of the field, score and give them very little time to execute their own two-minute offense." Alabama moved to inside the Auburn 10-yard line but hit a snag, at least momentarily. After two running plays, the Tide faced a third down-and-4 situation and had another running play called when head coach Nick Saban called for a time-out with 1:29 left to play. He changed the play, switching to a pass. "Honestly, it's a play we ran about 100 times," McElroy said. "We faked a quick dive and rolled out and hit Roy Upchurch right in the numbers for the touchdown. It was a great feeling, an incredible moment, just overcoming our rivals the way we did."

McElroy was 12-0 as a starting quarterback at Alabama and, including his time as a starting quarterback in high school, was undefeated as a starter. He was about to face his toughest test as a starter, certainly as a starter at Alabama. Florida not only had a formidable defense, but also it was strong in all phases of the game. McElroy not only would have to manage the game, but also he would be required to make plays. Florida would likely center its attention on stopping Ingram and Richardson while also keeping a close watch on receiver Julio Jones. It would be up to McElroy to produce enough plays that would keep the Gators' defense honest and prevent it from loading up on any particular aspect of the Alabama offense.

As kickoff approached and emotions and adrenaline were running high, McElroy called some of his teammates together on Alabama's sideline. He pulled them in close and offered a final directive.

"Let's go be champions, boys!"

• • •

Alabama's game plan was to deliver an immediate message, not just with its stellar defense, but with its offense as well. It managed to do both. As if to prove its intentions, Alabama won the coin toss and elected to receive, stepping away from the usual practice of starting on defense if given the choice. The move enabled the Crimson Tide to make good on its game plan while also setting the table for what would follow.

Starting on its own 22 after the opening kickoff, McElroy and the offense gave the Gators a preview of what they would witness over and over again—a completed pass right over the middle, right through the heart of Florida's defense. McElroy dropped back and fired a bullet to Julio Jones that was good for 18 yards and a first down at Alabama's 40-yard line, and the scoring drive was on.

An Ingram run produced a six-yard gain, and McElroy carried the ball for seven more. Ingram picked up two around left end in front of a McElroy-to-Marquis Maze pass for eight yards and another first down at the Gators' 37.

A three-yard pass, plus a three-yard run and incomplete pass, left the Tide at the Gators' 31 facing a fourth down-and-4 situation. Leigh Tiffin was called on to attempt a 48-yard field goal, which he made, giving Alabama a 3-0 lead less than five minutes into the game.

The Crimson Tide defense forced Florida into a three-and-out possession. The Gators punted, and Alabama's offense was back on the Georgia Dome's artificial surface, ready to score again. McElroy decided to stick with what was working—a pass over the middle on the first play of the drive, this one a 19-yarder to Colin Peek. Ingram followed with runs of seven and 15 yards, respectively, and Richardson tacked on a three-yard run to the Florida 32. An incomplete pass was followed by a 15-yard throw to Maze to the Gators' 17, good for another first down.

Ingram and penalties would be front and center the remainder of the drive. Gaining seven yards on first down, Ingram was thrown for a two-yard loss on second down, but Florida accepted a five-yard penalty against the Tide for illegal formation, giving it another second-down try. McElroy was sacked for a loss of three, but Florida was charged with a holding penalty that moved the ball to the Florida 7 and gave the Tide a first down. Only one down would be needed as Ingram burst up the middle and into the end zone. The Tiffin point-after attempt failed, and Alabama led 9-0, with 5:33 left in the first period.

In a little more than eight minutes of possession time, Alabama had scored nine points and gained 123 yards on 12 plays. Florida had the ball for just 68 seconds and three plays, but would reverse that trend with its next possession. Brandon James returned the ensuing kickoff to the Gators' 26, but a personal foul penalty against Florida on the first play of the drive moved the ball back to the 13. A Chris Rainey run collected eight yards, and Tebow connected with Deonte Thompson for 19 yards to the Gators' 40. An incomplete pass, three-yard Tebow run, and nine-yard pass from Tebow to James moved the Gators into Alabama territory at the 48.

Tebow threw an incomplete pass, ran for seven yards, then hit Riley Cooper with a 12-yard strike, moving the Gators to the Alabama 29. After a one-yard loss, Tebow found David Nelson with a pass, but it also lost a yard. An incomplete pass left Florida facing a fourth-and-12 at the Tide 31, so Caleb Sturgis was called on to attempt a 48-yard field goal, which he successfully kicked, trimming Alabama's lead to 9-3 with 28 seconds left in the first quarter.

The second period would be a fans' delight. Alabama and Florida would combine for 20 points, 23 offensive plays and 275 yards on four consecutive possessions. The offensive streak would send an electrical charge throughout the Georgia Dome and create an anything-can-happen atmosphere, one that would seem to indicate the game would go down to the last possession, the last play.

That wouldn't be the case, but in the second quarter, when the offensive units, directed by McElroy and Tebow, proved what they could do—and it was quite a show indeed—the matter of which team would emerge with the victory seemed up for grabs.

Following Florida's touchdown the teams swapped punts, and Alabama began a drive on its own 15-yard line. Richardson produced a six-yard run, and McElroy added an 11-yard pass to Maze. An incomplete pass led to a seven-yard Richardson run that was followed by a big 34-yard pass from McElroy to Maze that positioned the Tide at the Gators' 27. A Richardson five-yard run and nifty McElroy five-yard run were sandwiched around an incomplete pass. Ingram was held for no gain, and McElroy was sacked for a 10-yard loss back to the 27 before Upchurch gained 10 yards on third down. From there, Tiffin booted a 34-yard field goal, and Alabama led 12-3.

Florida's answer was swift. A 26-yard kickoff return by James left the Gators at their own 30, where Jeff Demps picked up nine yards on a first-down run. Tebow then slipped around left end for 23 before producing a 15-yard run on the next play to the Alabama 23. That's where Tebow covered the rest of the yardage with a strike to Nelson. Four plays, 70 yards, 92 seconds, 12-10 game, 4:31 left in the first half.

The Crimson Tide would better Florida's quick score in plays, yards and time of possession. Javier Arenas returned the ensuing kickoff 28 yards from the end zone. McElroy, again making hay on the first play of a possession, tossed the ball to Ingram on a screen pass. The player who would become Alabama's first Heisman Trophy winner turned the short pass into a 69-yard play all the way to the Florida 3. Since he had put the Tide there, Ingram got the ball again on the next play on a handoff from McElroy. He covered the remaining three yards for the touchdown. Two plays, 72 yards, 59 seconds, 19-10 game, 3:31 left in the half.

Back came the Gators. A touchback of Tiffin's kickoff placed Florida at its own 20. On the first play of the drive, Tebow connected with Copper on a 59-yard pass play, pushing the Gators quickly onto Alabama's side of the field. Tebow then rushed for two yards and threw two incomplete passes, leaving the Gators at the Alabama 15. After a time-out and with 1:21 remaining in the half, the Gators opted to attempt a field goal. Sturgis made the 32-yarder, closing the Crimson Tide's lead to 19-13. The half ended after a pair of three-yard runs by Ingram.

• • •

Florida head coach Urban Meyer felt at halftime that his team had not only gotten back in the game, but also had seized the momentum, an intangible that would pay dividends in the second half. "There was some energy, some juice, some confidence in that locker room [at halftime]," Meyer, now the head coach at Ohio State after a short stint working at ESPN, said. "Because we did have a good second quarter. The first quarter was not very good, but the second quarter, the momentum kind of bounced back in our lap, other than a screen pass. We kind of expected—I kind of expected us to come out and play very well in the third quarter, and we didn't do that."

Of course Meyer expected Florida to bounce back in the second half. That's what had happened the previous year, in the same game, against the same opponent.

Alabama's coaches and players—and its fans as well—had to live with that game for a year. It served to drive the Crimson Tide throughout summer workouts, preseason drills, and game after game of the 2009 season. This time, Alabama would be the team that made a statement in the second half. This time, Alabama would be the team that won the game and earned the right to play for the national championship.

This time, Alabama would be the team that dominated the second half. And that domination would begin right away.

• • •

Florida received the kickoff to start the second half and advanced the ball just nine yards in a three-and-out possession, punting to Alabama. Starting at its own 26, Alabama struck quickly. Ingram had runs of seven, two, and five yards to the Alabama 40. McElroy found Maze again, this time for 28 yards. A 15-yard roughing the passer penalty against the Gators moved Alabama to the Florida 17, and on the next play McElroy threw a touchdown pass to Peek. The Gators' momentum was lost in just five Alabama plays and 74 yards. It took just more than five minutes of play in the second half for Alabama to reclaim the "juice," as Meyer called it, scoring a touchdown and in effect said to the Gators, "Match that."

Florida would not be able to answer that call.

The Gators' offense was good for 12 yards on its next possession, leading to another punt . . . and another Alabama touchdown.

Again, the Tide struck gold on the first play, Richardson bursting off left tackle for a 25-yard gain to the 37. The drive almost halted there, but a five-yard offsides penalty against Florida on a third-and-7 play gave Alabama a third-and-2 opportunity, and Ingram gained five yards for the first down. He then picked up three on first down, and after an incomplete pass McElroy hit Jones for a 10-yarder and a first down at the Florida 37.

Upchurch rushed for five yards on first down, and Ingram took over from there. He managed runs of four and two yards, respectively, to the Gators' 26. A team fumble led to a loss of five yards, but from there Ingram had back-to-back runs of 10 yards to the Florida 11, where he picked up a yard on the final play of the third period. McElroy ran for eight yards to the 2, and a pair of Ingram one-yard runs gave Alabama another touchdown and a 32-13 lead.

The previous year, Florida owned the fourth quarter. That would not be repeated. Owning a 19-point lead and with a firm grasp of the game's momentum, the Alabama offense moved to conservative play and the defense let the Gators know they should give no thought to a big, last-quarter comeback. But that's not to say the Gators didn't try.

Tebow, directing Florida's first possession of the final period, moved the Gators from their 35 to the Alabama 6. He started with a second-down pass to Aaron Hernandez for 8 yards and a run for 7. An incomplete pass was followed by a 22-yarder to Hernandez to the Alabama 28. That was followed by a 22-yarder to Nelson to the Alabama 6. Looking to pass again, Tebow had a receiver open in the back of the end zone, but Arenas made a leaping interception of the pass well in front of the intended receiver, and the threat was halted.

"They ran a play we see a lot, even from our offense," Arenas said later. " . . . I had to be on my Ps and Qs, [and] when he came out, I read him, saw him. I went up and made the play."

The Tide ran three plays and punted back to Florida where the Gators took over at their 31. Again, they advanced deep into Alabama territory but came up empty-handed with 7:28 to play.

Alabama's offense would not give the Gators' offense another chance. Richardson ran for a combined eight yards on two plays before Ingram produced a five-yard run for a first down. Richardson had runs of five, seven, and eleven yards, respectively, followed by Upchurch runs of nine, two, one and 29 yards, the latter putting Alabama at the Gators' 12. Only a short time remained. McElroy took the snap and dropped to a knee on back-to-back plays that ran the final seconds off the clock, giving Alabama the victory and a spot in the BCS national championship game against Texas in Pasadena.

"It was kind of surreal in a certain extent," said McElroy, who was 12-of-18 passing for 239 yards, one touchdown and no interceptions and earned the game's Most Valuable Player Award. "We really kind of went out there and we knew it was going to be like a boxing match. It was going to be 15 rounds. . . . I think those last couple of minutes, that drive, the heart showed by the offensive line and the running backs. And I think it all came full circle in the sense that all the things we've done—all the 110s we've run and blood, sweat, conditioning, all the reps in the weight room—that's what it's all for: taking a knee against Florida to win the SEC championship."

Still undefeated as a starter, McElroy had gained something as tangible as the MVP trophy; he was the leader of the Alabama offense, the director of the offense, the player who had patiently waited for his time and then grasped that responsibility fully and with authority. He had earned a spot in Alabama football lore.

• • •

The success of Alabama's offensive game plan is magnified by the fact that Florida entered the game having allowed the fewest points and the fewest yards in the country. The Gators' defense was statistically superior, and it was the strength of that defense that some expected would lead Florida to the SEC championship game crown and another BCS national championship game appearance. Instead, Alabama's offense was the story. Ingram rushed for 113 yards and three touchdowns, and Richardson added 80 yards, with Upchurch running for 57. McElroy's passes were crisp and on target, and his receivers were active. Maze caught five passes for 96 yards, Peek had three catches for 39, Jones made two catches for 28 yards, and Ingram added two catches for 76 yards, giving him a total of 189 offensive yards against the Gators. The Crimson Tide couldn't be stopped when it mattered most—it was 11 of 15 in third-down conversions, keeping the football and keeping drives alive.

McElroy said the working of the guys on the offensive line was just as important as that of himself or any of Alabama's running backs and receivers. "You can't say enough about the work our offensive line did," he said. "It's not what I did or Julio or Marquis or any of those guys; it's about the fact that I was kept off my back for the majority of the game."

Defensive leaders? That would be Alabama in this case. The Gators would finish with just 88 yards rushing, 63 of that gained by Tebow on 10 carries. Tebow passed for 247 yards, but was forced to throw 35 times, one of those throws good for a touchdown, another was intercepted. Seven players caught at least one pass, but Hernandez had twice as many catches as the second-leading receiver, Nelson. The Gators were successful on just four of 11 third down conversion attempts. It simply wasn't Florida's night on either side of the football. This game belonged to Alabama.

The Alabama defense, like the team all season long, had beat the odds. It stopped college football's toughest one-man offensive show in Tebow, and it refused to allow the Gators to gain any momentum. Most importantly, this time around, unlike the previous season, Florida was unable to take over in the fourth quarter.

"I didn't think about it until we won the second national championship [for the 2011 season]," linebacker Nico Johnson said, "but all the adversity we went through was something. Nobody thought we were going to beat Florida in Tim Tebow's last year. They thought we were going to get beat by Auburn, but we ended up coming back and winning that game. It seemed like there was adversity after adversity that we fought through and we were able to get where we needed to be. . . ."

• • •

Several Alabama players held up two fingers on each hand during the on-field celebration after the victory. They were not declaring themselves No. 2, not after the convincing win they had just secured. Instead, they were announcing their membership in Alabama's long and proud football tradition and history.

"The two fingers signifies 22; this is our 22nd SEC championship for the University of Alabama," McElroy explained. "It's something that's important. It's a big reason why a lot of people come here, to play for the tradition. Our fullback said it best tonight, Baron Huber. He said, 'If you could write a page in history, what would you want it to say?' . . . And we wrote our page tonight and I think that's just a tribute to the teams that have come before us."

Much was added to Alabama's history in the game. Ingram, who rushed for 113 yards and three touchdowns on 28 carries and also added two receptions for another 76 yards, set the school record for most rushing yards in a season in the game. He became the first Alabama running back to rush for more than 1,500 yards in a season. The win gave Alabama a 5-0 record against Associated Press Top 25 teams that season. The record would improve to 6-0 in the Crimson Tide's next game. The 13 victories tied the school record for most wins in a season, a record the Tide would break in the next game. Tiffin moved into second place in SEC history for kicking points and field goals made.

Defensive back Chris Rogers explained, "It was like one of those movies, like *The Godfather* or *300*. When you have them, you've got to knock them out. . . . We broke their will."

"I think that was one of the most gratifying experiences of my entire life," McElroy said of the win. "I think walking off the field, understanding what we had just accomplished, getting revenge on a team that we had wanted to beat so bad for the past year leading up to it and just having that feeling, knowing I was walking off the field with a rose in my hand having accepted an invitation to the [BCS title game at the] Rose Bowl, with the game ball and the MVP trophy and a SEC championship game hat on, I think [that's] something that I'll remember the rest of my life."

McElroy and his teammates weren't finished. There would be one more big night, one more big accomplishment, one more championship to further cement the team's season and its place in the school's proud football tradition and history.

After that game, members of the team would celebrate by holding their hands in the air, a single finger pointing skyward to indicate their place in the 2009 season.

CHAPTER TWENTY-THREE

2010 BCS National Championship

Alabama 37, Texas 21
January 7, 2010
Rose Bowl
Pasadena, California

What started out as a joke advanced to a dare of sorts and eventually moved into the planning stages. It was silly at first, an I-will-if-you-will challenge. Then, a nonrefundable hotel reservation was made and the cross-country drive of a lifetime was set in motion. That was just the start of a crazy, adventure-filled, Phenix City-to-Pasadena road trip for friends Roy Dixon Jr., Shawn Taylor, and Jimmy Messick.

The trio of friends and Alabama football fans are always trying to push each other's buttons in a good-natured way. Once it was announced Alabama would play Texas in the 2010 BCS national championship game at the Rose Bowl, the friends started toying with the idea of finding tickets and heading west to see the game. One of them suggested they could drive out there to cut down on expenses.

The idea wouldn't go away and the more it was tossed around in casual, what-if? conversations, the more it moved toward possibility. The next thing the guys knew, they were seated around a kitchen table, mapping out the more than 2,300-mile driving route.

"My birthday is December 29th," Taylor said, "and we were all together at my house, just sitting around the table, myself, Roy and Jimmy and our significant others. We were just hanging out and talking about going to the game. It was one of those things like, 'I'm in, are you in?' and everybody said, 'Yeah, I'm in.' . . . We sat there and looked at each other and said, 'I'm serious, I'm going to the game.' We thought about that for a few more minutes and then we said, 'We can actually pull this off.' That's how it started. We were back at my house on New Year's Eve and that's when the planning started."

Messick added, "The next thing you knew, we had a hotel room and a plan on how we were going to travel to this, that and the other. It was just counting down the days until we left."

It wasn't exactly that simple. First of all, while they indeed had a hotel room and had mapped out their route of travel, they did not have something of even more importance: tickets to the game. They scanned the Internet hourly, looking for anyone selling tickets, and they also had a budget. The two were not coming up as a match.

They left on a Sunday, right after going to church then having lunch together with their families. Once they piled into Messick's Yukon, complete with coolers of leftovers and sandwich items so they could save money on meals, they were off. When word spread of the trip, friend Craig Howard, who at one time owned the city's weekly newspaper, *The Citizen of East Alabama*, had told Columbus, Ga., *Ledger-Enquirer* newspaper editor Chuck Williams, who was in California to cover the game, about the trio and their plans. Williams asked for a phone number to call so he could do a daily blog entry on their trip, which the guys agreed to do.

Working with Williams and the blog would pay dividends. Williams mentioned the road trip to Paul Finebaum, host of a Birmingham-based sports radio talk show. Finebaum asked for a phone number to call the group and have them as guests on his show the next day. The guys agreed to the interview, which noted the length of their drive and the fact they did not have tickets to the game. At the end of the program, Finebaum, whose show is syndicated throughout the state and is now available nationally, mentioned that someone should step forward with some tickets for the guys. Someone did—former Alabama All-SEC defensive lineman and NFL star Bob Baumhower, who lives on Alabama's Gulf Coast. He had heard about the trip and contacted Finebaum to inform him he had four tickets, which he would mail overnight to the trio. Soon after arriving in California, the guys had their tickets and a spare, which Dixon said was given to a man he knew of from his Internet ticket search whose father had recently died. The man was also making the trip without a ticket, hoping to buy one once he arrived.

They also discovered they had obtained celebrity status since departing Phenix City. "We were all out the day before the game waiting for the team to show up for a team photo, and I eavesdropped on another conversation a family was having nearby," Messick said. "They said they were listening to the Paul Finebaum Show and said, 'Can you believe those guys drove all the way out here without tickets?' I started nudging the other guys. 'Are y'all listening to these people? They're talking about us.' We introduced ourselves and all of a sudden we were like rock stars. People wanted to take their picture with us. That was kind of a neat experience."

The entire trip was an experience. An adventure too. After driving all day and night the first day of the trip, the trio rolled into Texas about 3 AM and pulled over to check the rates and availability of a room. The hotel wanted $100 for the stay and Taylor said, "Guys, the easy thing would be to stay in a hotel, but anybody can stay in a hotel. Let's keep going." And so they did, driving another 36 hours straight until they reached Phoenix, Ariz., where they would rest at the home of a friend. Soon afterward coming upon a sign on the interstate that read: EL PASO 893 MILES. "I didn't think we'd ever get out of Texas," Messick said.

They shared driving duty, though Dixon admits his time behind the wheel was much less than that of Messick and Taylor. They pulled over at state lines to take a photo. To defeat boredom, they even pulled the car over once and did a little rock climbing. They told stories, talked football, and just kept driving. The adventure was just getting started.

• • •

Alabama's journey was now 13 games old. The Crimson Tide had weathered a season of close games, including wins over Tennessee, LSU, and Auburn. Now Alabama had a chance to win the program's 13th national championship.

Playing against the team from his home state, at the Rose Bowl, for the national title and in his first year as Alabama's starting quarterback, it seemed everything had fallen into place for Greg McElroy. Energized by his performance against Auburn and in the SEC championship game, but also nursing a rib injury, McElroy set out to ready himself, physically and mentally, for the biggest game of his life.

"The preparation started the day after the SEC championship game for me," he said. "I suffered broken ribs in that game so I started rehabbing immediately, doing x-rays, getting everything checked out and just trying to get healthy. That was my first priority. . . ."

Playing against Texas added a little extra fire and incentive to McElroy's preparations and his desire to be ready for the game.

"The fact that we drew Texas for that game was kind of a dream come true for me," he said. "They were a team that never offered me [a scholarship out of] high school. They recruited me, but never pulled the trigger on an offer. So they passed on me. That's what it came down to. I'm glad they did, believe me, because I'm happy to have been at the University of Alabama and to have accomplished everything that I have. Texas, that would have been the school for a lot of guys growing up there in Texas, and after taking my visits to both places I still think I would have ended up at Alabama."

McElroy spent hour after hour watching game film, so much so that he had to make himself stop watching and do other things, knowing it was an aspect of his preparation that could be overdone. He managed to take breaks, visit with friends, clear his head for a little while, only to come back and study some more the next day. Physically, he was limited in what he could do to prepare so he made up for that with extra mental preparation.

When he and the team arrived in California after a few days of intense practices and preparation in Tuscaloosa after Christmas, McElroy said he wasn't the only player on the team ready to play; his teammates had taken the same approach. They took care of their obligations as a team leading up to the game in California and had some practices aimed at polishing the work done in Tuscaloosa, but there was no doubt the Tide players and coaches were ready for kickoff.

"The day of the game I woke up and I felt great," McElroy said. "I went down to breakfast and I sat down next to William Vlachos and he said, 'Do you realize we're playing for the national championship tonight?' I don't think I could respond. I really started getting excited. . . . I went down for the pregame meal and sat next to William again and he said to me, 'I literally just sat in a chair in my room looking out the window at the mountains. I could not think or process anything.' I said, 'Buddy, I did the same exact thing.' I think that lightened the mood a little bit."

• • •

The guys from Phenix City were ready too, though their game day plans took an unexpected turn. "We're going to head out to the Rose Bowl at about 9 AM to tailgate and take it all in," Dixon, whose son Brodie is named for former Alabama quarterback Brodie Croyle, said. "We go busting out to the parking lot at the hotel and the passenger side window had been busted out." Gone was a deputy's badge (Taylor's brother is the Russell County sheriff), Dixon's camera and some smaller items. The window had to be replaced. Locals helped them locate a place that could do the work right away. While that was taking place, Taylor, whose back problems had him walking around town hunched over the night before, received a massage in an effort to alleviate some of the discomfort. They made it to the Rose Bowl in time for the game and headed to their seats, which were split up—two on the 50-yard line and two in one of the end zones. Taylor told Messick and Dixon to take the seats on the 50 and he'd take the end zone seat.

"You could walk out there in an empty stadium and pick and I'm not sure you could pick better seats than we had," Messick said. "Just a couple of seats in front of them was then-Governor Bob Riley. "Here's Roy and I, just two guys from Phenix City, and we're sitting in the middle of all this. It was kind of neat. We were thinking, *these people can sit on their hands if they want to, but we're going to be standing up and screaming and hollering the whole game.* And of course, all the coats and ties and politicians, they were into it as much as we were. That just made it all the more fun."

Taylor wasn't left out of the fun at his seat. When he sat down he noticed he was sitting next to former Alabama player Siran Stacy, who was seated next to another former Alabama player, Mark McMillian. "How cool was that?" Taylor said. "To make the trip with no tickets, get free tickets, get in the park and sit by two former players, it was tough to put into words. It was one of the most amazing trips I've ever been on."

• • •

The team that had fought adversity all season, winning games in a variety of ways, would produce perhaps its worst start of the season. Starting on its own 37-yard line after choosing to receive when winning the coin toss prior to kickoff, Mark Ingram was held for no gain on first down. A false start penalty moved the Crimson Tide back five yards, McElroy was sacked for an eight-yard loss and then threw an incomplete pass on third down and 23 from the 20. And those plays weren't the worst things that happened on the drive. That came on fourth down, when punter P. J. Fitzgerald, instead of kicking to the Longhorns, attempted a pass. He actually had Dre Kirkpatrick open, but the pass was short of its mark and Texas' Blake Gideon intercepted it at the Alabama 37.

The Longhorns would suffer a bigger loss on the ensuing drive. Quarterback Colt McCoy, a Heisman Trophy finalist, threw a five-yard pass to his favorite target, Jordan Shipley, on first down, and followed with a four-yard pass to Malcolm Williams on the next play. Those would be the only two passes McCoy would throw. Cody Johnson picked up a yard on a third-and-1 play for the first down, and Tre' Newton rushed for 16 yards on the following play, moving the ball to the Alabama 11.

That led to one of the game's biggest plays. McCoy started a run around left end, but finding defensive traffic heavy, he cut back toward the middle. It was there that Marcel Dareus, who hit McCoy hard on his right arm and shoulder, greeted him. It wasn't a devastating blow, but when players untangled after the play McCoy signaled to the Texas sideline that he needed to come out of the game, and he jogged to the Longhorns' sideline. Texas called a time-out to allow some extra time to evaluate McCoy, but his arm was numb, and true freshman quarterback Garrett Gilbert was sent onto the field. He would be Texas' quarterback the remainder of the game.

"As much as I enjoy winning," Alabama head coach Nick Saban would say later, "you hate to see a great competitor who's had a great career not be able to be a part in a game he's worked his entire career to be a part of."

An injury to his right shoulder would not allow McCoy to return to the game. He was emotional after the loss, but spoke with the media regarding his injury.

"That's a hit I've taken over and over in my life," he said. "And playing this game, you know you're going to get hit. But I guess I got hit the right way. I'm not in pain, but my arm's dead. It feels like I slept on my arm, woke up and it's just dead."

Texas would see how it went with Gilbert at quarterback. On his first play, D. J. Monroe rushed for 10 yards to the Alabama 1, with Mark Barron making the tackle that kept him out of the end zone. On first and goal there was a Texas penalty for illegal formation that moved the Longhorns back four yards to the 5, but a personal foul penalty against Alabama moved the ball up to the 2. From there, Cody Johnson gained a yard on two carries and a Gilbert pass to Antwan Cobb fell incomplete. On fourth-and-1, the Longhorns decided to kick a field goal. Hunter Lawrence connected on the short 18-yarder to give Texas a quick 3-0 lead.

Less than 90 seconds later, the Longhorns would score again. Texas attempted a short kickoff that hit the ground untouched, and the Longhorns recovered it at the Alabama 30. Newton rushed for a yard, then four yards, and a Gilbert pass fell incomplete. That set the stage for Lawrence once again, who made the field goal from 42 yards out to increase the lead to 6-0.

The teams swapped punts, and Alabama took over possession late in the first quarter at its 43. It was there that the Crimson Tide offense would start to click. Ingram had runs of eight and nine yards to start the drive. Roy Upchurch followed with a five-yard run in front of a McElroy-to-Julio Jones pass play for 23 yards to the Texas 12.

He wouldn't admit to it until several days after the game, but McElroy was injured on the pass play. Hit after he released the pass to Jones, McElroy said the tackle broke his ribs again. He would remain in the game.

"Immediately, pain just started going everywhere," he recalled. "It was absolutely brutal. I remember thinking, *I'm going to have to play the rest of this game with these ribs broken again*. Fortunately, we didn't have to do a lot through the air. We were lucky to be able to run and rely on our great offensive line and our great running backs and just wear them down. That was really all she wrote as far as the game."

After the pass to Jones, a nine-yard Ingram run moved Alabama to the 3, and he would get the call twice more. He gained a yard on second-and-1 for a first down, then covered the remaining two yards for the score thanks to a blocking escort by defensive lineman Terrence Cody and tight end Preston Dial. It was an easy score, and Leigh Tiffin's extra-point kick gave Alabama the lead at 7-6.

On the ensuing possession, Texas would face a fourth-and-15 play that led to a punt. Alabama could do nothing with the ball and in fact faced a fourth-and-12 situation that required the Crimson Tide to punt as well. The Longhorns would do no better on their next try, running three plays without a gain from its 15 and punting back to Alabama once again. Alabama's offense set up at the Texas 49 and called on Trent Richardson, who was ready to respond. On his first run, Richardson was stopped without a gain. But the second time, he burst through a huge hole on the left side and outran the Texas defense, untouched, for a 49-yard score. Just that quickly, the Crimson Tide had grabbed a 14-6 lead with 7:59 left in the first half.

That would be enough time for Alabama to tack on a couple more scores.

After starting its next possession with a 28-yard pass play from Gilbert to Monroe, Texas moved from its 40 to the Alabama 32. A five-yard run by Foswhitt Whitaker advanced the Longhorns to the Alabama 27. A Gilbert incomplete pass preceded a Javier Arenas interception at the 25, halting the scoring threat. "The thing about this team is that when a guy has a play to make and everybody else does his job, that guy always makes that play," Arenas told ESPN.com's Chris Low. "That's the way it's been all year."

The Tide offense moved to Texas' 39 but stalled there and punted. The Longhorns would engage in a three-and-out offensive series. Punting from its 7, Texas produced a 34-yard punt that was returned 12 yards by Arenas, giving the Tide great field position at the Longhorns' 29.

Ingram had runs of six, five, and two yards, getting the ball to the Texas 16, at which point Alabama called a time-out with 1:24 remaining in the half. Richardson gained a yard, and McElroy ran for six. Another Alabama time-out led to Tiffin attempting a 26-yard field goal with 29 seconds left. The kick was good. Marquis Goodwin returned the kickoff 23 yards for Texas to its 28, and Newton gained nine yards on first down to the 37. The Longhorns called time-out, and when they returned Gilbert attempted a shovel pass. But the pass was bobbled up in the air, and Dareus picked it off and returned it 28 yards for a touchdown with two seconds left in the second quarter. Alabama had a 24-6 lead that it would take to the locker room at halftime. It also had confidence and momentum.

The cushion provided in the waning moments of the first half would prove valuable in the second half.

•••

The combined first six possessions of the third period all ended the same—with a punt. Neither offense could generate much movement, and Alabama's three possessions had them punting from their own 25, 15 and 19. The last of those punts set Texas up at its 41 with 3:15 left in the third quarter. Newton rushed for two yards, then was held for no gain. Gilbert found Goodwin on a 13-yard pass play, but his next throw fell incomplete. It was there, at the Alabama 44 on second down, that Gilbert found Shipley again—Shipley had 10 catches for 122 yards and two touchdowns—the two players connecting on a 44-yard scoring pass with 1:31 left in the period. The touchdown trimmed Alabama's advantage to 24-13.

The Longhorns would get the ball right back when a short kickoff was fumbled by Alabama and recovered by Texas at its 42. A Gilbert pass to Shipley missed its mark, and on second down the two tried again, Shipley catching the throw but losing a yard. Another incomplete pass, this one to Williams, forced Texas to punt. John Gold boomed a 53-yarder that was downed at the Alabama 6. One play later, a three-yard Richardson run, the third period was complete.

The Alabama offense would get some movement on the drive. Richardson had runs of nine and three yards, respectively. An incomplete pass set up a third-and-7 play in which McElroy completed an eight-yard pass to Richardson for the first down. A pass interference penalty against Texas on the throw from McElroy to Maze put Alabama at the Longhorns' 44. A five-yard personal foul penalty against Texas moved the Crimson Tide to the 39, where Richardson had runs of one yard and four yards. An incomplete pass left Alabama facing a fourth-and-5 situation at the 34. Tiffin was called on to attempt a 52-yard field goal, but the kick failed.

Taking over at their 35, the Longhorns' offense got back on track. Gilbert passed to Shipley for three yards and to Newton for six. An incomplete pass was wiped out by an Alabama offsides penalty that gave Texas a first down. Gilbert ran for a yard, then threw for five to Shipley, a gain that was erased by a false start penalty on the next play from scrimmage. Gilbert threw his next three passes to Shipley, completing the first for 13 yards and, following an incomplete pass, adding a 12-yarder on the third pass.

Now at Alabama's 25, a Gilbert pass to Dan Buckner lost three yards, so Gilbert looked to Shipley again, this time for 28 yards and a touchdown. A two-point conversion pass from Gilbert to Buckner was successful. With 6:15 left to play, the Longhorns had trimmed Alabama's lead to 24-21, and the momentum clearly seemed to be in Texas' favor.

The Crimson Tide offense generated little on its next possession and was forced to punt to Texas. Starting at its 7, the momentum would switch sidelines quickly. Gilbert threw an incomplete pass on first down, but a defensive holding penalty against Alabama pushed the ball to the 17. Gilbert wanted to pass on second down, but Eryk Anders sacked him, jarring the football loose. Courtney Upshaw recovered for Alabama at Texas' 3.

Ingram was handed the ball on three consecutive plays, picking up a yard each time. The third time was good for a touchdown that, combined with Tiffin's extra-point kick, gave the Crimson Tide some breathing room in the form of a 31-21 lead with 2:01 remaining.

Arenas sealed the victory a few minutes later. On second down, Arenas picked off a Gilbert pass at the 30 and returned it three yards to the 27. Richardson rushed for 17 yards on the Crimson Tide's first play, and a facemask penalty against Texas moved the ball five more yards to the Longhorns' 5. Richardson had a three-yard run, followed by a two-yard scoring run with 47 seconds left in the game to seal the game. Tiffin's point-after try was unsuccessful, leaving the score at 37-21.

Gilbert hit Goodwin with an 18-yard pass to the Longhorns' 48 to start Texas' ensuing possession, but his second effort was intercepted by Tyrone King at the Alabama 31. McElroy and the Alabama offense returned to the field for one play, McElroy taking the snap then taking a knee, as the final seconds disappeared.

Alabama had its 13th national championship.

"After we scored the touchdown to go up 37-21 we knew it was over at that point," McElroy said. "Really, when we scored the touchdown to go up 31-21 with very little time left, we felt like we had it in the bag. We felt pretty good about our chances.

"We passed out the national championship hats and shirts [in the waning moments] on the sidelines. Our defense was on the field, and Texas was still trying to throw it. And sure enough, we get an interception. We're all scrambling [on offense]. We're trying to put our hats in safe places so no one would take them. We're running everywhere trying to find our stuff. I couldn't find my helmet for a couple of minutes. I finally found it, went out on the field and took a knee and that was just an incredible feeling. . . . That's why I signed up at Alabama, to try and win a national championship. The fact I was able to do that with that team was extremely gratifying and I'm extremely happy."

• • •

McElroy, who had directed Alabama to the win over Florida in the SEC Championship Game and helped lead the charge in the comeback win over Auburn, had provided solid play at quarterback, but not big numbers. His leadership was the key, as he completed just 6-of-11 passes for 58 yards. But he had no interceptions. Ingram carried the ball 22 times for 116 yards and two touchdowns, and Richardson had 19 carries for 109 yards and two scores. They combined for four receptions for another 31 yards. Julio Jones caught just one pass for 23 yards.

For Ingram, it also meant defeating the Heisman jinx. Having become Alabama's first-ever Heisman winner a few weeks before the game, Ingram was made aware of the so-called jinx that went to the winner who would go on to play in the national championship game—six of the previous Heisman winners who played in that game were on the losing team.

Not this time. Not only did Alabama win, but its Heisman-winning running back was a key contributor to the victory. Ingram told ESPN.com's Chris Low he never gave any thought to the jinx. "When I won the trophy, it was a great honor to win it, but it was more than just a trophy to me," Ingram said. "It was overcoming adversity. All throughout my life, me and my family sticking together and overcoming obstacles and people that tried to hold us back. A lot of emotion came from that."

Javier Arenas had a strong performance, returning three punts for 19 yards to go along with his five tackles and two interceptions. Dareus was named the defensive MVP, more for his disruptive abilities than total tackles, of which he had just one. He also had the interception he returned for a touchdown that may have been the game-breaker. Anders had seven tackles, including a sack and two tackles for a loss, with Barron and Robby Green getting six stops each. Arenas was next in line, followed by Rolando McClain.

Gilbert, called to action in the Longhorns' biggest game of the year, in a difficult situation and against one of the country's top defenses, was 15-of-40 for 186 yards and two scores, but he was intercepted four times, sacked once [losing the ball on a fumble], and he lost six yards on five carries. McCoy was 2-for-2 for nine yards and he had one carry for no gain, a carry that led to him being sidelined for all but the first few minutes of play.

Upchurch said after the win, "Some people dream and never get to accomplish that dream," he told *Press-Register* of Mobile beat writer Gentry Estes. "Tonight, my dreams came true. It's a great feeling."

• • •

In the final seconds of the game, Saban found himself on the receiving end of what has become a ritual for the winning coach of a big game—a Gatorade dousing. It may have been Alabama's worst execution of the night as the players delivering the Gatorade bath unintentionally bumped their coach. The Gatorade turned a portion of his white shirt pink.

"I wish they'd do water," he said later. "The Gatorade is awfully sticky. But I'm a lot happier with a bath than if I didn't get one, I'll tell you that."

Alabama players and fans were happy to have Saban as their coach. In just his third season at the helm he had led the Crimson Tide program back to the top of the college football mountain. "The process," his description of what was necessary in order for Alabama to return to prominence, worked. The BCS title was all the proof of that.

Having Saban in charge—he would lead Alabama to another national title in the 2011 season—was the one move that brought everything else together. Tiffin said he wasn't just the right man for the job that season, he has been the right man for the job, for the program, since the day he arrived.

"The one thing I can say about Nick Saban as a head coach, and I played for him for three years, is I never once—and I mean never one time, not even his first year—stepped on the field thinking we were going to lose. You always know that's a possibility, but every time I had a confidence and a feeling that we were going to win. I think that's a huge factor." Tiffin emphasized his statement was not a criticism of any other coach, but instead was a testament to Saban's abilities in running a program and coaching the game.

• • •

It was a special team, a team that seemed to will its way to victory week after week, challenge after challenge. There was talent on the roster to be sure, but Tiffin said there was something more, something extra the 2009 team possessed.

"I think it's even more special when you look back upon it and you have time to reflect on what happened and how special those things that transpired really were," Tiffin said.

"We went out there every week and worked hard. Everybody carried their own weight, everybody felt a certain amount of responsibility to their teammates for their own self-determination and for their own ability to execute and do their job. And people did it. To me, the big takeaway that I can carry from that in my own life is that average performers and high performers don't really coexist. You kind of have a critical mass and you have a group that takes over and we had a critical mass of high performers. . . .

"Did we have the best offense of all time or the best defense of all time? Did we have the best punter and kicker of all time? No. Not even close. We just were undefeated, and we found a way to beat everybody we played in a very competitive league and I think we had probably some of the greatest intangibles of any team you'll ever see."

• • •

The trip had been worth it for Dixon, Messick, and Taylor. All the miles, the sore back, the break-in of the car, the loss of sleep. Everything. Alabama had won another national championship at the Rose Bowl, and the best friends had been there to witness it—with free tickets and great seats. When the trip was first considered seriously, none of the three men could have imagined it would turn out as it did. They certainly imagined Alabama winning, but they didn't figure into all the planning what would happen on the journey itself.

"Would I do it again? Absolutely," Messick said when the question was posed. "We all said if we'll drive to California to watch them play, any other trip will be a cakewalk. So when Alabama was getting ready to play [in the

The trio of Phenix City friends pose for a photo in front of the Rose Bowl: (left to right) Roy Dixon, Shawn Taylor, Jimmy Messick. (Photo courtesy of Shawn Taylor.)

BCS national championship game against LSU in New Orleans in January, 2012] everybody kept asking, 'Are y'all going to make the trip?' We actually threw it out there with each other. But we said, 'New Orleans? That's a short drive. We'll wait until they go back to California again.' But I'd do it in a heartbeat."

Messick pressed the point that the purpose of the trip was to see Alabama play in a national championship game. All the other things were by-products of the original intent. "We weren't trying to get the recognition and the publicity we got. We didn't set out for any of that. We just wanted to go to the game. It just happened the way that it did. But it was a great trip, one for a lifetime and one that we can tell our grandkids about one day."

CHAPTER TWENTY-FOUR

2012 BCS National Championship

Alabama 21, LSU 0
January 9, 2012
Mercedes-Benz Superdome
New Orleans, Louisiana

Every team and season seems to adapt its own theme, its own personality. Alabama's 2011 season would be personal. Very personal.

It would be more personal than any one game, more personal perhaps than any other season in the school's tradition-rich history. Preparation was a hallmark of this Crimson Tide team, having learned lessons from the previous season and learned about itself along the way. And yet nothing could prepare the team for the role it would be asked to play, a role it readily accepted.

This would be a season that could not be defined by one game, by one occurrence, though one day would forever be associated with the team and its drive to a national championship. Alabama would be a team that proved itself on the field and off, in difficult games and difficult situations. It would be a team that overcame adversity over and over again, a team that some felt wasn't deserving of a chance at a national championship, only to prove those critics wrong. This would be a team that had great talent and maybe a greater desire; a team that was fundamentally strong, but also possessed an "it" factor; a team that was astute at the Xs and Os of the game, but made equal use of the intangibles and instincts that are often part of a successful team's DNA.

Most notable about Alabama's 2011 team, a team that would win the school's 14th national championship, was its heart. It was a heart that would be wounded and tested and would in all cases remain strong. How else to explain that a team that didn't win its conference championship—heck, didn't win its divisional championship—would win the national title? How else to explain that a team that was asked to lift up a university and community in the aftermath of a terrible tragedy? How else to explain a team that used a regular-season loss, one that might have floored other teams, as incentive to get better? How else to explain the path of a season and its outcome that no one could have predicted?

Heart. Alabama's 2011 team had that quality, and it would certainly need it.

• • •

April 27, 2011, is a date that will never be forgotten in Tuscaloosa. It is the day that a EF-4 level tornado ripped through the city and the hearts of those who live, work, and attend school there. It cut a three-to-four-mile swath through the heart of the town, especially the McFarland Boulevard and 15th Street areas, leaving behind millions of dollars in destruction and millions of tears.

"It's the most devastating thing I've seen in my life," Alabama head coach Nick Saban would say. He and his wife Terry spent many days visiting shelters and Red Cross facilities, handing out bottled water and offering encouragement and hope at a time when both were needed. Alabama football players played a key role in helping the city in its recovery in a variety of ways. Players, coaches, and fans of other schools sent supplies and funds and in many cases drove to Tuscaloosa to offer their help in clean-up and repair efforts.

As he made stop after stop, Saban maintained the same message: "We will build a better place," he said on more than one occasion.

The tornadoes that swept through portions of the state left 53 dead in the Tuscaloosa area and 253 dead across the state. Saban introduced a plan called "13 for 13," in which 13 homes would be built for residents who lost their homes, the number representing one home for each national championship the football team had won. When they won their 14th title at the end of the season a 14th home was added to the list. The aid and inspiration offered by the Alabama football team during that time was noted by President Barack Obama when the team was honored for winning the national title on a visit with the president at the White House.

At one visit to the city's largest shelter, instead of working in line, helping to feed people, Saban signed autographs, posed for photos and listened. Gould recognized that was exactly what those there needed.

It wasn't a chore, Jones said of his work and the work of others on the football team, in helping with the recovery and repairs. Instead, it was what they wanted to do. "I don't think it was a burden at all," the 2011 Outland Trophy winner said. "I think that tragedy brought our team together. We had a chance to spend time with each other in ways that we wouldn't have [under normal circumstances]. We got a chance to spend time while we were serving, and we really became a family. Tuscaloosa had supported us for so long, and we just felt like it was our chance to kind of support them and show them that we love them and we're grateful for all the support that they had given us over the years."

Linebacker Nico Johnson said, "It was a shocker. It's hard to explain, but it's a day that no one who was around that day is ever going to forget. So we wanted to give some kind of hope to the community that we're still here. We're not going anywhere. Tuscaloosa's still strong; Alabama's still strong.

No player on Alabama's roster understood the loss that took place on April 27 as deeply and as personally as deep snapper Carson Tinkler. He and his girlfriend, Ashley Harrison, took shelter in Tinker's apartment when the tornado approached Tuscaloosa. When the tornado struck, Harrison was pulled from Tinker's grasp, the force and power of the winds sweeping her away, as it did Tinker himself. Friends found Tinker, who was taken to a hospital having suffered a concussion, a broken wrist, a deep cut on his right ankle, and other injuries; Harrison died.

Tinker, whose story was told often in the days and weeks that followed, represented the Alabama team when it was awarded the Disney Sports Spirit Award after the season. While he said he was honored to represent his team, it wasn't a spotlight he sought. "I don't really relive it anymore," he said prior to the presentation of the award in early December of 2011. "I don't talk about stuff. . . . I wouldn't have chosen this role for myself, so I can't say that I like it. But I know it comes with a responsibility. A few days after the tornadoes, Coach Cochran, our strength coach, told me God places the biggest burden on those who can carry it. I feel like God isn't going to put me through something that He isn't going to help me get through. My faith has definitely gotten stronger through all of this. . . . If I can have a positive impact on anybody, that excites me. That's what I'm trying to do. I'm trying to be a blessing."

When the day of Alabama's season-opener against Kent State at Bryant-Denny Stadium arrived, the emotional charge was palpable. "It was humbling," Jones said. "The first time we came back on the field it kind of felt like that was the first time our community had been all together again since that terrible tragedy. It was a special feeling, just to take our minds off of it for a few minutes and then return to what we feel is normal."

Those feelings continued throughout the season.

• • •

The Game of the Century had everyone's attention. Alabama had settled into its role as the face and heart of a community while earning a No. 2 national ranking with its 8-0 record. The Crimson Tide would entertain No. 1-ranked and unbeaten LSU in front of more than 100,000 fans on Alabama's home field. LSU was in the midst of an outstanding season too. The winner would be the No. 1-ranked team in the country and have the inside track for the SEC West Division title and would be favored to win the SEC championship. Just as important, the winner would be on track to earn a spot in the BCS national championship game in New Orleans.

As most everyone expected, it was a close game; so close, in fact, that an overtime period was needed to decide the winner. But the game didn't play out as most had expected. Both teams were led by strong defenses, which would shine. That would also be true of the offenses, both of which struggled. The most important regular season game of the year would be handed over to the kickers. Alabama had its chances but failed to cash in. In the first quarter, kicker Cade Foster missed field goal tries of 44 and 50 yards. Jeremy Shelley attempted a 49-yarder early in the second period that was blocked, and with 3:53 left in the half he made a 34-yarder to give Alabama a 3-0 lead. LSU matched that score on the final play of the half when Drew Alleman booted a 19-yarder.

Foster returned to make a 46-yarder for Alabama late in the third quarter, and early in the fourth quarter Alleman made a 30-yarder that tied the game at 6-6. Alabama started a drive after LSU's field goal that took it from its own 23 to the LSU 28, thanks to a Trent Richardson run of 24 yards. It was there that Alabama tried a trick play; with Marquis Maze at quarterback in the wildcat formation, he attempted a pass to Michael Williams at the goal line. LSU defensive back Eric Reid went up for the ball along with Williams, and the official ruled he made the interception at the 1. The call was upheld by a video replay. The offenses continued to struggle, and the game was tied at the end of regulation.

In the overtime, Alabama had possession of the ball first, and that possession ended with Foster missing a 52-yard field goal try, Alabama's fourth missed field goal attempt in the game. LSU drove from the 25 to the

8, where on a third-and-goal play, Alleman kicked a successful 25-yard field goal for the 9-6 win, allowing LSU to hold on to its No. 1 national ranking and leaving Alabama's future for the season uncertain.

There would be another Game of the Century. Alabama would win the remainder of its games and, even though it didn't play in the SEC championship game, when the BCS poll came out after all the conference title games had been played, LSU was ranked No. 1 and Alabama had moved back to No. 2 ahead of teams such as Oklahoma State, Stanford, and others. The rematch, which created a division among college football fans, some of whom did not agree with a team that didn't win its league or division crowns playing for the national championship, would dominate sports talk radio for the next month. This time, the teams would play in Louisiana.

• • •

This would be a rematch, but not a rerun. It would more closely resemble, at least on this night, a mismatch. Alabama's offense would show LSU something more than a steady dose of Trent Richardson runs; it would employ a conservative but effective passing game too. The defense would be its usual, stingy self, but with a little something extra; LSU would find its way onto Alabama's side of the field only once, that coming in the fourth quarter and ending with a fumble that Alabama would recover and parlay into the game's only touchdown.

No, this would be a rematch, but it would not be a replay; the regular season game was close from start to finish and required an extra quarter to decide the outcome. This time one team would dominate from start to finish and claim the national championship.

It would be a Louisiana night with a serious Alabama flavor.

The dominance of the Alabama defense would be evident at the start. LSU received the opening kickoff and ran three plays for a total of six yards before punting to Alabama. The Crimson Tide ran seven plays on its first possession for 36 yards, but punted the ball back to the Tigers. LSU again ran three plays and punted the ball to Alabama. Punter Brad Wing of Australia, who had been a huge factor for the Tigers all season, boomed a 54-yard punt to the Alabama 25, but Marquis Maze provided the game's first big play, returning the punt 49 yards to the LSU 26-yard line, setting up the Crimson Tide's first score.

Quarterback AJ McCarron was ready. He tossed a 16-yard strike to Darius Hanks on first down, moving the Tide to the LSU 10. From there, Richardson was held for no gain on a run, and two incomplete passes brought

Jeremy Shelley on for the first of his seven field goal attempts. He made the kick from 23 yards out, giving Alabama a lead that it would not surrender the rest of the day.

LSU picked up one of the only two first downs that it would produce in the first three quarters of play on its ensuing possession, but still the Tigers moved the ball a collective 17 yards and was forced to punt yet again. Alabama took over at its 11 after a fair catch. A slow start improved as McCarron completed a nine-yard pass to Brad Smelley on a second down-and-5 play and followed with an eight-yard strike to Chris Underwood. Following a three-yard Eddie Lacy run, McCarron took to the air once more, teaming with Kevin Norwood on a 26-yard play that moved the Crimson Tide to the LSU 38. It was the final play of the first quarter, a quarter in which Alabama's defense held the Tigers' offense to a mere 28 yards on 11 plays.

After an incomplete pass, McCarron and Smelley hooked up on a seven-yard throw, and Lacy gained one yard on a carry. On a fourth-and-4 situation from the LSU 32, Alabama decided to go for the first down, which it picked up with a four-yard McCarron-to-Norwood pass to the 28. From there, Alabama would gain just three more yards and Smelley would be called on to attempt a 42-yard field goal. The kick was blocked by Michael Brockers, and LSU took possession at its 25.

The LSU offense followed a familiar pattern: three plays and a punt. Alabama, taking over at its 25 after a 47-yard Wing punt, embarked on another drive. McCarron tossed to Richardson for five yards, Richardson lost a yard on a carry, and McCarron got nine yards on a throw to Hanks. Richardson rushed for seven yards, McCarron hit Smelley for five, and Richardson clicked off a 20-yard run to the LSU 25. An incomplete pass preceded a nine-yard Lacy run, but Lacy lost a yard on third-and-1. Smelley got the call again, this time for a 34-yard attempt, which he made to give Alabama a 6-0 lead with 4:18 remaining to play in the first half.

LSU followed its trend offensively—three and out. Alabama took over after a fair catch of a punt at its 24 and started another scoring drive. McCarron and Richardson combined on a six-yard pass on first down, with Richardson producing runs of two and five yards, respectively, for a first down at the 37. McCarron connected with Smelley on a pass that lost two yards, followed by completions of 20 (to Norwood), four (to Michael Williams), eight (to Norwood) and nine (to Hanks). Using time-outs to preserve the clock, Alabama had methodically moved to the LSU 24 with four seconds to play in the half. It was Shelley time again. This time, he connected on a 41-yarder on the final play of the first half, giving Alabama a 9-0 halftime advantage.

The advantages didn't stop there. The Crimson Tide had collected 225 yards, compared to only 43 for the Tigers. It held a 13-1 edge in first downs, 21:15 to 8:45 edge in time of possession and was simply dominating the game. The only thing Alabama had failed to do in the first two periods was score a touchdown, but with its defense owning LSU and keeping Tigers quarterback Jordan Jefferson guessing as to what was coming next, touchdowns hadn't been required. The game's momentum was dressed in crimson, and it didn't appear a change was near.

It certainly didn't appear to be the case when LSU couldn't find its way onto Alabama's side of the field, which it failed to do in the first half and would only do once (in the fourth quarter) in the game.

"We didn't realize it," linebacker Nico Johnson said of keeping LSU from crossing the 50-yard line in the first half. "We were so tuned into the game. We felt like we didn't finish the first game. We started strong, but we didn't finish that game. . . . But we were so focused in, it was like we weren't worried about the game. All we were worried about was executing our game plan to perfection. When they told us [at the half] that they didn't cross the 50, it wasn't a shocker because our defense was good. It wasn't a surprise that we did that. It happened the way it happened, and it showed that we were ready."

• • •

As if scripted, McCarron reminded LSU what it had experienced in the first half and what Alabama had planned for the remaining two quarters. On the half's first play from scrimmage, he teamed with Hanks on a 19-yard pass play that moved Alabama from its 32 to the 49. On the next play, he teamed with Kenny Bell for 26 yards, reaching the LSU 23. Richardson was held without a gain on a run, but Hanks caught a short McCarron pass for five yards to the 18. An incomplete pass on third-and-5 forced Alabama to once again call on Shelley. He delivered again, kicking a 35-yard field goal that pushed Alabama's lead to 12-0 just two minutes and 11 seconds into the third period.

LSU would double its first-down production on the ensuing drive, but the end result would be the same: punting to Alabama and remaining on its side of the field. Starting at its 24, Jefferson tossed a 19-yard pass to Odell Beckham on second-and-10 to the Alabama 43. Spencer Ware gained two yards on the next play, Jefferson was sacked by Courtney Upshaw for a loss of five yards, and Jefferson rushed for seven yards. That left the Tigers with a fourth-and-6 situation at their 46. Wing punted 43 yards to Alabama's 25.

"After halftime, those guys came out with not as much fire as they had when they came in," linebacker Dont'a Hightower said. "From there, it was kind of downhill for those guys." Toward the end of the game, the demeanor of the LSU players had only decreased. "I could tell they really didn't want to play against us any longer," defensive end Jesse Williams said.

The Crimson Tide started the ensuing possession well. McCarron hit Norwood for 24 yards to the 49, but the drive quickly stalled and Alabama punted back to the Tigers. LSU kept the ball only a few moments, as Jefferson was intercepted by C. J. Mosley on a second-and-11 play, returning the pick one yard to the LSU 27. Richardson lost two yards on first down and then gained six more yards on second down. McCarron's pass to Bell fell incomplete, opening the door for another Shelley field goal try. This one, from 41 yards out, missed the mark, and the turnover failed to produce any points.

Another LSU three-and-out series resulted in Alabama gaining possession at the LSU 47, thanks to a 15-yard punt return by Christion Jones. Lacy manufactured back-to-back 11-yard runs, putting the Tide at the LSU 25. He was then held for no gain, and McCarron subsequently threw an incomplete pass and was sacked for a loss of two yards on third down. Back came Shelley, who was good on his attempt from 44 yards, giving Alabama a 15-0 lead with 22 seconds to play in the third quarter.

Alabama had possession of the ball for 30 minutes (two entire quarters) of the first three quarters. LSU's offense, which had managed just 66 total yards and two first downs, still had not ventured onto Alabama's side of the field. It was as if there was a brick wall at the 50-yard line that the Tigers could not scale. Wing had punted seven times, and Alabama had five field goals. Jefferson had thrown for just 24 yards on 13 tries and rushed for only three yards on nine attempts. That averaged out to little more than a yard per play.

The teams swapped punts to start the fourth quarter. One of the LSU players receiving a lot of pregame attention, Tyrann Mathieu, a player expected to have a great impact on the outcome as both a defensive back and punt returner, fielded the 54-yard Will Lowery punt. Instead of the "Honey Badger'" making a play that would change the momentum of the game, as he had done several times during the season, he returned the punt for one yard. Defensively, he fared much better, making six solo stops, including one tackle for a loss, and he broke up two passes.

LSU needed more. Lots more.

On the plus side, the Tigers would finally find their way across the 50-yard line, if only for a few moments, on its second possession of the fourth quarter. Starting at the Tigers' 35, Ware gained five yards in front of a Jefferson three-yard run and a seven-yard rush by Kenny Hilliard, who started the quarter with five yards on two carries. That placed the Tigers at the 50, where Jefferson ran for 18 yards to the Alabama 32. Just as it appeared the Tigers might make a move, their fortunes changed dramatically.

Michael Ford was stopped for a three-yard loss, and LSU was called for a false start penalty prior to its second-down play. Incomplete passes on second and third downs left LSU with a fourth-and-18 situation at the Alabama 40. Trailing by 15 points and with time rapidly running out, the Tigers had no option but to go for the first down, if not more. Hightower sacked Jefferson on the play, resulting in a loss of 10 yards. Jefferson also fumbled the ball on the play, and Alabama's Nick Gentry recovered it at the 50.

LSU's lone visit to Alabama's side of the field would only serve to set up the Crimson Tide's—and the game's—only touchdown drive. Richardson burst off left guard for two yards, and McCarron tacked on a 13-yard run to the LSU 35. Richardson then produced a one-yard run before sealing the victory with a classic 34-yard scoring run that bumped the score to 21-0. The 50-yard drive took just four plays and erased any thoughts of a late LSU comeback. Shelley, who had provided five Alabama field goals along with a blocked attempt and a miss, missed the extra-point attempt, but with 4:36 left to play, it didn't matter.

LSU received the ensuing kickoff and repeated a familiar theme: three plays and a punt. It was the official waving of the white flag, the sign that this was Alabama's night, and as a result, Alabama's season.

"The goal today was you control your own destiny, you control what you do; the outcome of the game, as good as LSU was, will be determined by how we play and what we do," Saban said in the postgame press conference. "And I think the players really responded well to that."

Alabama had avenged the regular season loss to LSU, proved it belonged in the national championship game, and collected its 14th national championship. LSU had beaten Alabama in overtime on the Crimson Tide's home field; Alabama had defeated the Tigers in what was basically their backyard, New Orleans' Superdome.

"It was a blessing," Johnson said of the outcome and the experience. "It was a lot of guys' second championship. We wanted to take every advantage of being in that game. When we won, it was like—honestly, it still hasn't hit me yet [six months later] that we won."

• • •

How dominant was Alabama's defense? Let us count the yards. In order, here is each of LSU's offensive possessions, where it started and ended: 1. LSU 28, LSU 34; 2. LSU 21, LSU 21; 3. LSU 27, LSU 44; 4. LSU 25, LSU 28; 5. LSU 21, LSU 28. Second half: 1. LSU 24, LSU 47; 2. LSU 20, LSU 19; 3. LSU 24, LSU 18; 4. LSU 22, LSU 39; 5. LSU 35, Alabama 40; 6. LSU 23, LSU 24.

The defensive performance only solidified Alabama's national standing as the country's best defensive team. It was not a one-game trick for the Crimson Tide; it was a season-long performance, one that stands out as among the game's best ever. Alabama finished the season ranked No. 1 in the country in total defense (allowing just 183.62 yards a game; No. 2 LSU allowed 261.50), scoring defense (8.15 points per game), rushing defense, passing defense, passing efficiency defense, red zone defense and first down defense. It is one of only two teams to ever finish a season ranked No. 1 nationally in the top four defensive categories: total defense, scoring defense, rushing defense, and passing defense.

"Look at that!" strength and conditioning coach Scott Cochran yelled as he approached defensive coordinator Kirby Smart after the game, pointing at the scoreboard. "That's a goose egg, baby!"

It was more than a shutout; Alabama's defense, earning consideration as the top defensive team in college football in the modern era, had shut down LSU. Completely. Totally. Thoroughly.

"I feel we're one of the greatest of all time," defensive back Mark Barron said of the Alabama defense to *Birmingham News* reporter Jon Solomon after the game. "Hopefully we proved that to everyone else tonight. We have so many playmakers, such great chemistry. We didn't want to give anything up."

Interestingly, Johnson said it wasn't success that drove the defense. It was quite the opposite. "Being failures in 2010," he notes as the reasoning. "We failed three times [three losses]. We let our team down three times. Because we go out, no matter what position the offense puts us in, we're the defense and that's what we're there for, to stop the opponent. Even if we're on the one-yard line. It doesn't matter. The failure we had in 2010, we didn't want that."

• • •

There was every reason for AJ McCarron to be happy. In his first season as Alabama's starting quarterback, he had led the Crimson Tide to a national championship. Not only had he managed the offense, but on the night when the offense needed him most he played his best game of the year. In the national title game, with the offense geared toward him completing passes, especially on first-down plays, he took care of business. Most expected Alabama to place the brunt of its offensive attack with Richardson, but instead offensive coordinator Jim McElwain came up with a different attack, one that required McCarron to be the offensive trigger. He was ready for the responsibility.

McCarron completed 23-of-34 passes for 234 yards and was not intercepted. He was sacked twice, but he also had four carries for 11 yards. His throws were accurate and sharp and his control of the offense smooth and without hesitation. "To watch his development throughout the year and then to culminate it with the performance he had against LSU [in the national title game], to me that was one of the bigger themes of the game," Savage said.

McElwain agreed and wasn't surprised by the play of his quarterback. "I thought AJ played well, but he's a good player." McElwain, who left Alabama after the game to become head coach at Colorado State, said. "I think his ceiling is way high. We're going to see a lot of football out of AJ McCarron. He's a sponge. . . . He loves to learn and do anything he can to win ballgames."

• • •

And so they celebrated, for a variety of reasons, influenced by a variety of emotions. The 2009 Alabama team won a national championship, and the 2010 team was the prohibitive favorite going into the season to win the national crown again. That didn't happen. Regardless of what was placed in front of them, they found a way to push forward. That was true in the aftermath of the tornadoes, it was true in dealing with the death of a teammate, and it was true in overcoming a regular-season loss. In short, they believed in themselves and what they could accomplish, even when it seemed that reaching their goals would not be possible.

Those who played on that team, especially those who won a national title in 2009, were determined not to let anything stop them in 2011. They didn't. They played for themselves and for their coaches; they played for their community and for their school and fans. They played with purpose and intensity and with a lofty goal in mind, just as they played with enthusiasm and creativity and with the idea of having fun.

"The celebration was amazing," Gould said. "It felt it was more football-related at that point. They had the disappointment of 2010. You could argue the offense in 2010 was stacked and they still lost three games and ended up playing in the Capital One Bowl. What I took away from the experience [of the 2011 season] was the team learned from its mistakes in 2010 and never lost sight of what the goal was in 2011, which was to go out, dominate their opponents, and win a national title.

Through it all—rematch and recovery, rebuilding and rebirth, resolve and redemption—Alabama's football team performed with heart and with purpose. With each week, each game, the Crimson Tide defined itself not with words, but with actions.

"I think the entire tornado tragedy, that really brought the team together and gave them a purpose maybe bigger than themselves because they felt like they were playing for Tuscaloosa and for the state of Alabama," Savage said. "No doubt, that was an inspiration for them. And they played so well."

CHAPTER TWENTY-FIVE

2013 BCS National Championship

Alabama 42, Notre Dame 14
January 7, 2013
Sun Life Stadium
Miami Gardens, Florida

As he stood on the Sun Life Stadium field, confetti falling all around, his teammates, coaches, and thousands of fans in full celebration, Alabama quarterback AJ McCarron found himself standing next to the crystal football trophy that goes to the team that wins the BCS national championship.

As is customary with most players, the first thing to come to his mind was that he wanted to share his feelings and the moment with his family. But at that moment, it wouldn't be enough just to find them in the stands. He would have to take along a symbol. Something special.

So when McCarron, who now had his hands on the crystal football, which had made its way into the grasp of several teammates since the final horn sounded on Alabama's 42-14 smacking of No. 1-ranked Notre Dame, glanced at the man in charge of keeping tabs on the Waterford trophy, he let him know he was taking the crystal on a short trip. It was more a pronouncement than a request. "I looked at the guy in charge of it and said, 'I'm taking it,' and he was like, 'That's fine,'" McCarron recalled. "He really wasn't going to tell me 'no,' I don't think. So I took it over to [my family] and they enjoyed it more than I probably did. I like having them be a part of the process and seeing everything happen. After every big game—after every game, period—I'll go find them and hug them wherever we're playing and tell them I love them, whether we win or lose. They always tell me they're proud of me. It just makes me realize that football is just a game at the end of the day, it's not life. And family is a lot more important."

There have been many happy reunions following Alabama football games for the McCarron family and all family members of Crimson Tide football players. The 2013 national championship was Alabama's second straight and its third in four years, the 15th in school history. After the LSU game earlier in the season, when a late drive by Alabama gave the Crimson Tide the win, the McCarrons celebrated. After the loss to Texas A&M, when it appeared the Tide's national title hopes may have been dashed, the family was there for McCarron. The same was true the remainder of the season, just as it had been at the start of the season. Wins would be family celebrations; losses—and they have been few in McCarron's time at Alabama—would lead to family support.

"My family and my family's closest friends, guys who are close to my mom and dad and any family member that helped raise me growing up—family has always been a big part of my life and I love having family members around me at all times," McCarron, who now has three national championship rings, said. "They keep me grounded and help me whenever I need help. They're always there. . . . I'm playing because I have fun playing, but they love watching it and being there and I guess seeing history being made at the same time."

There was a lot to celebrate on this particular night, in this particular victory. McCarron had led a potent Alabama offense that scored touchdowns on its first three possessions. The Crimson Tide, ranked No. 2 coming into the game, dominated the Fighting Irish in every phase of the game. Cheering every big play, every score, was the McCarron family, led by mother Dee Dee Bonner and her husband Derek Bonner and AJ's dad, Tony McCarron, as well as several others.

"The first thing I thought," Dee Dee said when she spotted her son, crystal football in hand, headed toward them, "was is he about to get tackled coming over here with the football? Is he going to get in trouble? So he comes over—he calls me Ma—and he's calling, 'Ma! Ma!' and I look down and that little goober kid's got the crystal football and he says, 'Get a picture of me holding it.' I'm thinking, there's 12 million cameras around you baby, people are getting pictures of you with the football. But he wants me to take a picture of him with my iPhone. I take the picture with the iPhone and he kisses the football. My iPhone picture, of course, is the one he wanted, not all the magazine covers and everything else. It was funny to me. We were asking him, 'Are you excited?' and he was just grinning. He was so excited."

Tony McCarron was concerned at first his son might try something risky with the trophy. "It's like living a dream," he said of the game and moment. "He comes running over there to us and we're on the front row but not where he could get to us. He's holding the crystal football and it looks like he's going to toss it up to us. . . . Just to see from a dad's point of view—you know, we tell our kids all the time that if you work hard it will pay off for you. It's good to see that really happen. I know how much time he puts into it every day and how hard he has worked to get to where he's at now."

Derek Bonner said the moment still lingers for him and the family. "That's one of the surreal moments in my life," he said. "Obviously, I've been blessed in life to have met Dee Dee and get married and become a part of AJ's and Corey's lives and to have experienced a lot of great moments in the past ten years. The first championship [with McCarron as the starter] was special, but that one in Miami, I'll hold on to a lot of great memories and moments from throughout that entire week we were down there. And to see his face—I think one of the best things a parent can see is a glow on their kid's face—and to be able to share that moment with them, it was amazing. I was happy to be a part of it."

That sentiment was shared throughout the Bama Nation. It was a moment that continues to be a celebration for the loyal fan base, a point of pride. There were many reasons to be excited, many performances to be celebrated. McCarron, Eddie Lacy, T. J. Yeldon, an All-America offensive line, Amari Cooper, and Kevin Norwood were leaders on offense, while defensively the play of C. J. Mosley, Robert Lester, Deion Belue, Dee Milliner, Vinnie Sunseri, Nico Johnson, and many others was key to stopping the Irish offense.

But before the national title was secured, Alabama had to get past LSU in Baton Rouge, which it did with a brilliant last drive and a devilishly good play call of a screen pass for the game-winning score; the Tide had to overcome a loss to Texas A&M the following week; it had to collect wins over West Carolina and Auburn and then outlast Georgia in the SEC Championship Game and, with other contenders losing, pushing Alabama to No. 2 in the BCS standings, make the most of its second chance. Alabama did all those things, in most cases with a little gusto and some drama.

The drama began at LSU, where Saban led the Tigers to the national title in 2003. Early in the fourth quarter, LSU took a 17-15 lead, but with 51 seconds to play, McCarron tossed a screen pass to Yeldon, which resulted in a 28-yard scoring play for the win. After the score, McCarron could be seen on the Alabama bench, crying.

"I think it was everything," McCarron said when asked if his tears were the result of the pressure to win or the emotions of pulling out the victory in the final seconds. "Being raised in the state of Alabama—I mess with my dad because he's one of those fans that when the quarterback didn't make the right throw or whatever he was the first one to scream at the TV and the quarterback. I can remember telling Tyler Watts and Brodie [Croyle, former Alabama quarterbacks], 'You don't know how many times my dad was yelling at you.' But I think my view's a lot different than a lot of quarterbacks that come through here because there's only a few that are from the state."

The comeback win added to McCarron's confidence, which was growing. The previous year in the BCS game against LSU, the offensive game plan was to put the ball in McCarron's hands, and he had handled the task well in the victory. Now, more and more, the coaching staff put the ball in his hands and allowed his play to dictate the pace of the offense and in many ways, its success. They would put the ball back in his hands again in Miami Gardens against unbeaten Notre Dame for the national championship. It would be a good decision.

"I never really know how he's feeling until the day of the game," Tony McCarron said. "He'll usually say something to me when we start to say goodbye [before a game]. In Miami I got ready to walk out of this little conference room where we had all spent some time together. He looked at me and he said, 'Where are your seats at?' I said, 'I don't know, we won't know until we get out there.' He laughed and said, 'Make sure you get a good seat because I'm going to put on a show.' I said, 'OK,' and then he said, 'I'm serious.' I said to him, 'Oh, I don't doubt you.'"

• • •

Notre Dame won the coin toss. It would be the only victory of the night for the Fighting Irish. Alabama started its first possession at its own 18-yard line. The Crimson Tide would need just five plays and less than three minutes to score, giving it a lead it would not surrender. Lacy began the drive with a one-yard run and McCarron followed with a 29-yard pass to Norwood. Now at the Alabama 48, Lacy rushed for 10 yards and an extra 15 was tacked on to the play because of a facemask penalty against Notre Dame. Another penalty against the Irish, this one for offsides, moved the ball five yards closer to the end zone. After Yeldon rushed for two yards, Lacy covered the remaining 20 for the touchdown.

It was just that simple, just that quick. And it was just the start.

"Whenever he threw the first couple of passes, I looked at Dee Dee and said, 'He's on,'" Derek Bonner said. "You could just tell he was on. It was just amazing."

The Alabama defense held Notre Dame to a three-plays-and-out possession and following a 43-yard punt and a 15-yard penalty against the Irish for interference, the Crimson Tide took over at its own 39. Lacy rushed for three yards and added six more on a pass from McCarron before gaining eight on another run. After an incomplete pass, Lacy ran for five yards and on third down-and-5, McCarron threw a seven-yard pass to Marvin Shinn for a first down at the Notre Dame 32. Lacy, finding running room throughout the game, picked up five more yards, McCarron threw to Cooper for four, and on a third-and-1 play Lacy pounded the Notre Dame defense for 20 yards and a first down at the 3. That's where McCarron would throw a strike to Michael Williams for a touchdown and a 14-0 lead.

Notre Dame's offense would get a first down on the ensuing possession, but only one. After five plays and 15 yards, the Irish punted to Alabama. The Crimson Tide offense went back to work with 4:22 remaining in the first period at its 20-yard line. Yeldon picked up seven yards and McCarron followed with a 25-yard strike to Norwood, quickly moving the Tide into Notre Dame territory at the 48. McCarron and Cooper connected on an 11-yard pass play and after Yeldon lost two yards on a run, he followed with a six-yard pickup. On third-and-6, McCarron and Cooper connected again, this time for 27 yards to the Notre Dame 6. Yeldon rushed for five yards on the last play of the first quarter to the 1, then covered the final yard on the first play of the second quarter. It was 21-0 and there were a lot of people across the country—none of them Alabama fans, of course—clicking the TV remote in search of other viewing options. Notre Dame wouldn't escape that easily.

In its first three offensive possessions, Alabama had run 23 plays, moved the football 223 yards, and scored 21 points while maintaining possession for 12 minutes and 12 seconds. The Alabama defense had allowed Notre Dame a sole first down, eight plays, 23 total yards and less than three minutes of possession time in the first quarter.

"Coming in, watching film on Notre Dame, we knew they were good up front," McCarron said. "Their front seven, their box, was extremely good at stopping the run. They were like top three in every category in the country on defense and number one on most of them and so we knew they could stop the run. We knew play-action passes were going to be a big part of the ballgame. We knew we were going to have to hit some explosive plays and get them off-balance. . . . We knew if both cylinders of our offense were hitting, we would be hard to stop."

Phil Savage, executive director of the Senior Bowl, former general manager of the Cleveland Browns and the radio color commentator for

Alabama football games, said he knew Alabama would have a big night against the Irish. He had seen the signs weeks before the game and leading up to game day.

"After Bama beat Georgia to get into the BCS game, probably a week later, I got my Notre Dame tapes and put them on and honestly, after watching five games of the Irish, I put down the clicker and walked into the other room where my wife was and said, 'If we don't beat these guys by two touchdowns or more I'm going to be disappointed,'" Savage said.

Alabama's offense hit a brief lull after the third score, but the defense continued to play strong, refusing to allow the Irish a chance of getting back into the game. The offenses swapped short, unproductive drives until the 3:43 mark of the quarter, when Alabama took over possession at its 29. In its previous two possessions of the quarter, Alabama had produced just nine plays and 27 yards. Instead of sitting on the 21-0 lead and working to run out the remaining time in the first half, Alabama's offense went on the attack.

Yeldon had rushes of two and 10 yards, and following a rare McCarron incomplete pass, Yeldon produced runs of seven and 10 yards, moving Alabama to the Notre Dame 42. A pass from McCarron to Yeldon produced no gain and Lacy followed with a four-yard gain that set up a third-and-6 situation from the 38. McCarron hit Christion Jones for 27 yards to the 11, and on the next play McCarron tossed an 11-yard touchdown pass to Lacy with 31 seconds to play in the half that gave the Crimson Tide a 28-0 lead at halftime.

Everyone watching could see that Alabama was dominating Notre Dame and the game. What Alabama head coach Nick Saban saw was the possibility of complacency taking hold of his team. "It was funny because at halftime, the younger guys, the freshmen that had come in, guys who had never experienced anything like that, they come in [to the locker room] and they're celebrating and saying we're going to win a national championship," McCarron recalled. "Coach Saban comes in and yells and rips and you automatically—I remember that like it was yesterday, him doing that in '09 in Pasadena [at the 2010 BCS national championship game], coming in at halftime and ripping everybody, telling them it's not over, that the score is 0-0, just the usual stuff. But to the younger guys it's a bigger deal because Coach Saban is speaking and he's telling you what you really need to understand. The older guys understood that, hey, we can be happy about it, but we can't be satisfied."

They wouldn't be satisfied, even though the stat sheet indicated the Crimson Tide was unquestionably in charge—Alabama had 309 total yards, 28 points, and 16 first downs compared to 124 yards, no points, and just five first downs for Notre Dame. So Alabama hit the field for the second half with the aim of adding to its advantage. It didn't have to wait long to achieve that goal.

After a six-play, 39-yard possession and punt by Notre Dame to start the third quarter, Alabama took possession at its own 3. Lacy had runs of four and 16 yards to give the Crimson Tide breathing room, and McCarron hit Norwood for a 12-yard gain. Yeldon added a six-yard run and McCarron threw a 13-yard pass to Jones for a first down at the Notre Dame 46. Yeldon ran for gains of five and three yards, Lacy added runs of one and three yards, and McCarron delivered again, this time on a 34-yard strike to Cooper for the touchdown. Ten plays, 97 yards, five minutes and 37 seconds. It was now 35-0 with 7:34 left in the third quarter and, as Savage had declared much earlier, the game was over. There was simply the matter of running the remaining time off the clock before the crystal football would be handed to Saban and his team for the second-straight year and third time in four years.

The Irish responded to Alabama's score with its first touchdown. Notre Dame put together a nine-play, 85-yard scoring drive that included a 31-yard pass from Everett Golson to T. J. Jones on a third-and-16 play. The pass moved the Irish to the Alabama 17, where four plays later Golson scored on a two-yard run.

How would Alabama respond? By scoring another touchdown, of course. Starting at its 14, Yeldon had four consecutive carries, good for eight, three, 10, and six yards respectively. Lacy picked up from there, rushing for six and four yards. McCarron followed that run with a 10-yard pass to Cooper on the final play of the third quarter, moving Alabama to the Notre Dame 49. After Lacy lost three yards on a run, McCarron threw a five-yard pass to Kelly Johnson and an eight-yard pass to Williams. An incomplete pass to Cooper was followed by a completion of seven yards to Shinn. Facing third-and-3, Lacy burst through with a 13-yard run to the Irish 19 and that's where McCarron threw a strike to Cooper for a touchdown, capping a 14-play, 86-yard drive that gave Alabama a 42-7 lead and placed an exclamation point on the evening.

Notre Dame would follow with a meaningless touchdown on its ensuing possession, with Golson throwing a six-yard scoring pass to Theo Riddick with 7:51 to play, but it was window dressing and nothing more. The confetti guns were at the ready with crimson and white paper for the celebration to follow. And yet there would be one more head-to-head battle of interest— McCarron vs. teammate Barrett Jones.

Right in the middle of the field, in the middle of a rout of Notre Dame, only minutes from winning a second consecutive national championship,

McCarron and Jones were arguing. In the midst of the argument, Jones shoved his quarterback and road game roommate. With gusto.

"No, I wasn't surprised he did it," McCarron would say later, smiling as he recalled the moment. "You ask anybody, me and Barrett got into it at practice all the time and they would have to break us up or whatever. That's just me and him. We're the same type [of] personality and always wanting everything on the field to go right, but go our way too. We had done that numerous times on the practice field too. We roomed together before every game and we have been always so close. It wasn't a surprise to me, though it probably was to fans and other people because they'd never seen us in practice. But it's been worse at practice, so that's a positive of it."

Jones also said the shove meant nothing, that it was merely two competitive guys who believed they were right, "discussing" exactly who was right. "We did that all the time, so there was nothing to it," Jones said. "Besides, he knows I was right."

Coach Saban noted the dust-up the following morning during the press conference in which he was presented with a number of national championship trophies and said he liked what he saw because of what it represented to him. "You watch [AJ] and Barrett in the fourth quarter with five minutes to go in the game, you can see what kind of competitors they both are, the kind of respect for each other and the kind of standard of excellence they're trying to play to," Saban said. "We're always trying to get players to play for 60 minutes and be the best they can be and not worry about the scoreboard, and I think their reaction to each other was an indication that they're still out there competing and playing the way you'd like them to."

When the starting team was called to the sidelines, Jones went straight to McCarron and lifted him off the ground in celebration. The countdown was on; the school's 15th national championship was in hand. And McCarron was only a few minutes away from getting his hands on that crystal football.

McCarron's stats, just as was the case for others, were strong. He completed 20-of-28 passes for 264 yards, four touchdowns, and no interceptions. He ran the offense with precision and emotion. Cooper caught six passes for 105 yards and two scores, Lacy carried the ball 20 times for 140 yards and a touchdown and he also caught two passes, one for a touchdown. Yeldon had 21 carries for 108 yards and a score as the Crimson Tide offense, behind the best offensive line in the country in Jones, D. J. Fluker, Chance Warmack, Cyrus Kouandjo, and Anthony Steen, piled up 529 yards in an even split—264 yards passing, 265 yards rushing.

"Any quarterback you talk to, they're going to say they want the ball more," McCarron said. "I truly do. I love having the ball in my hands, especially in key moments in a game and especially in big games. I've always been that way, ever since I was a little kid. I think it pushes you to be the best player you can be if you always have the ball, even if you're not always successful making plays in big-time games. I believe you grow, not only as an athlete and a competitor, but as a person. You really, truly find out what type of person you are under pressure. So I've always wanted to have the ball in my hands in big situations."

McCarron has already cemented his place among the best quarterbacks in Alabama's long history. His name belongs alongside the greats such as Namath, Stabler, Steve Sloan, Richard Todd, and Pat Trammell. He has three national championship rings and has a chance to pick up one more. He has broken several school passing and offensive records and is close to grabbing others. He is driven to improve on what he has already accomplished.

"AJ has really, really done a great job of becoming a player," Savage said. "People thought they were going to have to harness him in when he got there and he has taken to the coaching that he has received there. He knows when to go for it and when to back off and he's become a game manager. But I think it's a mistake for people to label him as a game manager, because he's so much more than that. He throws the outside post corner route as well as anybody in the country. And with him being able to do that, it really keeps the defense honest."

Television analyst Charles Davis, who covers college football and the NFL, also noted the "game manager" tag is unfair to McCarron.

"I'm a big believer that the term 'game manager' is damning someone with faint praise," Davis said. "But I'm also a big believer that people understand what it takes to be a game manager and that's a lot tougher proposition than we give it credit for. . . . You know, [Michael] Jordan didn't make every last-second jumper, but he was willing to take it. AJ is willing to take it. . . . Look how early they started slinging the ball against Notre Dame in their own territory. That pass to start the game set a big tone as far as I was concerned. If we didn't have that idea before that, you had the idea right then that Nick Saban trusts this guy, no ifs, ands, or buts."

Indeed, McCarron has Saban's complete trust, and his respect. He has earned this not only with his play on the field, but also in how he has handled himself since arriving in Tuscaloosa and his willingness and desire to accept a leadership role on the team. But as with most things, that was a trust that had to be developed. Saban said he and the coaching staff recognized McCarron's talent when they recruited him. Turning that raw talent into the polished player he has become took some prodding at times. That was especially true when McCarron first arrived.

"AJ has done a fantastic job in his development," Saban said. "I remember the first scrimmage AJ was in, we made him play with the threes [third team]. He was hot behind the collar and fussing out on the field and he stormed up to my office when the scrimmage was over and said, 'How come you made me play with the threes? I thought I was going to be with the twos.' I said, 'We're only evaluating your leadership today and you failed,'" Saban said, smiling at the memory.

"He has come a long way. Now he is the best leader on our team, and has been, and is one of the best quarterbacks in the country. We're certainly pleased and proud to have him being our quarterback."

In return, McCarron says Saban is the reason he decided to play football at Alabama.

"It was Coach Saban, strictly him," McCarron, who grew up a Miami fan and during the recruiting process seriously considered schools such as Oklahoma and Georgia, said when asked—about the deciding factor in his decision. "Coach Saban was the guy who mainly recruited me. Every time they came down and saw us at school, it was always Coach Saban."

The closeness of the relationship could be seen near the end of the win over Notre Dame, when McCarron found Saban on the sidelines and gave his coach a celebratory hug. "At the end I just told Coach I loved him and congratulations and he told me he loved me and he was proud of me," McCarron said. "I know he gets hounded and he had to go shake hands [with Notre Dame's Brian Kelley], so I just tried to get him real quick like I did last year [in the 2012 BCS title game]. . . . I just try to cherish every moment. It's not always going to be here. I've been playing since I was four, and you don't always win championships. To be starting for two years and have two [national championships] in a row is something very special to be a part of, and I'm glad I get to experience it with Coach."

• • •

Someone uttered that word, the "D" word, in the press conference following Alabama's convincing victory over the Fighting Irish. After all, the win gave Alabama its second consecutive national title and its third in four years. So, the individual asked Saban, considering the program's success the past four seasons, would it be appropriate to use the word "dynasty" when referring to the team and program?

"I don't think words like 'dynasty' are really words that I'm much interested in," Saban said. "You know, we're interested in accomplishments and consistency in performance, and we want to continue to try to do that in the future. So those are for other people to talk about."

"Pride" is a word that Saban was comfortable using, though, especially when speaking of his 2012 team. "I would say that regardless of the result that this team achieved, that they certainly exceeded every expectation that we had for them with the number of guys we graduated last year, the number of new roles, young players, injuries, the adversity that this team had to overcome," he said. "These guys really battled. And people talk about how the most difficult thing is to win your first championship. Really, the most difficult is to win the next one, because there's always a feeling of entitlement, and the commitment that these guys made two days after we played LSU last year in the national championship game to be a team, to set a goal to accomplish something of significance, is really special for what they were able to accomplish.

"So I've never been prouder of a group of young men for what they were able to do. Their legacy as a team certainly gets sort of defined by what they were able to accomplish this entire season, but especially in what they were able to accomplish tonight."

• • •

The pride factor was strong with the McCarron family too. They knew that not only had AJ been playing with a lot of pressure all season, but also he had played Alabama's final seven games with broken ribs, suffered in a win against Mississippi State. The public wasn't made aware of that fact until weeks after the BCS title game. The public does know that McCarron could leave Alabama after his senior season of 2013 as one of the most decorated players in the school's tradition-rich history. It knows he could leave with four national titles rings if the Crimson Tide wins the 2013 crown. Many know that no quarterback in history has been the starter on three consecutive national championship teams. Some Alabama fans undoubtedly know McCarron's career stats—5,956 career passing yards, 49 career passing touchdowns, as well as a record of 25-2 as the Tide's starting quarterback. And two national championships as the starter.

What the McCarron family knows is the internal drive that will push him in the 2013 season. They know the little boy who always hated to lose, the little boy who played catch with anyone and everyone at his dad's fire station until they couldn't throw anymore and another fireman had to join the game of catch, the young man who wants to be great, wants his team to be great, and isn't afraid to work as hard as necessary to make that happen.

"When AJ was born I was in the Air Force and I always told everybody that my boy was going to grow up and be the quarterback at Alabama," Tony McCarron said. His son has grown up to be one of the best quarterbacks in the school's history, but for mom, in many ways, he's still her little son . . . on a big-boy stage.

"For a parent—I know for Derek and I and Tony—we're just so happy for him and proud of him because we feel he's carried himself and handled himself with a grace beyond his years," Dee Dee said. "People have doubted him and said some things about him where my Mama Bear claws have come out. Even at the level of ESPN some people have said some things about him, and that had to hurt, but he's never let it show. . . . And he was able to prove his doubters wrong."